CORNISH STUDIES

Second Series

TWO

INSTITUTE OF CORNISH STUDIES

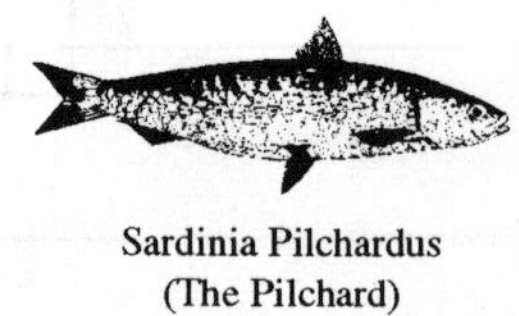

Sardinia Pilchardus
(The Pilchard)

EDITOR'S NOTE

Cornish Studies (second series) exists to reflect current research conducted internationally in the inter-disciplinary field of Cornish Studies. It is edited by Dr Philip Payton, Director of the Institute of Cornish Studies at the University of Exeter, and is published by the University of Exeter Press. The opinions expressed in *Cornish Studies* are those of individual contributors and are not necessarily those of the editor or publisher.

PUBLISHER'S NOTE

The publisher wishes to thank the following for items supplied for the cover design: Brian Edwards, *The Western Morning News*, Ian Murphy, 'Fishes' (Fishmonger, Exeter), Jon Mills, Camborne School of Mines, Robin Wooten, Sharron Robinson, The Trevithick Society, Exeter Postcard Society, Earth Resources Centre (University of Exeter) and the Director of the British Geological Survey (1:50,000 map sheets 351 and 258). The cover was designed by Delphine Jones using a photograph by John Saunders.

CORNISH STUDIES

Second Series

TWO

Edited by

Philip Payton

UNIVERSITY
of
EXETER
PRESS

First published in 1994 by
University of Exeter Press
Reed Hall, Streatham Drive
Exeter, Devon EX4 4QR
UK

British Library Cataloguing in Publication Data
A catalogue record of this book is available from the British Library

ISBN 0 85989 454 1
ISSN 1352–271X

Printed and bound in Great Britain
by Short Run Press Ltd, Exeter

Contents

INTRODUCTION

The launch of this second series of *Cornish Studies* at the end of 1993 attracted widespread interest, and amongst the chorus of approval were favourable reviews in journals and newspapers, appreciative letters from Associates of the Institute of Cornish Studies, and enquiries from other readers anxious to learn more about the Institute's activities. Perhaps the most pleasing of these responses to *Cornish Studies: One* was a review article by Cornish novelist and poet, Alan Kent, in the magazine *Cornish Banner*. Catching the spirit of *Cornish Studies*, Kent wrote that it provided 'the necessary kick-start for the new kind of enquiry being completed in the Cornish context'. The establishment of this second series was, he said, 'a massive step forwards in the commentary on Cornish issues'. Flattering words indeed, but also evidence that *Cornish Studies: One* had been successful in its attempt to reflect the recent broadening of the academic base of Cornish Studies as an area of scholarly enquiry, not least in emphasising its international scope and its rapidly developing social science.

This present volume, *Cornish Studies: Two*, aims to perpetuate this approach, with a balance of disparate themes and an international team of contributors. In an article which shows how local history, particularly in culturally distinct Cornwall, can have wide contextual and comparative importance, David Cullum and Peter Wardley chart the diffusion of the Hindu-Arabic numbering system in West Penwith in the seventeenth century, a time of technological and linguistic change. Ronald M. James returns to the familiar topic of the Cornish in America but draws on recent work in immigration and ethnic studies to suggest that on the nineteenth-century mining frontier the Cornish nurtured their separate ethnic identity as an economic strategy. Similarly, Hörst Rossler, in focussing on the experience of emigrant Constantine stonemasons, further emphasises the importance of local place-specific micro-research while also demonstrating the significance of (and relationship between) craft tradition and ethnic identity. There is also a piece on radical politics in Cornwall from the Third Reform Act until the eve of the Second World War, a synthesis which draws together several strands of recent research but which also suggests the need for further work on the relationship between Cornish political parties, political culture and the changing nature of the Cornish identity.

Moving to more contemporary themes, Charles Penglase tackles the thorny issue of 'authenticity' in the revival of the Cornish language, questioning the wisdom (and method) of the Phonemic revision and suggesting that in the current climate of change in the language movement, Modern Cornish may be the best model for the future. Paul Thornton assesses the current state of research into the fortunes (or otherwise) of Cornish tourism, and indicates some of the problems and prospects of the industry. Tourism is also the theme of John Lowerson, who examines the 'Celtic' literary-religious constructs that underpin many current perceptions and images of Cornwall. Alys Thomas, in a discussion of Cornwall's regional aspirations, exposes the inherent tension between a Cornish identity based on the salience of territory and a functional approach to regional planning focussed on the 'Westcountry' or 'South West', suggesting that although Europe offers Cornwall many potential opportunities the lack of Cornish institutions makes them difficult to grasp. Prompted by the work of Allen Ivey and facilitated by recent Cornish research in the social sciences, there is also a preliminary attempt at defining a Cornish identity theory, arguing that the development of such a theory is now both timely and essential. Finally, in an introductory comparison of the wildlife of Brittany and Cornwall, Adrian Spalding reminds us that the similarities between the two regions are by no means confined to history and human culture.

Acknowledgement is again due to the University of Exeter Press for its continuing support, and at the Institute of Cornish Studies thanks go to the secretarial, administrative and academic staff who have helped make this volume possible, especially Sarah Clayton who with considerable skill and good-humoured dedication has so expertly type-set *Cornish Studies: Two.*

Philip Payton,
Director,
Institute of Cornish Studies,
University of Exeter,
Redruth, Cornwall.

THE DIFFUSION OF THE HINDU-ARABIC NUMERICAL SYSTEM: NUMERACY, LITERACY AND HISTORICAL ANALYSIS OF WRITING SKILLS IN SEVENTEENTH-CENTURY WEST CORNWALL

David Cullum and Peter Wardley

INTRODUCTION

As the title of this article suggests, the work presented below is concerned primarily with the 'diffusion', in early modern West Cornwall, of the Hindu-Arabic numerical system, which, over the course of the seventeenth century, appears to have supplanted entirely the Roman numerical system used previously. This phenomenon is regarded here as an example of the diffusion and eventual dominance of a new technology, with West Cornish communities, or rather their documentary remains, providing a case-study of the process of technological diffusion in a local context. The West Cornwall region, shown on Map 1 below, has particular features which render it appropriate as the focus of such a case study. It is not only geographically remote and peripheral, but also possesses some clear sub-regional characteristics – almost surrounded by the sea and separated from the rest of Cornwall and Britain by the River Hayle and its isthmus, the Land's End peninsula is distinctly formed by a massive granite outcrop rising to 800 feet above sea level. The historical landscape of the region is remarkably transparent to the contemporary observer, with field and land-use patterns established in the prehistoric era still operating in the late twentieth century.[1] The Cornish language was still spoken on the Land's End peninsula in the seventeenth century, making the region culturally distinct from most of the rest of Cornwall and from England.[2] The region proved, perhaps, resistant to new industrial technologies,[3] and to the penetration of consumer goods observed elsewhere,[4] in this period.

Roman numerals retain some considerable and potent symbolism in the design culture of the late twentieth century, perhaps most notably where timepieces are concerned, signifying the old and the traditional, connoting an elegant classicism. The Roman numeral is used today for its redolence of the 'past', of a time that was not modern. This aesthetic function, however, is but the vestigial remnant of a system of numerical representation which formed the parameters and provided the 'programming language' of mathematics and calculation throughout Europe until the adoption of the Hindu-Arabic numerical system – which inherently possesses 'enormous advantages for accounting, measuring, and calculating'[5] over its forerunner. Given the symbolic attributes of the Roman numeral in modern society, and a close correspondence between the European adoption of Hindu-Arabic numerals and economic and technological progress, the process of transition from Roman to Hindu-Arabic numerals might possibly be considered as analogous to a transition from the medi val to the early modern world. As will be shown below, the transition

Map 1: The West Cornwall Region

from Roman to Hindu-Arabic numerals occurred in West Cornwall alongside other significant social and economic transformations.

This article will attempt to establish the experience of the geographically remote and insular communities of the Land's End peninsula and place it in a wider context, informed by similar studies of other communities – notably Clee in Lincolnshire and the major port of Bristol.[6] The discussion is divided into five distinct sections. The first, *Problems: historical literacy, numeracy and numbering systems*, takes as its focus the issues raised by the historical study of numeracy and literacy. This focus shifts, in the second section *The evidence: probate inventories*, onto the source materials consulted and the rationale which informs the subsequent analysis. This section also includes a close examination of the systems of numerical representation employed in two illustrative documents. Section three, *Analysis and method: West Cornwall's numerical systems*, is concentrated on the methodology employed in this work, and outlines quantitative indicators derived from a large corpus of evidence relating to West Cornwall in the seventeenth century. Section four, *The nature and experience of numerical change*, examines closely documents in which both numerical systems are employed, to demonstrate the process of transition. Here, the practices adopted by specific praisers and scribes to construct probate inventories are scrutinised to reveal aspects of this transformation. The fifth section *The 'national' context of local change* will place the process as observed in the wider context afforded by other recent studies. Technological assimilation has a social and economic context, and section six, *Echoes and feedbacks: concomitant regional trends*, explores the wider socio-economic environment in which the assimilation of Hindu-Arabic numerals occurred, and points to ways in which the process of assimilation may be shaped by, but may also itself shape, this environment. The seventh and final section, *Summary comments*, offers some tentative conclusions regarding the diffusion of the Hindu-Arabic numerical system in the region.

PROBLEMS: HISTORICAL LITERACY, NUMERACY, AND NUMBERING SYSTEMS

Of the so-called 'three R's' of reading, writing, and arithmetic, the basic and vital skills which modern societies attempt to inculcate in all their citizens, 'arithmetic', or, more strictly defined, numeracy, is very much the poor relation in terms of the attention it has received from historians. Whilst historical studies of literacy have been many and various the apparent judgement of the historical profession has been that 'there is no prospect of ever being able to map degrees and forms of numeracy, regionally or socially, in the way that some have attempted to map literacy'.[7] Such a capitulation seems extraordinary, especially when the extent to which numbers and numerical concepts pervade all aspects of modern life is considered. Modern perceptions of time and space are defined by numbers, on clocks and calendars, roadsigns and odometers; structures of work, exchange and reward operate in a numerical environment of prices, wages and balances – in a world dominated increasingly by information technology, money itself exists commonly only in numerical form and possesses no tangible reality; the fluctuating and nebulous political opinions of modern electorates are expressed as percentages, which themselves, perhaps regrettably, can be seen to drive government decision and policy making. An understanding of the modern world demands high levels of numeracy from its inhabitants, and, in the age of televisual media and computers, the numerate disciplines may, arguably, be gaining hegemony over the literate in everyday life for the mass of people.

More particularly, the community of historical scholarship has engaged increasingly with numerical concepts, perhaps most prominently in the disciplines of economic and demographic history – which depend on numerical data, numerical expression and numerical awareness in their attempts to elucidate and communicate past experience. For Peter Laslett, one of Britain's most eminent and respected social historians, 'the discovery of how great a proportion of the population could read and write at any point in time is one of the most urgent tasks which faces the historian of social structures, who is committed to the use of numerical methods'.[8]

The urgency of this task is predicated on the assumption that the literate in early modern Britain possessed a number of advantages over their illiterate peers. The ability to absorb and retain written and printed information could provide enhanced economic opportunities, allow social advancement and foster the development of political awareness.[9] However, whilst Laslett discusses the potential of numerical enquiry for investigating levels of literacy his argument is, ironically, not extended to encompass the issue of historical numeracy. His discussion provides no sense of the possible advantages of the numerate, nor of the disadvantages of the innumerate.

Despite the all-pervasive nature of the number, or perhaps because of it, the historic character of the adoption of systems of numerical representation has not received the attention of historians which its evident importance demands. The ubiquitous nature, or indeed tyranny, of numbers in modern societies makes it imperative that some attempt be made to chart the penetration of numerical concepts into everyday life.

Hindu-Arabic numerals are first recorded in Europe in 976 AD, in the manuscript *Codex Vigilanus*,[10] but their assimilation into everyday usage was a slow process, as this study will show, and Roman numerals were the established and predominant form of numerical representation employed throughout Europe in the mediæval era. The adoption of the Hindu-Arabic numerical system must be seen in the context of wider technological advances occurring in the Europe of the sixteenth and seventeenth centuries, an age of previously unparalleled technological creativity and application in agriculture, industry, commerce, and communications. The economic and intellectual climate of early modern Europe was one in which new, appropriated, and adapted technologies flourished, leading Joel Mokyr to assert that the Hindu-Arabic numerical system provides an example of European appropriation and adaptation, as 'In the later Middle Ages the Europeans first saw, then learned, then imitated, then improved, then eventually took over the field, so that modern mathematics is by and large a European product'.[11]

The advantages of this infidel numbering system lay in its use of 'place-values', the fact that its ten characters could represent any number, and the presence of a zero. This combination of attributes, not found in the Roman system, facilitated the practice of arithmetic calculation. It allowed the figures to be arranged in vertical columns for addition and subtraction, and the efficient and consistent expression of large numbers within the framework of a limited set of symbolic characters.[12] Arithmetic calculation was a skill recognised by contemporaries such as William Kempe as being of great importance throughout many facets of life in the early modern period:

> Take away arithmetic [and] ye take from all sorts of men, the faculty of executing their functions aright. Arithmetic then teacheth unto us matters in divinity, judgeth civil causes uprightly, cureth diseases, searcheth out the nature of things created, singeth sweetly, buyeth, selleth, maketh accompts, weigheth metals and worketh them, skirmisheth with the enemy, goeth on warfare, and setteth her hand almost to every good work, so profitable is she to mankind.[13]

As was noted above, whilst studies of the literacy of the historical community have proliferated only scant attention has been paid to the issues surrounding the numeracy of people in the past – any attempt to trace the historiography of studies of numeracy is destined to stimulate only a brief and limited debate. Historians of mathematics have generally engaged with the issue of the adoption of the Hindu-Arabic numerical system, and there was a brief flowering of interest in this question in the early years of the twentieth century.[14] Such investigations have only cursorily examined the geographical spread of the Hindu-Arabic numerical system, and have not engaged at all with issues of social diffusion, or the extent to which Hindu-Arabic numerals were utilised within societies. Traditionally, of course, the historian has been primarily concerned with words and their meanings – perhaps explaining the evident disparity in historical enquiry between the issues of literacy and numeracy.

It is instructive at this point to consider the origin and nature of the evidence which informs many studies of the penetration of the skills of literacy into the historical community. It was a provision of the so-called Hardwicke's

Marriage Act of 1753 that the marriage record should include an indication of the assent to marriage of the two nuptial partners. Brides and grooms could either 'sign' the marriage register, by writing their name, or 'mark' the register with some distinctive symbol. The ability, or otherwise, of newly-weds to 'sign' their names has provided historians with an index of basic literacy. This methodology is far from perfect, as it is thought that more people could read than could write and further that an individual may be able to write only their name, but has become the standard method used in the elucidation of patterns of literacy.[15] The methodology employed in this study of the employment, penetration, and incidence of numerical systems, with inevitable caveats, may match the rigour of the accepted index of literacy.

THE EVIDENCE: PROBATE INVENTORIES

This study is based upon on an examination of 617 probate inventories, detailing the estates of individuals living on the Land's End peninsula in the seventeenth century. Probate inventories have proved to be a most versatile data-source, comprising a listing and valuation of a deceased individual's 'accumulated possessions and holdings whether purchased in a market, produced within the household, or received in kind through barter or as pay'[16] and were intended to supplement the deceased's will in order to 'safeguard the deceased's executors from excessive claims upon the estate, and to protect the next-of-kin from fraud'.[17] Many aspects of early modern life have been identified and examined in the light of information extracted from individual probate inventories, or from collections of these documents.[18] Such studies range from examinations of rural credit networks to investigations of economic imperatives in household production, from 'material culture' and the development of the consumer society, to patterns of leaseholding and the 'consumption of rental property'.[19] Inventories have also formed a vital data-source for major studies of the English agricultural economy in the early modern period, while James Whetter's study of the economic history of seventeenth-century Cornwall derives much of its data from Cornish probate inventories of the period.[20] For local historians in Cornwall, the probate inventories have long been recognised as an invaluable source.

As can be seen from the examples below, probate inventories listed and valued the contents of the dwelling of the deceased, and the accoutrements of his or her work. Inventory appraisers, who constructed these documents, were drawn from amongst the local community, the 'friends and neighbours' of the deceased,[21] and thus the resulting document is informed by close local knowledge of both prevailing market conditions, which determine the values ascribed to assets, and the deceased individual.[22]

The focus of this study is on the systems of numerical representation employed, by 'friends and neighbours', in the compilation of the probate records, charting the diffusion 'on the ground' of the new numbering system at the very periphery of Europe. Such documents as probate inventories, compiled to a standard but flexible format and surviving in large numbers, afford the historian an invaluable glimpse of the everyday experience of the historical community, and lend themselves particularly to the concerns of this article. As the *raison d'être* of the document was the itemisation and valuation of goods and assets numerical systems were necessarily employed. The structure of the documents remains consistent over a long period of time, throughout the seventeenth century and beyond in West Cornwall, allowing longitudinal analyses and comparisons to be made with some confidence. The documents were not, in rural areas, drawn up by professional scribes or appraisers but by diverse and 'amateur' members of the local community, and thus represent the experience of a wider community than that of the professional bureaucrat – 83 appraisers were involved in drawing up 60 inventories from Paul parish between 1600 and 1699. The type of numerical representation to be used in probate inventories was never prescribed by a central authority, and thus the choices made were those of the specific appraisers and scribes. Of course, any study based on probate inventories does not equate with a study of a whole community, but must be selective. Not everyone in any given community made a will or had their estate inventoried, and any 'probate sample' will be biased toward the older and wealthier members of the community; at least one of the appraisers involved in the construction of a probate inventory would have been, necessarily, literate, and thus, in this sense at least, not typical of the whole community.

Two documents, one dating from the beginning and one from the end of the seventeenth century, illustrate the changing nature of documentary numerical representation in seventeenth century West Cornwall. Figure 1 shows the inventory of John Alsa, of Paul parish, drawn up in November 1606, Figure 2 the inventory of John Favell, also of Paul parish, compiled in 1693.[23]

Figure 1 may be regarded as typical of probate inventories from West Cornwall in the first decade of the seventeenth century, as Roman numerals are used to represent the large majority of numerical terms employed, in dating – '*xvii*th daie' – quantification – '*iii* lyttle pannes' – and valuation – '*iis vi*d'. Hindu-Arabic numerals occur in the preamble of the document, where the regnal year given for dating is supplemented by *1606*, and in the valuation column, where the Hindu-Arabic *4*, *6*, and *13* can be observed. This usage of Hindu-Arabic numerals in the valuation column is not consistent, as the use of *iv*, *vi*, and *xiii* demonstrate. Words are occasionally used, as in the '*fourth* yere' and '*one* old tabell bord'.

In Figure 2, the construction of which was undertaken some 87 years after Figure 1, no Roman numerals are employed. The predominant form of numerical expression, particularly in the valuations, is the Hindu-Arabic numeral, which has allowed values to be arranged in headed columns. Hindu-

An Inventorie of all the goodes and Chattels of John Alsa of the pish of Pawle late decessyd prysed by Indifferent men whose names foloweth the xviiith daie of November In the fourth yere of the raigne of our soveraigne Lord James by the grace of god Kyng of England Scotland France and Ireland defender of the fayth 1606

prysed by William Roberts
Arthur Berryman &
Richard Parsons

Item first an old tabell bord & an old form prysed .... iis vid
Item a lytle Crock of brase prysed .... iiis 4d
Item iiii lytle pannes an old lyttle Cawdron & ii lytle skyllet .. xiid
Item iiii platters a pogger a sawser & a tynning candelstick .... iis 6d
Item ii old coffers without lockis prysed .... iis
Item iii lytle tubbes a barell iii dishes & erthing platters .... iis vid
Item a spade a batock a pigooll & a brandish .... xviiid
Item iii bordes or plannckis .... xiid
Item an old canvis sheett a blanket & an old coverlet or cloth . iiiis
Item vi shepe prysed .... xiis
Item a lytle horse prysed .... vis viiid
Item a Cowe a heyfeart of iii yeris old & a
styrre of ii yeres old prysed to .... xlvis
Item a hog & a pig prysed to .... vs
Item iiii hynnes & a cock .... xiid
Item the third of a mowe of Corne & a
lytle corne more prysed to .... iiili 13s 4d
Item the third pt of ii ackers of whet in ground prysed .... xiiis 4d
Item the hocks of a young styrre or oxe prysed to .... xviiis
Item the third pt of the plow & that belonging to it .... xxd
Item the third pt of an harow prysed .... xiid
Item the third pt of a lytle mare prysed .... vis viiid
Item some farshis & canvis prysed .... vs

Summe is .... xli xiid

FIGURE 1

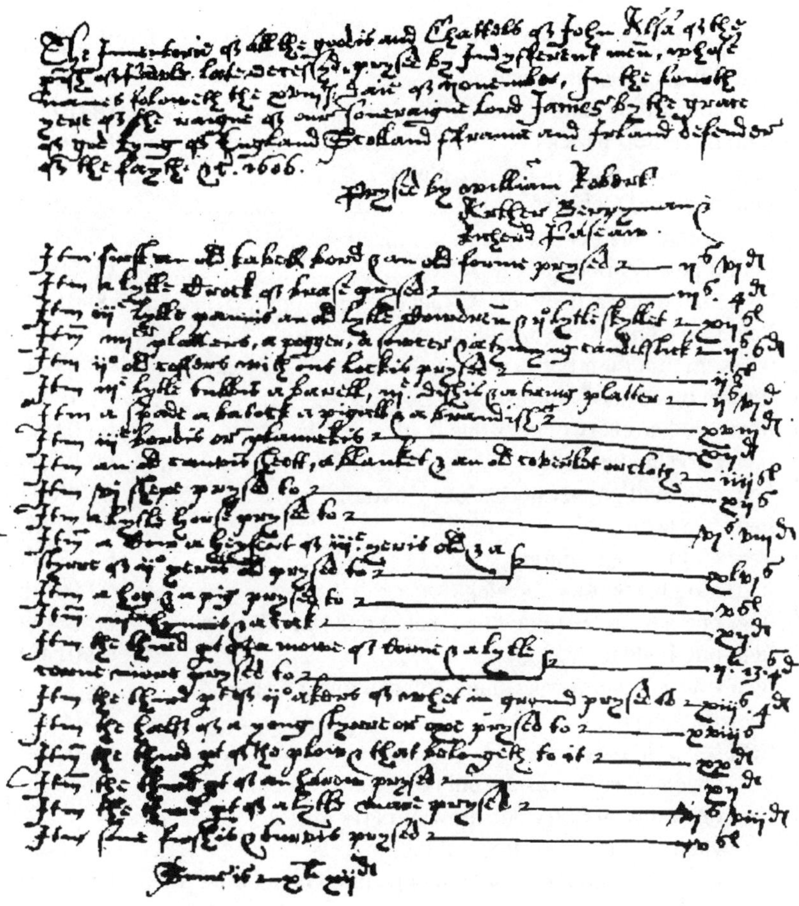

FIGURE 1A:
The inventory of John Alsa of the parish of Paul, 1606. Reproduced courtesy of Cornwall Record Office.

An Inventorie taken the xxvith daye of September 1693 of All the goods and Chattells whcsoever John Favell of Pawle pish in the County of Cornwall yeoman Decessed praysed the day & yeare Above writen by Sampson Huchens and Thomas marrack and other

	£ - s - d
first All his Aparell valued at	01-00-00
Item fowar bras pans valued	01-10-00
Item three bras Crocks	00-10-00
Item 6 pewter platters & three plates	00-02-00
Item one ould Cobbard	00-10-00
Item tenn trenchers	00-00-04
Item 6 pewter spoones	00-00-06
Item som ould earthen pots & som earthen Cops	00-01-00
Item two Chaires one tabel bord one forme & som other tember	00-03-00
Item two bedsteeds furnished	01-10-00
Item two barrels two tobes one boule one Cheese vat	00-03-00
Item two Candlesticks	00-01-00
Item one ould pewter bocar & one bottall	00-00-03
Item one layar & three seefes	00-02-06
Item all his tabell linning	00-03-00
Item too glas bottols obe glas Cop	00-00-02
Item one harrow one plow two matox one shovell hous	00-06-00
Item one Laddar	00-01-00
Item fowar Cows fowar young bolocks fowar Calves & 17 sheepe	12-00-00
Item fowar horses	06-00-00
Item seven piges 7 gees & som other pultry	00-16-00
Item one mow of barly one mow of barly & wheat one mow of otes	10-00-00
Item one small tenement of land depending on an ould life	05-00-00
Item a paire of panyars & some Reings	00-01-00
Item for things forgoten	00-01-00
Total	**39-18-09**

FIGURE 2

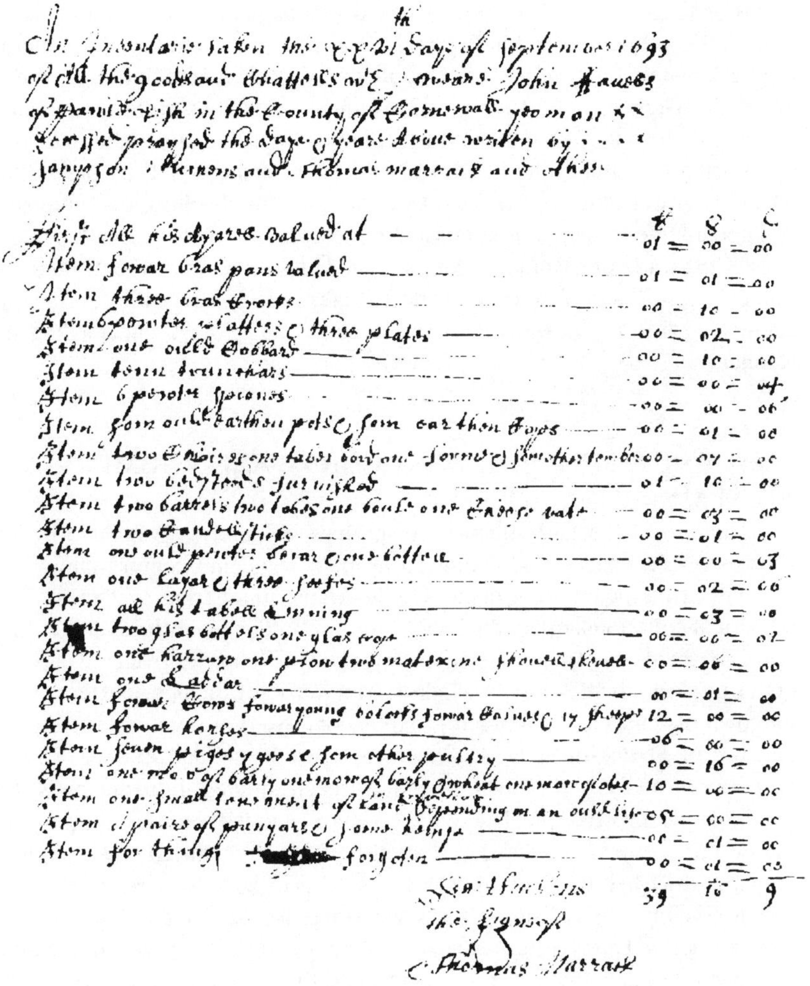

FIGURE 2A:

The inventory of John Favell of the parish of Paul, 1693. Reproduced courtesy of Cornwall Record Office.

Arabic numerals have also been employed in the dating schedule of the document, with the calendar year being expressed as '1693', which contrasts with the 'number-word' expression of the regnal year, supplemented by *1606*, observed in Figure 1, and the day as '26th'. There is a continued use of 'number-words', such as '*fowar*' and '*three*'. It is also notable that the term 'one' is far more frequently employed in Figure 2 – '*one* boule *one* cheese vat' - than in Figure 1, where the use of 'a' is favoured – '*a* spade *a* batock *a* pigooll & *a* brandish'. The zero is used in Figure 2 to indicate no pounds, shillings, or pence – retaining the integrity of the vertical columns for arithmetic addition as well as ensuring the future integrity of the values ascribed to assets by preventing the insertion of further digits. These two examples thus display the common use of three distinct systems of numerical representation in seventeenth century West Cornwall, the Roman numeral, the Hindu-Arabic numeral, and the 'number-word', and, further, indicate changes in usage over the seventeenth century – with the 'new' Hindu-Arabic numbering system superseding the Roman.

ANALYSIS & METHOD: WEST CORNWALL'S NUMERICAL SYSTEMS

Examination of the large quantity of probate inventories generated by the peoples of the Land's End peninsula in the seventeenth century allows the charting of the penetration of the Hindu-Arabic numbering system into the numerical consciousness of the local community. The inventories are divided into two groups, the first group consisting of the inventories from the parishes of St Buryan, Gulval, St Levan, Madron, Morvah, Paul, Sennen, and those from the town of Penzance. A second group is comprised of inventories from the parishes of St Just-in-Penwith, Sancreed, Towednack, and Zennor. For the purposes of analysis the inventories have been divided into four parts: the preamble, which gives the date of the inventory and the names of the praisers; the descriptive text, which describes the goods inventoried; the valuation column, which lists the individual values of items in the inventory; and the total, which gives the sum value of the inventoried assets. For the first group of parishes defined above, the systems of numerical representation employed in each part of the documents in parishes from the first group are outlined in Tables 1a, 1b, 1c, and 1d which clearly demonstrate the replacement of the Roman numerical system by its Hindu-Arabic counterpart over the course of the seventeenth century.

In the following tables:
The ***Roman*** *column shows the number and proportion of inventories which display exclusive use of Roman numerals, which may be supplemented by number-words;*
The ***HinAra*** *column shows the number and proportion of inventories which display the exclusive use of Hindu-Arabic numerals, which may be supplemented by number-words;*
The ***both*** *column shows the number and proportion of inventories which employ both Roman and Hindu-Arabic numerals, a combination which may also be supplemented by number-words;*
The ***only word*** *column shows the number and proportion of inventories which display the exclusive use of number-words;*
The ***also words*** *column shows the number and proportion of inventories which display number-words as well as Roman and/or Hindu-Arabic numerals (****one*** *or* ***a*** *or* ***an*** *are not counted as an 'also-word');*
The ***total*** *column shows the total number of inventories examined.*

TABLE 1a:
Inventory preambles (St Buryan, Gulval, St Levan, Madron, Paul, Penzance, Sennen)

decade	Roman		HinAra		both		only words		also words		total
	n	%	n	%	n	%	n	%	n	%	n
1600-09	1	6.3	5	31.3	10	62.5	-	-	3	18.8	16
1610-19	-	-	6	37.5	10	62.5	-	-	4	25.0	16
1620-29	3	14.3	10	47.6	8	38.1	-	-	4	19.0	21
1630-39	-	-	17	68.0	8	32.0	-	-	3	12.0	25
1640-49	-	-	18	56.3	14	43.7	-	-	5	15.6	32
1650-59	-	-	13	92.9	1	7.1	-	-	4	28.6	14
1660-69	1	1.7	51	86.4	6	10.2	1	1.7	19	32.2	59
1670-79	-	-	44	89.8	2	4.1	3	6.1	11	22.5	49
1680-89	-	-	60	95.2	-	-	3	4.8	18	28.6	63
1690-99	-	-	82	90.1	2	2.2	7	7.7	28	30.8	91
total	5	1.3	306	79.3	63	16.3	14	3.6	99	25.6	386

Table 1a, which is concerned with the inventory preambles, shows clearly that Roman numerals were only rarely the sole system of numerical representation used in the dating of the documents, although they were used in combination with Hindu-Arabic numerals and/or number-words, as was the case in the inventory of John Alsa. In most cases where both systems were used the Roman numerals described the day part of the date, with the Hindu-Arabic system being almost exclusively used in the representation of the year – this practice being apparently well established by the beginning of the seventeenth century. In the few cases in which a praiser used Roman numerals exclusively in the preamble the calendar year is not given, the regnal year being preferred, as in the example of the inventory of Edmond Pewis, of Paul, drawn up on '*xx*th day of September in the fyth yere of the raigne of our sovereign Lord James'.[24] The use of Roman numerals in combination with the other numbering systems becomes increasingly uncommon over the seventeenth century, although they do occasionally appear in the later decades, as in the inventory of John Edwards, of Paul parish, which was compiled on the '*xxiiii*th day of June' in 1696.[25] The decline in the usage of Roman numerals in inventory preambles corresponds with an increase in the use of number-words, which are usually employed to enumerate the day of the month but occasionally delineate the whole date, with the year written out longhand 'One thousand six Hundred sixty-three'.[26] Number-words are also used for clarification – 'Anno domini 1689 Eighty nine'.[27]

TABLE 1b:

Inventory descriptive text (St Buryan, Gulval, St Levan, Madron, Paul, Penzance, Sennen)

decade	Roman		HinAra		both		only words		also words		total
	n	%	n	%	n	%	n	%	n	%	n
1600-09	11	68.7	2	12.5	1	6.3	2	12.5	4	25.0	16
1610-19	7	43.8	3	18.8	2	12.5	4	25.0	6	37.5	16
1620-29	5	23.8	8	38.1	4	19.0	4	19.0	4	19.0	21
1630-39	3	12.0	15	60.0	1	4.0	6	24.0	8	32.0	25
1640-49	-	-	20	62.5	1	3.1	11	34.4	11	34.4	32
1650-59	-	-	5	35.7	-	-	9	64.3	-	-	14
1660-69	-	-	8	13.6	-	-	51	86.4	5	8.5	59
1670-79	-	-	9	18.4	-	-	40	81.6	4	8.2	49
1680-89	-	-	16	25.4	-	-	47	74.6	9	14.3	63
1690-99	-	-	22	24.2	-	-	69	75.8	9	9.9	91
total	26	6.7	108	28.0	9	2.3	243	63.0	60	15.5	386

Two distinct transitional processes can be observed from Table 1b, which shows the systems of numerical representation employed in the descriptive text of the inventories, where assets and goods are quantified. There is a marked decline in the use of Roman numerals, which were predominant only in the first decade of the century and which do not appear at all beyond the 1640s. However, whilst Hindu-Arabic numerals achieve an ascendancy in the 1630s and 1640s it is notable that it is number-words which become the favoured form of numerical representation in these descriptive parts of inventories – 'thirteene sheepe and Lambs'[28] – being exclusively employed in over three quarters of inventories from 1660 onwards, and occasionally being used in combination with Hindu-Arabic numerals.

The analysis of the descriptive text of the inventories shows the very widespread use of 'number-words' in this part of the document, particularly in the later decades of the seventeenth century. Local worthy William Borlase noted, in the mid-eighteenth century, the litigious nature of the Cornish people, engendered, he believed, by the fact that 'in mining as well as fishing there are very numerous and minute subdivisions of property'.[29] The use of number words in the inventories may reflect this litigious nature, longhand expression being utilised to avoid confusion, error, and fraud, as is the case in the writing of cheques today.[30]

TABLE 1c:
Inventory valuation columns (St Buryan, Gulval, St Levan, Madron, Paul, Penzance, Sennen)

decade	Roman		HinAra		both		only words		also words		total
	n	%	n	%	n	%	n	%	n	%	n
1600-09	11	68.8	2	12.5	3	18.7	-	-	-	-	16
1610-19	9	56.3	1	6.3	6	37.4	-	-	-	-	16
1620-29	7	33.3	10	47.6	4	19.1	-	-	-	-	21
1630-39	5	20.0	17	68.0	3	12.0	-	-	-	-	25
1640-49	3	9.4	28	87.5	1	3.1	-	-	-	-	32
1650-59	4	28.6	9	64.3	1	7.1	-	-	-	-	14
1660-69	-	-	55	93.2	4	6.7	-	-	-	-	59
1670-79	1	2.0	46	94.0	1	2.0	1	2.0	-	-	49
1680-89	-	-	63	100.0	-	-	-	-	-	-	63
1690-99	-	-	91	100.0	-	-	-	-	-	-	91
total	40	10.4	322	83.4	23	6.0	1	0.2	-	-	386

Hindu-Arabic numerals appear to have been slower to pervade the valuation columns of inventories than they were the preambles and descriptions, as is shown in Table 1c, first occurring in more than half of inventories in the decade 1620-29. The valuation column, or rather the entries within it, form the basis of the calculation, and the numerals the 'programming language', by which the total value of the inventoried estate is determined. This contrasts with the preambles and descriptions, where numerals are used merely to *express* a number or date, and do not, usually, form part of a calculation. The somewhat retarded trend which can be observed in valuations may indicate that praisers more readily adopted the new numerical system as a 'shorthand' than as a calculating tool. Certainly there are examples in which the praiser adopts Hindu-Arabic numerals in the valuation column to replace numbers whose expression is perhaps 'inefficient' under the Roman system, as in the inventory of John Alsa. Number-words are extremely rare in the valuation column of these inventories, found only in the inventory of Richard Luddra, whose sheep, for example, were valued at 'One Pound, Twelve shillings and sixpence'.[31] Another anomalous case is that of the inventory of Thomas Clyes of Penzance, in which valuations are expressed in both Roman and Hindu-Arabic forms – the Hindu-Arabic form being given to the right of the description, the Roman to the left.[32] By the end of the seventeenth century Hindu-Arabic numerals were the only form of numerical system employed in the valuation part of inventories.

TABLE 1d:
Inventory totals
(St Buryan, Gulval, St Levan, Madron, Paul, Penzance, Sennen)

decade	Roman		HinAra		both		only words		also words		total
	n	%	n	%	n	%	n	%	n	%	n
1600-09	14	87.5	2	12.5	-	-	-	-	-	-	16
1610-19	11	68.8	4	25.0	-	-	1	6.4	-	-	16
1620-29	9	42.9	12	57.1	-	-	-	-	-	-	21
1630-39	6	24.0	18	72.0	1	4.0	-	-	-	-	25
1640-49	4	12.5	18	87.5	-	-	-	-	-	-	32
1650-59	4	28.6	10	71.4	-	-	-	-	-	-	14
1660-69	-	-	57	96.6	2	3.4	-	-	1	1.7	59
1670-79	1	2.0	48	98.0	-	-	-	-	-	-	49
1680-89	-	-	62	98.4	-	-	1	0.6	-	-	63
1690-99	-	-	91	100.00	-	-	-	-	-	-	91
total	49	12.8	322	83.4	3	0.8	2	0.5	1	0.3	386

Table 1d shows that the total value of inventoried assets was expressed in Hindu-Arabic numerals in the majority of cases from the 1620s onwards, and that the new numerical system is more rapidly assimilated in totals than in the valuations, with a number of inventories displaying valuations in Roman numerals and totals in the Hindu-Arabic system. This tends to support the contention above, that the Hindu-Arabic system was adopted initially for ease of expression and was only later adopted as a 'programming language', as the given total is an expression of a result of a calculation, and does not itself form part of a calculation. Word-number expression is very rare in the 'total' part of inventories – the inventory of Richard Trevailer of Gulval gives the total in the form 'the whole thirty eight pounds', whilst Thomas Jenkin's inventory, which extends onto a second page, shows a sub-total of 'twenty-five pounds five shillings & eightpence' at the foot of the first page.[33]

The data from the second group of parishes is not as full as that from the first group, as it was taken from transcripts in which the numbers in the valuation column had been standardised on the Hindu-Arabic system in the process of transcription.[34] It was possible, however, to augment this investigation into the nature of numerical representation by examining the numbering systems used in the descriptive body of the inventories, the results being shown in Table 2.

TABLE 2:
Inventory descriptive text
(St Just-in-Penwith, Sancreed, Towednack, Zennor)

decade	Roman		HinAra		both		only words		also words		total
	n	%	n	%	n	%	n	%	n	%	n
1600-09	9	36.0	7	28.0	7	28.0	2	8.0	10	40.0	25
1610-19	3	14.3	9	42.9	5	23.0	4	19.8	7	33.3	21
1620-29	1	8.3	8	66.7	1	8.3	2	16.7	1	8.3	12
1630-39	-	-	14	63.6	2	9.1	6	27.3	3	13.6	22
1640-49	1	4.4	17	73.9	1	4.4	4	17.4	13	56.5	23
1650-59	-	-	-	-	-	-	2	100.0	-	-	2
1660-69	2	7.4	9	33.3	-	-	16	59.3	5	18.5	27
1670-79	-	-	8	38.1	-	-	13	61.9	5	23.8	21
1680-89	-	-	12	38.7	-	-	19	61.3	10	32.3	31
1690-99	-	-	22	46.8	-	-	25	53.2	11	23.4	47
total	16	6.9	106	45.9	16	6.9	93	40.3	65	28.1	231

THE NATURE & EXPERIENCE OF NUMERICAL CHANGE

The diffusion of the Hindu-Arabic system was the result of a series of decisions made by a number of scribes who wrote out the individual probate inventories. Although it is probable that the numerical system chosen in each case reflected the preference of the individual writer, it is possible that the scribe acted in accordance with the collective wish of the praisers, of which he was usually one.[35] Deeper insight into the process whereby Roman numerals were supplanted in this context can be obtained only by investigating the techniques employed in the construction of these documents and the practises of individual scribes who created them.

Aspects of the nature of the process of transition may be illuminated by a close examination of certain of the inventories from the first three decades of the seventeenth century, this period being identified as the period of changeover in numerical systems. The proportion of inventories displaying, in all parts of the document, the exclusive use of Roman numerals shrinks from decade to decade. In the decade 1630-39 two-thirds of inventories display the consistent use of Hindu-Arabic numerals in preambles, descriptions,[36] valuations and totals. The following section of this discussion is based on the eighteen of the 53 inventories from the first three decades of the century which employ both

Hindu-Arabic and Roman numerals in their descriptions, valuations, or totals – four from 1600-09, eight from 1610-19, and six from 1620-29 – these documents embodying the fulcrum of change as the praisers or scribes demonstrated varying degrees of facility and familiarity with both numerical systems. The use of numerical systems in the descriptions and valuations in each of these 18 inventories can be seen on Table 3.

The four inventories written in the first decade of the seventeenth century share two important features: first, the zero was not used at all; and, second, the valuations were not listed in directly vertical columns. All seven occurrences of Hindu-Arabic number expression in descriptions in the four inventories from the first decade of the century are found in one document, that of Thomas Carne of St Buryan, from 1605,[37] which also includes five numbers expressed in Roman numerals but no word- numbers. Whilst Carne's inventory is the only one of the four to employ Hindu-Arabic numerals in the descriptive text it is also the only one *not* to employ Hindu-Arabic numerals in the valuations. The most commonly used Hindu-Arabic numeral in the four documents is the 4, which occurs 9 times[38] in valuations, 8 is used four times in the inventory of John Bodiner, with 6 and 13 making single appearances in the inventory of John Alsa. Further evidence of the transitional nature of this period is the inconsistency of the scribes who drew up these documents, all using both systems to express the same numbers within each document – in John Bodiner's inventory *iiii* is used twice and *viii* twice, for example.[39]

In the second decade of the century , the most marked development in the use of numerical systems was the use of the zero, which occurs thirty times, accounting for nearly half of all Hindu-Arabic numerals used. Other Hindu-Arabic numerals were employed alongside Roman numerals in the descriptive texts of six of the eight inventories from the second decade of the century, although Roman numerals were dominant in most cases. Hindu-Arabic numerals were used commonly in combination with Roman numerals in the same value expression '*xxvis* 8d',[40] as well as on their own 'one oxe & ii steeres *6*li 1*10*s'.[41] The most marked development in the use of numerical systems over the earlier decade can be seen in the use of the Hindu-Arabic zero, which occurs thirty times, accounting for nearly half of all Hindu-Arabic numerals used. Other than zero the most commonly used Hindu-Arabic numeral is the *4*, used on fifteen occasions in five inventories; *8* is used five times, in two inventories; *6*, *10*, and *18* are all used four times each,[42] with *5* occurring three times, in two inventories.[43]

The choice of Roman or Hindu-Arabic numerals appears to have been made in a more consistent manner in the second decade of the century than was the case in the first, with four inventories showing, for example, the exclusive use of *4*. One other document displays the Hindu-Arabic *4* fives times and the Roman *iv* twice. However, only one inventory displays more Hindu-Arabic than Roman numerals in the valuation column – that of Michael Thomas (Paul,

TABLE 3:
Inventories which use Roman and Hindu-Arabic numerals 1600-29 (St Buryan, Gulval, St Levan, Madron, Paul, Penzance, Sennen)

				Numeric expressions in:				
				descriptive text			**valuations**	
				Roman	**HinAra**	**words**	**Roman**	**HinAra**
inventory				**n**	**n**	**n**	**n**	**n**
CARNE, Thomas	St Buryan	1605		5	7	0	16	-
BODINER, John	Paul	1605		9	-	7	29	9
ALSA, John	Paul	1605		12	-	-	25	5
PEWIS, Edmond	Paul	1607		9	-	2	29	1
1600-1609				35	7	9	99	15
MORISHE, Richard	Madron	1611		2	1	1	12	2
SAMPSON, John	Penzance	1612		3	24	50	32	25*
ARGOLLS, Jennet	Madron	1612		2	3	-	13	5*
RICHARDS, John	Paul	1614		18	1	-	15	7
TRESIZE, Walter	Penzance	1618		2	-	-	5	3
THOMAS, Michael	Paul	1618		18	2	8	11	24
PERSE, Margaret	Paul	1619		13	4	2	19	10
CLEMMOWE, John	Gulval	1619		3	-	19	49	-
1610-1619				61	35	80	156	76
GREENE, William	Penzance	1621		17	2	-	29	3
BODINER, Martin	Paul	1621		5	4	3	12	22
GALE, Katherine	Paul	1624		4	-	1	2	18
HARRIE, Richard	Paul	1624		3	2	5	2	18
BAGGES, Thomas	Penzance	1628		-	27	-	34	39
HARRIE, Marten	Paul	1629		1	13	6	-	89a
1620-1629				30	48	15	79	189
1600-1629				134	90	104	334	280
* - all zeros								
a - 51 zeros								

A numeric expression is defined as a single number, which may form part of a value expression e.g. the **iis vid** on the sixth line of the John Alsa inventory consists of two numbers **ii** and **vi**.

1, **i**, **one**, **a**, or **an** are not counted.

1618), where there are 24 Hindu-Arabic numbers and 11 Roman. It is notable that all of the 11 Roman numerals are found in the upper part of the valuation listing, not occurring at all below the eleventh line of a 31 line listing, the praisers or scribe having apparently abandoned the old system and adopted the new in the process of drawing up this inventory.[44] There appears to have been no systematic attempt, in any of the eight inventories, to arrange the valuations in dedicated vertical columns.

By the third decade of the century Hindu-Arabic numerals had become the dominant form of numerical representation, being more commonly employed than either Roman numerals or word-numbers, though a degree of inconsistency remained. In only one case, that of the inventory of William Greene, are there more Roman numerals than Hindu-Arabic. Its scribe used Hindu-Arabic numerals for 4 on three occasions and the Roman *iiii* once. In Thomas Bagges' inventory 39 Hindu-Arabic zeros outnumber 34 Roman numerals. In the four remaining inventories' valuation columns Roman numerals are the minority form of numerical expression, being used for just 16 out of 163 (9.8%) numerical expressions.[45] The most commonly used Roman numeral in these four inventories is *ii*, occurring six times in two inventories. The praisers were consistent within documents in their expression of *two*, which occurs 13 times in the four inventories, making exclusive use of one form or the other. This consistency of use is reflected throughout the range of numbers expressed, and on only four occasions are both systems used in the same valuation listing.[46] Of seventeen numerical values which were expressed as Hindu-Arabic numerals eleven were rendered exclusively in the new format, while only fifteen was represented as the Roman *xv* – once in this collection of documents.

The patterns outlined above suggest a creeping advance in the usage of Hindu-Arabic numerals over the first three decades of the seventeenth century. Praisers adopt Hindu-Arabic numerals as alternatives to the Roman for some numbers, such as four and eight, with the alternative Hindu-Arabic expression becoming a replacement for the Roman over the early decades of the seventeenth century. This replacement process may have had a purely ergonomic rationale initially, with the Hindu-Arabic forms *4* and *8*, for example, requiring fewer pen strokes than their Roman counterparts. Praisers with the facility to make use of both numerical systems increasingly favoured the Hindu-Arabic system, and used it to express a widening variety of numerical terms, thereby reaping the other benefits of the system – such as the arrangement of values in vertical columns facilitated by the 'place-value' attributes of Hindu-Arabic numerals, and by the zero.

Inventory appraisers usually worked in pairs, sometimes in threes, and very occasionally there were four or more appraisers. The documents give no indication of which of the praisers actually wrote, or scribed, the inventory. However, it has proved possible to identify eight praiser-scribes who were active in the first three decades of the seventeenth century, and who were also responsible for scribing more than one inventory. Where inventories have a common praiser and the same handwriting it is assumed that the common praiser wrote both documents. Details of these scribes, and the numerical systems they employed, are given in Table 4 below.

Three of the identified praisers, Tudgio, Ford, and Trithall, employed no Hindu-Arabic numerals at all, using Roman numerals, word-numbers, or a combination thereof in their descriptions of the estates and Roman numerals only in valuation. Inventories drawn up in the manner employed by Robert Trithall, making exclusive use of Roman numerals, were in the minority when he scribed the inventory of Thomas Drewe in 1626. Marrack and Berryman used a few Hindu-Arabic numerals in their respective documents, and the inventory of John Alsa, given in illustration, is typical – displaying, for example, the use of *4* as an alternative expression of *iiii*. The documents drawn up by these five men suggest that they had only a slight familiarity with the Hindu-Arabic numerical system. They made marginal use of its expressive attributes and did not exploit its possibilities in arithmetic.

The remaining three inventory praisers, Chergwin, Dunking, and Keigwyn, all showed a facility for both numbering systems. The first of Chergwin's inventories, of John Sampson's estate in February 1612/13, displays his awareness of the Hindu-Arabic system. He numbered each line in the inventory, at its left margin, with Hindu-Arabic numerals, also using them within the descriptive text. In the valuation column he employed Roman numerals with zeros. It appears that Chergwin was in the process of assimilating the Hindu-Arabic numerical system when he drew up the 1612/13 document, using it confidently for expression and having grasped the function of the zero. In the second inventory scribed by Chergwin, some 21 months later in November 1614, all numerical expressions are in the Hindu-Arabic form, Chergwin having adopted the new system of arithmetic as well as the new system of expression.[47] John Dunking made exclusive use of Roman numerals in 1616, much later exclusively employing, in 1628, Hindu-Arabic numerals. Richard Keigwyn was not so coherent in his use of numerical systems, being responsible for the inventory of Michael Thomas in March 1618/19, in which the numerical system changes a third of the way down the valuation. Later the same year Keigwyn mixed, seemingly randomly, Roman and Hindu-Arabic numerals throughout the inventory of Margaret Perse. He used no zeros in either inventory, did not organise valuations in direct columns, and employed both systems, apparently indiscriminately, to represent numbers from throughout the value range.

TABLE 4:
Inventory praisers' careers 1600-29 (St Buryan, Gulval, St Levan, Madron, Paul, Penzance, Sennen)

		Numeric expressions in:				
		descriptive text			valuations	
		Roman	HinAra	words	Roman	HinAra
praiser	inventory (CRO Prob.)	n	n	n	n	n
TUDGIO, Thomas	ALGAR, W. Mad. 1605	2	-	5	14	-
	MULFRA, J. Mad. 1605/6	-	-	5	13	-
MARRACK, Richard	BODINER, J. Paul 1605	9	-	7	29	9
	PEWIS, E. Paul 1607	12	-	-	25	5
BERRYMAN, Arthur	ALSA, J. Paul 1606	12	-	-	25	5
	TREGERAS, J. Paul 1614	18	1	-	15	7
FORD, Richard	FORSE, T. Gul. 1611	-	-	9	28	-
	MORTEN, J. Gul. 1612	6	-	25	54	-
CHERGWIN, John	SAMPSON, J. Pz. 1612	3	24	50	32	25
	SAMPSON, K. Pz. 1614	-	63	-	-	159
DUNKING, John	GAME, R. Pz. 1616	5	-	-	28	-
	THOMAS, J. Pz. 1628	-	5	-	-	18
KEIGWYN, Richard	THOMAS, M. Paul 1618/9	18	2	8	11	24
	PERSE, M. Paul 1619	13	4	2	19	10
TRITHALL, Robert	CLEMMOW, J. Gul. 1619	3	-	21	55	-
	DREWE, T. Mad. 1626	2	-	5	23	-

THE 'NATIONAL' CONTEXT OF LOCAL CHANGE

The general trend which can be observed from the evidence presented here is one in which the use of Roman numerals became increasingly infrequent, the period of transition from Roman to Hindu-Arabic systems being focussed in the early decades of the seventeenth century. Indeed, it was only in the first decade of the century that Roman numerals appear in a majority of inventories from both sample groups. This trend mirrors, broadly, those observed elsewhere for Lincolnshire and Bristol although some differences may be observed in the detail. In the other regions examined the period of transition from the use of Roman numerals in inventories to the use of Hindu-Arabic numerals was rooted in the 1620s and 1630s, a decade or so later than appears to have been the case in West Cornwall, where the transition was focussed in the first and second decades of the seventeenth century. This suggests a slight 'technological lead' in West Cornwall, although the small size of the sample means that the existence of such a lead must remain a possibility only.

It is regrettable that just a single inventory survives for West Cornwall from the period before 1600,[48] frustrating the fuller elucidation of the process of transition which was possible for Clee and Bristol. The sample from West Cornwall also yields fuller data from the Interregnum period of the 1650s than do the collections from Clee and Bristol, particularly in the Table 1 group of parishes – which, further, show something of a 'recovery' in the usage of Roman numerals in this uncertain period of political dislocation.[49]

ECHOES & FEEDBACKS: CONCOMITANT REGIONAL TRENDS

An analysis of the structures of society and economy in West Cornwall in this period has suggested that this remote, upland and insular region of Celtic Britain was beginning to show signs of nascent 'modernisation', of structural economic change and of an increasing intrusion of the English language as it came to challenge Cornish in its heartland. Population was expanding rapidly, and communities were engaged increasingly in rural industry, particularly in the burgeoning tin mining sector. The region was becoming reliant on external markets – for corn and textile goods, for example, which had previously been supplied from local resources – with households adopting consumer imperatives in the provision of basic needs as the communities' endeavours were focussed in specialised pastoral agriculture, and in the tin, fishing and service industries. Marriage registers from the region's parishes show that what had been rather 'closed' communities were becoming more open over the seventeenth century and beyond, with a growing proportion of local brides and grooms taking partners from outside their immediate area; further, the rhythms of the agricultural calendar were loosening their grip on the timing of marriage, suggesting changing patterns of local employment.[50]

Over the seventeenth century, and into the eighteenth, as noted above, there were some significant alterations in the nature of household economies in West Cornwall, most notably as a result of an increasing engagement with markets. When production is geared toward sale for profit rather than domestic consumption, and needs are met through purchase rather than domestic production, it may be the case that a more acute perception of value develops within the communities concerned. Indeed, money itself becomes a commodity in the region, with inventories revealing a proliferation of small scale lending and borrowing, and lending and leaseholding supplant the purchase of precious metals as the major investment medium for households over this period.[51] Such economic changes, it may be hazarded, would demand a level of numerical awareness and facility not demanded by a subsistence economy, such numerical awareness being, perhaps, both fostered and evinced by the spread of the Hindu-Arabic numerical system.[52] Where a community experienced increased engagement with numerical concepts, and where arithmetic manipulations became an evermore vital part of economic life there was, probably, an increased demand placed upon its literate and numerate elite. One response may have been an increased willingness amongst the elite to accept a simpler system and one which, in the long run, would prove to be more efficient. In this sense the transformation of numerical representation recorded in the documents which captured aspects of life and death may also have represented and facilitated some kind of 'democratisation' of the written use of numbers.

It would appear from the Tables 1b and 2 that the parish communities of St Just, Sancreed, Towednack and Zennor embraced the new numbering system rather more readily than did their neighbours. This feature might be explained by the economic structures which prevail across the two groups. Of the 83 seventeenth century inventories from the region which indicate engagement in the tin mining industry 69 are of estates in the parishes of St Just, Sancreed, Towednack and Zennor – accounting for almost a third of the sample from these parishes (32.2%).[53] Thus, whilst these four parishes provide 34.2% of all the inventories in the whole sample they also provide 83.1% of the inventories of industrial workers. Recent research has suggested that parts of the tin mining industry were rather slow to adopt new technologies over the seventeenth and eighteenth centuries[54] – whilst this may indeed be the case in West Cornwall where mining, smelting and organisational technologies are concerned this study suggests that these particular rural-industrial communities were more prepared to adopt the new numbering system than were the more determinedly agrarian communities in the same region – just 16.7% of inventories from the first group of parishes indicate any engagement in tin-mining.[55] Aside from the practicalities of mining and smelting tin mining had, by this period, developed into a most complicated endeavour, requiring the establishment of partnerships for the raising of start-up capital, corollary embroilment in complex networks of credit, speculation and debt, and engagement in somewhat arcane marketing structures.[56] A 'disembodied' technology such as a numbering system with 'enormous advantages for accounting, measuring, and calculating' could prove very attractive to communities engaged in the tin mining industry.

SUMMARY COMMENTS

To reprise, it appears that, over the course of the seventeenth century, the communities of West Cornwall fully adopted a new system of numerical representation, one which, arguably, gave greater access to the arithmetical skills of calculation than did the one it replaced. Whilst conditions in West

Cornwall may have been inimical to such 'embodied' technologies as were developing elsewhere in mining regions, and also, in this period, to consumer goods, this particular 'disembodied' numbering technology flourished. In the context of Europe the adoption of the Hindu-Arabic numbering system was 'late',[57] although perhaps not so tardy in West Cornwall as elsewhere. However, whilst the adoption of the Hindu-Arabic numerical system may have been late, its assimilation by communities was rapid, particularly so in West Cornwall. The process of change appears to have been one in which the expressive attributes of the Hindu-Arabic system were recognised first, its advantages for calculation being exploited slightly later. The penetration of this numbering technology in West Cornwall did not occur smoothly, with apparently varying rates of diffusion within the region conditioned by the wider economic concerns of communities. A glance at other documents shows that Hindu-Arabic numerals were 'available', and were used, in the region in the 1570s, for instance in the marriage register of Madron parish.[58] If this is taken, in the absence of any other evidence and for the sake of argument, to be the earliest usage of Hindu-Arabic numerals in the region it can be seen that within around six decades, from 1570 to 1630, the community had absorbed a new system of numerical expression, a new 'programming language' for the manipulation of numerical concepts. This sixty-year period represents, approximately, the passing of two generations. Those who learnt their 'three R's' in the late sixteenth century, and who were subsequently engaged as occasional scribes and praisers in the early years of the seventeenth century, favoured the Roman system. These individuals served as the educators of the next generation, and had to assimilate the 'new' technology of Hindu- Arabic numerals in order to pass it on to those who praised and scribed from the 1620s and 1630s. It is interesting to note that at least a few praisers retained a facility for the Roman system into the 1650s and beyond, suggesting that both systems continued to be taught for some time after the hegemony of the Hindu-Arabic system was established. The diffusion of the new system of numerical representation not only provided access to a technology which appears to have been more efficient, but it also allowed a choice of technique which has persisted to the present.

NOTES AND REFERENCES

1. See W. Balchin, *The Cornish Landscape*, London, 1983, pp.81-85.
2. The eleven parishes examined in this study were all recorded in the early eighteenth century as being 'the places in Cornwall that at this day retain the Ancient language'; E. Lhuyd, *Archaeologica Britannia*, 1707. He also notes that 'there's no Cornish Man but speaks good English', p.253.
3. R. Burt, 'The International Diffusion of Technology in the Early Modern Period: The Case of the British Non-ferrous Mining Industry', *Economic History Review*, XLIV: 2, 1991.

4. Goods such as books, pictures, looking glasses and table linen, for instance, are far less commonly listed in inventories from West Cornwall than they are in English inventories. A study of a 'national' sample of probate inventories has revealed that 43% of inventories from 1675-1695 list table linen, 27% list looking glasses, 18% list books and 8% list pictures. See L. Weatherhill, *Consumer Behaviour and Material Culture in Britain, 1660-1760*, London, 1988, Table 2.1, p.26. 18.8% of rural inventories from West Cornwall list table linen 1650-1699, 4.4% list books, one West Cornwall inventory lists a looking glass, with none listing pictures; see D. Cullum, 'Society and Economy in West Cornwall c1588-1750', unpub. Phd, University of Exeter, 1994, Table 2.21: Household Goods in Rural Inventories 1650-1699.
5. J. Mokyr, *The Lever of Riches: Technological Creativity and Economic Progress*, Oxford, 1990, p.74.
6. See P. Wardley, 'Dead Reckoning to Count the Change: Number and Numerical Representation in the Early Modern Period', unpub. paper presented to Economic and Social Research Council Quantitative Economic and Social History Meeting, University of York, September, 1993; P. Wardley, 'Quantitative Analysis, Numerical Data and Local History', in A. Brown, K. Schurer, P. Wakelyn (eds.), *New Directions in Local and Regional History: The Impact of Historical Computing*, Leicester, forthcoming.
7. K. Thomas, 'Numeracy in Early Modern England', *Transactions of the Royal Historical Society*, 37, 1987.
8. P. Laslett, *The World We Have Lost*, London, 1965, p.207.
9. As an example, the ability to read gave the farmer access to the 'greatly increased volume of agricultural literature which was published in the mid and later seventeenth century': C. Clay, *Economic Expansion and Social Change: England, 1500-1700*, Cambridge, 1984, Vol.I, p.131.
10. B. van der Waerden and M. Folkerts, *History of Mathematics: Counting, Numerals and Caluclation 3: Written Numbers*, 1976, p.54.
11. Mokyr, 1990, p.74.
12. For example, using Hindu-Arabic numerals any number between 100 and 999 can be represented by three characters – as opposed to the situation with Roman numerals. Consider the extreme example of the number 888, or dccclxxxviii.
13. W. Kempe, *The Art of Arithmeticke in Whole Numbers and Fractions . . .*, 1592; cited in J. Fauvel and J. Gray, *The History of Mathematics: A Reader*, London, 1987, p.289.
14. For example, G.F. Hill, *The Development of Arabic Numerals in Europe*, 1915; H. Jenkinson, 'The Use of Arabic and Roman Numerals in English Archives', *The Antiquaries Journal*, 67.
15. For example, R.S. Schofield, 'Dimensions of Illiteracy 1750-1850', *Explorations in Economic History*, 10, 1973; E.G. West, 'Progress in Artisan Literacy from 1790', *Economic History Review*, 31, 1978; R.C. Russell, *A History of Schools and Education in Lindsey, Lincolnshire, 1800-1902: The Foundation and Maintenance of Schools for the Poor*, Lincoln, 1965.
16. A. Hanson-Jones, 'Estimating the Wealth of the Living from a Probate Sample', *Journal of Interdisciplinary History*, 13.
17. M. Havinden (ed.), *Household and Farm Inventories in Oxfordshire 1550-1590*, London, 1965, p.1.

18. See M. Overton, *A Bibliography of British Probate Inventories*, Newcastle, 1983.
19. See, for example, C. Clay, 'Lifeleasehold in the Western Counties of England 1650-1750', *Agricultural History Review*, 29, 1981; P. Frost, 'Yeomen and Metalsmiths: Livestock in the Dual Economy of South Staffordshire 1560-1720', *Agricultural History Review*, 29, 1981; B. Holderness, 'Credit in English Rural Society Before the Nineteenth Century, with Special Reference to the Period 1650-1720', *Agricultural History Review*, 24, 1976; M. Overton and B. Campbell, 'Norfolk Livestock Farming 1250-1740: a Comparative Study of Manorial Accounts and Probate Inventories', *Journal of Historical Geography*, 4, 1992; C. Shammas, *The Pre-industrial Consumer in England and America*, Oxford, 1990; M. Spufford, *Contrasting Communities: English Villagers in the Sixteenth and Seventeenth Centuries*, Cambridge, 1974; A. Urdank, 'The Consumption of Rental Property: Gloucestershire Plebeians and the Market Economy 1750-1800', *Journal of Interdisciplinary History*, 21, 1990; D. Vaisey, 'Probate Inventories and Provincial Retailers in the Seventeenth Century', in P. Riden (ed.), *Probate Records and the Local Community*, Gloucester, 1985; Weatherill, 1988.
20. See E. Kerridge, *The Agricultural Revolution*, London,1967; J. Thirsk (ed.), *The Agrarian History of England and Wales: Vol.04:1540-1640*, Cambridge, 1967, *Vol.5 1640-1750*, Cambridge, 1984; J. Whetter, *Cornwall in the Seventeenth Century: An Economic History of Kernow*, Padstow, 1974.
21. Havinden, 1965, p.1.
22. For a more detailed discussion of the nature of probate inventories see J. Cox, 'Probate Inventories: The Legal Background - Parts 1 and 2', *Local Historian*, 16:3&4, 1984; N. Cox and J. Cox, 'Valuations in Probate Inventories: Parts 1 and 2', *Local Historian* 16:8, 1985, and 17:2, 1986.
23. Cornwall Record Office (CRO hereafter) probate, ALSA, John, Paul parish, 1606; CRO Probate, FAVELL, John, Paul parish, 1693.
24. CRO Probate, PEWIS, Edmond, Paul parish, 1608.
25. CRO Probate, EDWARDS, John, Paul parish, 1696.
26. CRO Probate, TRESILGAN, James, St Buryan parish, 1663.
27. CRO Probate, HUTCHENS, John, Paul parish, 1689/90.
28. CRO Probate, LUDDRA, Richard, Madron parish, 1674.
29. W. Borlase, *The Natural History of Cornwall*, 1763, pp.306-7.
30. Italian authorities attempted to prohibit the use of Hindu-Arabic numerals in banking, in the late thirteenth century, on the grounds that they were more liable to fraudulent alteration than were Roman numerals. Mokyr, 1990, p.179.
31. CRO Probate, LUDDRA, 1674.
32. CRO Probate, CLYES, Thomas, Penzance, 1644. The total is given in Hindu-Arabic numerals only.
33. CRO Probate, TREVAILER, Richard, Gulval parish, 1686; JENKIN, Thomas, Penzance, 1662.
34. The transcripts were prepared for a project which had no relation to this study. The standardisation of the numbers in the valuation column provides on object lesson in transcription practice, the transcriber having failed to anticipate possible future uses of the transcripts and thus compromising veracity with expedience. The transcripts were prepared for eventual rendering into a machine readable form, and the conversion of Roman to Hindu-Arabic numerals in this process is an

example of 'pre-coding', described by Kevin Schurer as a 'necessary evil' as '[If] pre-coding has been carried out and the codes are all that the secondary researcher has at his disposal, then the data file will only be as good as the codes that have been used': K. Schurer, 'The Historical Researcher and Codes: Master and Slave or Slave and Master', in E. Mawdsley, N. Morgan, L. Richmond, L. and R. Trainor (eds.), *Historians, Computers and Data: Applications in Research and Training*, Manchester, 1990, pp.74-82. The guilty party in this case is Dr D. Cullum.

35. All the scribes identified here were praisers and were male.
36. Table 1b shows that just 60% of inventories employ Hindu-Arabic numerals exclusively in their descriptive text. However, only three-quarters of inventories from 1630-39 employ any system of symbolic numeric representation, with six of the 25 inventories using number-words only. Of the 19 inventories which use symbolic numerals, 15 (78.9%) use Hindu-Arabic numerals exclusively.
37. CRO Probate, CARNE, Thomas, St Buryan parish, 1605.
38. Five times in the inventory of John Bodiner, three times in that of John Alsa, once in the inventory of Edmond Pewis. CRO Probate, BODINER, John, Paul parish, 1605; ALSA, 1606; PEWIS, 1607.
39. Alsa's praisers use *iiii* once, *vi* four times, and *xii* once; Pewis' inventory includes three occurrences of *iiii.*
40. CRO Probate, TREGERAS, John, Paul parish, 1614.
41. CRO Probate, TREGERAS, 1614.
42. *6* in two inventories, *10* in three inventories, *18* in two inventories.
43. *3, 7, 30* each occur twice, *3, 9, 12, 16, 20,* and *24* each occur once.
44. CRO Probate, THOMAS, Michael, Paul parish, 1618.
45. Or 16/112 (14.3%) if the 51 zeros are excluded. CRO Probate, BODINER, Martin, Paul, 1621; GALE, Katherine, Penzance, 1624; HARRIE, Richard, Paul parish, 1624; HARRIE, Marten, Paul parish, 1629.
46. The praisers of Martin Bodiner used *6* three times and *vi* once, *10* four times and *x* twice; those of Richard Harrie used *3* twice and *iii* once.
47. Further evidence would be required to determine if this was the John Chergwin whose diverse economic interests, including a town house and extensive business and property holdings in Penzance, were recorded in a Sancreed inventory dated 1637. The Sancreed Chergwin was notable for experimenting with the wheel – a neglected technology in West Cornwall in this period – and the establishment of a link between 'embodied' and 'disembodied' technological assimilation could be highly revealing.
48. CRO Probate, WEAREN, Richard, Gulval parish, 1578/9.
49. Wardley, 1993; Wardley, forthcoming.
50. See Cullum, 1994, and A. Kussmaul, *A General View of the Rural Economy of England 1538-1840*, Cambridge, 1991, for the seminal elucidation of the links between marriage seasonality and regional employment structures.
51. See Cullum, 1994, Table 1.20, Table 2.20, 18.4% of inventories list debts owed to the estate in the period 1600-49, 36% list debts owed in the period 1650-99. A base 10 numbering system would appear to possess inherent advantages for the calculation of interest, perhaps rendering lending a surer proposition. Lending and leaseholding supplant the purchase of silver as the major investment medium for households over this period – an abstract investment replacing the tangible – facilitated by Roman/Hindu-Arabic shift?

52. This is not to suggest an inherent lack of arithmetic facility in subsistence economies, rather that such a facility – along with the ability to express it in writing – becomes a more vital attribute as the orientation of household economies shifted from subsistence to market imperatives.
53. That is inventories in which the deceased is described as a 'tinner' or which list some capital goods associated with tin mining.
54. Burt, 1991. Burt makes the case that various 'new', particularly German, mining technologies did not necessarily have utility in the tin mining sector, or were not, in fact, new, or were too expensive to implement in the early modern period. He notes, however, that whilst 'many [mines] remained small in scale and simple in their technology' a small number of mines 'grew large and used techniques as up-to-date as those found anywhere in the world'. West Cornwall appears not to have been one of those regions which possessed 'the new large-scale, high-tech, high investment enterprises', but one which, for a variety of possible reasons, was endowed with the 'older, smaller, traditional mines' – at least until the middle of the eighteenth century.
55. There is little substantive difference between the inventories of those engaged in tin-mining and those who were merely farmers. Almost a quarter of tinner inventories (19/83, 22.9%) are identified by qualitative indicators alone i.e. the deceased is described in the preamble as a 'tinner' but holds no capital associated with tin mining. In the vast majority of cases the monetary value of tin mining capital is slight, and forms only a small proportion of the inventoried value of the estate. There is some evidence which suggests that tin miners were often younger members of the community: see Cullum, 1994, Tables 1.16 and 2.16.
56. See R. Pennington, *Stannary Law: A History of the Mining Law of Cornwall and Devon*, Newton Abbot, 1973.
57. Fauvel and Gray, 1987, p.240.
58. G. Millett (ed.), *The First Book of the Parish Registers of Madron in the County of Cornwall*, Penzance, 1877. The frontispiece of this volume shows a photograph of the marriage register open at year 1571, with the year and dates entered using Hindu-Arabic numerals. Contrasting with this case is that of the Gulval parish register, where Roman numerals were employed at least until the first years of the seventeenth century. W. Bolitho and G. Millett (eds.), *The Parish Registers of Gulval (alias Lanisley)*, Penzance, 1893. The transcript registers in this volume show the use of Roman numerals up until the middle of 1600, with Hindu-Arabic numerals employed thereafter.

DEFINING THE GROUP: NINETEENTH-CENTURY CORNISH ON THE NORTH AMERICAN MINING FRONTIER

Ronald M. James

INTRODUCTION

Popular opinion in the Western United States during the nineteenth century held that immigrants from Cornwall were the most qualified of all miners. Sojourners from Cornwall also formed one of the region's better known ethnic groups, complementing a kaleidoscope of international representatives. North Americans, particularly those of northern European ancestry, used linguistic, cultural, and physical clues to distinguish immigrants from Italians and Greeks to Hispanics and Asians. Subjecting the new arrivals to stereotypes and prejudice followed all too frequently. The Cornish, as northern European, Protestant, native speakers of British English were not obviously distinct from the native Euro-American population, and so they could have avoided much of this process. They could have blended in easily, and yet they did not. How and why the Cornish retained an identity apart from the Euro-American population raises deeper questions about the nature of ethnicity and the immigrant adaptation to the mining West. In the case of the Cornish, it appears that they chose to perpetuate their ethnic character as an economic strategy to secure preferential employment in the mines.[1]

IMMIGRATION & ETHNICITY

In general, it is possible to see immigrant ethnicity in one of two ways. Expressions of ethnicity can be a response to the tension and anxiety associated with immigration. This interpretation maintains that newcomers undergo stress and need comfort, and are unable to face the new environment without support from other immigrants. They create little pockets of the Old World to soften the blow of transition. Hostility from others frequently promotes this segregation, underscoring the ethnic identity of the immigrants.

In contrast to this, immigrant associations and ethnic identity can be an economic strategy. In this analysis, immigrants work together to achieve success in the New World. Anxiety has little to do with asserting and promoting one's ethnicity. Immigrants came to America to profit, and ethnic identification and immigration associations merely make them more effective. These people are like the Honourable Patrique Oreille (pronounced O-re*lay*) of Mark Twain's *The Gilded Age* who provides an example of the economic and social exploitation of ethnicity. He returned from France with pretensions of aristocracy and so assumed a French accent and spelling of his name. Oreille began his American career as Patrick O'Riley, an Irish immigrant. In the early days, his Irish connections were an advantage to his career. But for Oreille, Irish ethnicity was something to discard when no longer useful after having ascended the social ladder, to be replaced with a more distinguished French persona.[2] Along this line, this interpretation characterises ethnicity in practical economic and political terms and regards immigrants as active exploiters, not victims.

Needless to say, the two approaches are not mutually exclusive. Whether taken together or separately, they can be useful in understanding Cornish and other immigrants. In addition, three major contributions – Rowe's *The Hard-Rock Men*, Rowse's *The Cornish in America*, and Todd's *The Cornish Miner in America* – provide a general description of the Cornish in the New World. Although specific assertions may differ and warrant investigation, these books furnish a framework within which to examine the issues of ethnic identification and acculturation of the Cornish.[3]

The importance the mining West attributed to Cornish miners, or Cousin Jacks as they were called, appears all the more striking considering the relative paucity of their numbers. Perhaps no more than one hundred thousand Cornish left Europe for America during the nineteenth century. This was significant from the point of view of Cornwall: the 1861 Census shows only 369,390 people living there at that time.[4] Indeed, it is possible that in the 1870s, up to a third of the miners of Cornwall emigrated.[5] This was hardly astounding from an American perspective, however, for millions were arriving in the New World in the last century. Spread over the course of one hundred years, the numerical effect of one hundred thousand Cornish in America is further diminished.

Most Cornish left their homeland out of economic necessity.[6] Fortunately, for the Cornish miners, they were accustomed to moving. Britain had a well developed history of internal migration,[7] and mining especially presented a unique economic environment that was particularly conducive to this movement, not least within Cornwall.[8] When the nineteenth-century Cornish depression deepened, it made sense to look elsewhere for work. Coincidentally, the discovery of lead and copper deposits in Michigan and Wisconsin in the late 1830s and early 1840s attracted considerable attention in Cornwall. The move there was natural for the Cornish, and America acquired the whimsical name of 'the next parish over'. The Cornish subsequently followed mineral strike after strike throughout the western hemisphere and indeed the world. The 1850s found them in California, and the 1860s brought them to Colorado and Nevada, making the Cornish miners a familiar group in Western American mining towns.

Of all the Celtic peoples of the United Kingdom, the Cornish were perhaps the most obscure,[9] the indigenous language having more or less disappeared by the end of the eighteenth century (albeit surviving in many dialect words)[10] but with the pressure of anglicisation resisted by a distinctive regional culture and ethnic identity based on industrial prowess and sharpened by geographical isolation.[11] Certainly, as immigrants in America, the Cornish tended to present an image that was often 'Cornish' rather than 'English'. This is significant, for central to literature on ethnicity and immigration is the assumption that sojourners cannot easily discard certain aspects of ethnicity but can employ or abandon other features as desired. In short, the projection of ethnicity in some cases can be a matter of choice.[12] The distinction is useful when dealing with the Cornish because they could not easily discard some attributes, while they appear to have adopted and perpetuated others intentionally. In addition, the non-Cornish community had the ability to reinforce ethnicity by the way it dealt with the immigrants. And yet, there was little about the Cornish that demanded immediate attention or made them obviously distinct in North America. They were not physically different from the Euro-American majority, and there were no other features that would identify them at a glance as Cornish.[13]

EXPRESSIONS OF CORNISH ETHNICITY

The two most obvious ethnic attributes of the Cornish were their dialect and surnames. Nineteenth-century America used a simple rhyme to identify the Cornish: 'By Tre-, Lan-, Ros-, Car-, Pol-, and Pen-; you may know the most of Cornishmen.'[14] The sojourner, however, could change his name. Occasionally, some members of the second generations anglicised their names so that they would be less distinct or less likely to be confused with other groups (Santo, Jago, Jose and other Cornish surnames were often mistaken as Spanish).[15] Thus although a name can function as a non-optional marker of ethnicity, it can also be a matter of choice. Similarly, the Cornish dialect functioned as an inherent marker of ethnicity,[16] although Cornish vowels were closer to North American English than those of London or Standard English.[17] Nevertheless, the Cornish dialect did arouse considerable interest in North America, probably more as a marker of ethnicity rather than because of any deviance from normal speech.[18] For example, the humour of many Cousin Jack tales was dependent upon the rendition of Cornish dialect:[19]

> Sime Ogg was there – Cousin Jack was up to Virginia to-day. Says he: 'I saw the Hodd Fellows' procession all through. The

> Hencampment was a fine set o' lads, and there was a big string of carriages. Sime Hogg of Gold 'ill, you know, 'ah the finest rig of 'em all. Hogg druv four fine 'orses, with 'is 'air all slicked down, and a nobby 'at on 'is 'ed. Some style about he'.[20]

Folklorist Richard Dorson outlines some of the issues central to immigrant dialect stories. He suggests that they contributed to 'a free and easy social interplay'. There is little doubt that this is correct, but it is also clear that a dialect helps distinguish an immigrant from others.[21] In the mining West, this was perhaps particularly an issue since the foreign-born were more numerous *per capita* in the region than elsewhere. As Mark Twain observed:

> as each adventurer had brought the slang of his nation or his locality with him, the combination made the slang of Nevada the richest and the most infinitely varied and copious that had existed anywhere in the world, perhaps, except in the mines of California in the 'early days'. Slang was the language of Nevada.[22]

Other manifestations of Cornish ethnicity were not 'innate' in the sense that surnames and dialect might be, but they were nevertheless entrenched in the immigrant's culture. Methodism (with many of the chapels in mining towns built by Cornish stonemasons)[23] and food (such as pasties and saffron cake)[24] were two additional markers of Cornish ethnicity. Also significant as an expression of Cornish ethnicity was their imported Old World folklore, their oral traditions, beliefs, and traditional crafts and habits.[25] Folklore, however, served only briefly as a distinct marker of ethnicity: the useful elements of Cornish occupational lore soon diffused among other miners, and most of it ceased to be the exclusive property of the immigrant, especially as other groups began to imitate Cornish mining techniques. As A.K. Hamilton Jenkin observed, the words of the Cornishman's specialised occupation 'have found their way into mining camps and the mining vocabulary of the world, where they may now be heard bandied about on the tongues of distant races who have never heard of Cornwall'.[26] As Todd points out, Cornish vocabulary became an important part of the Western mining industry, providing standard English with the means of dealing with the unique underground environment.[27] The diffusion was not restricted to descriptions of excavations: a 'lode' is an ore deposit; 'country', the rock around the ore; and a 'bal' is a mine. A bal is 'knacked out' when the lode is removed.

These are only a few examples of a much longer list of words and phrases that the North American mining population borrowed from the Cornish. Indeed, Raymond's mining glossary of 1881, which identifies thousands of industrial terms not found in Standard English, lists nearly a third of those ascribed as being of Cornish origin.[28] This is all the more impressive if terms associated with coal mining are excluded (these being largely Welsh or midland English in origin); then it becomes clear that the Cornish contribution represents over half the hard rock mining vocabulary. Although people often ridiculed Cornish pronunciation, the Cornish vocabulary diffused easily among other miners. This serves as one of the best examples of how the mining West responded to the traditional lore of the Cornish. Non-Cornish miners respected the Cousin Jack for his knowledge and found it useful to adopt as much of his know-how as possible.

Diverse aspects of Cornish folklore repeat the example that the mining vocabulary provides. Perhaps the most famous expression of Cornish folklore diffusing into the broader mining population of the American West is the 'Tommyknocker'. Most if not all pre-industrial miners have fancied the idea that underground spirits share their unnatural work environment. It was the Cornish Tommyknocker, however, that took hold in North America, diffusing among other ethnic groups. This aspect of Cornish folklore was so pervasive that no other underground mine spirits made the transition from Old to New World. Indeed, Tommyknockers appear to have survived longer in North America than they did in Cornwall.[29]

Other examples of Cornish occupational folklore include prohibitions against whistling in the mines and against allowing women below ground. The Cornish considered rats in the mines as good luck and gave them portions of meals. Gatherings of birds on the way to the mine were bad luck and could keep the miner who saw them from reporting for duty that day. A candle that went out three times or fell from its place in the wall signified that the miner's wife was with another man. A horseshoe hammered to the entrance of a shaft would bring good luck.[30] Much of this traditional lore diffused throughout the mining community, eventually preventing it from functioning as an indication of Cornish ethnicity.

Cornish immigrant culture included several features that signalled ethnicity to one another and to the community in general. These were more a matter of choice and so they are of particular interest in the context of selective ethnicity. The Cornish were reputed to be independent, often choosing not to join groups or unions,[31] relying on their skill, experience and reliability to find their way in the economic world.[32] Indeed, such was the strength of this individualistic self-confidence, there is some indication in nineteenth-century sources that other ethnic groups joined unions in order to counter preferential treatment afforded the Cornish by mine managers of the same background.[33] Rowse points out that in Michigan during the 1874 strike on the Marquette iron-range, the Cornish did not join the Scandinavians and that they similarly boycotted the 1914 copper strike of the unskilled Finns, Slavs, and Italians.[34] However, Cornish political action against their competitors was rare. It is easy to dispute, for example, the credit given the Cornish for the defeat of Henry R. Mighels, candidate for Lieutenant Governor of Nevada in 1878. The electorate perceived Mighels as supportive of Chinese labourers, and at least one historian suggests that this inspired the Cornish to rally to his defeat. Anti-Chinese sentiment, however, was not the monopoly of the Cornish (the Irish formed societies especially aimed against the Chinese), although it is interesting that in the public mind, both then and subsequently, such attitudes should have been attributed specifically to the Cornish.[35]

In contrast to their resistance to joining multi-ethnic organisations, the Cornish were well-known for their choral societies and bands.[36] In both Cornwall and North America, people often considered such groups as a community's best. They were particularly noted for their custom of singing deep within the mine on Christmas Eve. The tradition of singing and forming bands was strong among Cornish immigrants. As late as 1925, the 'Cornish Singers' and the 'Grass Valley Miners Band' from Grass Valley, California toured the West.[37]

The Cornish formed military guard units less frequently. This was a common practice among the Irish who saw it as a means to support nationalism, but the secondary literature dealing with the Cornish is silent on the subject.[38] Nonetheless, there is at least one example of the Cornish organising such a military unit. On 27 March 1873, the Cornish miners of Virginia City, Nevada formed the Washington Guard. It was neither the first nor the most impressive of the local units. Other guards there date to the early 1860s, and the Irish had four units before the end of that decade.[39] The Cornish, late in the game, formed a militia that the local *Territorial Enterprise* described as 'composed mostly of men of English birth, though there [would] also be in it several Americans'.[40] Whether described as English or Cornish (primary sources are occasionally ambiguous on this distinction), the surnames of the members indicate Cornish origins. Members elected Frank F. Osbiston as Captain, and the unit began a career of drilling, target practices, and competitions. The treasurer of the organisation stole the Guard's funds in 1880, however, and participation dwindled until there seemed little reason to continue. After an undistinguished career, the Washington Guard disbanded in 1883. Nonetheless, affiliation with the unit may have been a way to signal ethnicity to the rest of the community, the fact of belonging to a specifically Cornish organisation.

In addition, the Cornish expressed their ethnicity by participating in sports. Boxing and Cornish wrestling were common sources of entertainment in Western mining towns. Contests frequently pitted Cornish and Irish athletes, giving the event a sense of international conflict. Although the boxing conformed to Euro-American standards of the time, the Cornish brought their own rules for their own form of wrestling. These displays furnished the Cornish community with an opportunity to express identity, and the primary literature has numerous examples of the Cornish cheering their comrades and the Irish responding in kind.[41]

DEMOGRAPHIC CHARACTERISTICS

A demographic analysis and an assessment of residence patterns lend further insight into the Cornish experience. Nevada's Comstock Lode furnishes an example. The 1880, 10th United States Manuscript Census was the first to record street addresses, and so with a computerised version of the text it is possible to understand who the Cornish were and where they lived.[42] The first problem when dealing with Census data is assessing Cornish origin when the enumerator used only the generic term 'English'. Surnames are an important clue, especially those of Celtic origin, but others are less distinctive or exclusive and so one can only assess the probability of a subject being Cornish. It is possible, therefore, to divide Comstock residents listed with 'English' nativity or ancestry into three groups: those of likely Cornish origin (their number equals 539); those of possible Cornish origin (of which there are 861); and those listed as English who were probably not Cornish (numbering 1,020).[43] The surname criterion is not perfect, and misplaced people are likely appear in each group, but numbers are large enough to even out anomalies caused by misidentification. Women present another problem because many appear as Cornish by virtue of a married name. Conclusions about Cornish women, the Cousin Jennies of the mining West, are inevitably unreliable when based on Census data.[44]

A quick assessment of various demographic bench marks suggest that those with likely and those with possible Cornish affiliation are similar to one another and distinct from the non-Cornish 'English'. It appears, therefore, that the majority of both the first two groups are indeed of Cornish origin or ancestry (see Tables 1a and 1b). Based on this, it is possible to conclude that at the time of the 1880 Census there were over one thousand Cornish immigrants together with their families in Storey County, the principal county of the Comstock Mining District. This is far less than the 5,669 Irish and Irish-Americans who lived there in 1880, but it is nonetheless a significant slice of the overall population which numbered only slightly above fifteen thousand.

In general, the Cornish of the Comstock were younger than their English and Irish counterparts and much more likely to find employment in the mines. They were also, for the most part, directly from Europe: far fewer adult, second generation Cornish lived on the Comstock in relationship to first generation immigrants than was the case with English-Americans and Irish-Americans. It appears, therefore, that the Cornish on the Comstock were young immigrants looking for opportunity in the mines of the West.

The Cornish were also prone to living in neighbourhoods set apart from the Irish and others. While the Irish dominated parts of Virginia City, many of the Cornish settled in Gold Hill to the south and in the area known as the Divide, separating the two communities.[45] The tendency of the Cornish to live in their own neighbourhoods is repeated in the Comstock cemeteries. Both the Virginia City and Gold Hill burial grounds have sections where most or all of the tombstones discuss Cornwall as a place of birth or have surnames which appear to be of Cornish origin. The decision to select a residence in a predominantly Cornish neighbourhood and to bury one's dead in a similarly segregated section of a cemetery helped define the immigrants as a group.

TABLE 1a:

Cornish Ethnicity: Ratio of First to Second Generation Males aged 18 years or over

	Number of First Generation	Number of Second Generation	Ratio of First to Second
Probably Cornish	216	17	13:1
Possibly Cornish	313	21	15:1
English (not Cornish)	309	107	3:1
Irish	1,241	415	3:1

Source: 1880 10th U.S. Manuscript Census for Storey County, Nevada.

TABLE 1b:

Cornish Ethnicity: Involvement in the Mining Industry First Generation

	Adult Males	Miners and Associates	% of Adult Males working in mining
Probably Cornish	216	168	77.8%
Possibly Cornish	313	252	80.6%
English (not Cornish)	309	167	54.0%
Irish	1,241	697	56.2%

Source: 1880 10th U.S. Manuscript Census for Storey County, Nevada.

Adult males are defined here as 18 years or older. Table 1b above uses only first generation because the American-born Cornish are so poorly represented. All groups appear to show a decline of miners in the second generation, proportional to the number of their group who followed the occupation in the first generation.

Complementing the mechanisms used by the immigrants to define their ethnicity, the non-Cornish community also contributed to a sense of group and ethnicity among the Cousin Jacks. The immigrants could not directly control these efforts, but if the non-Cornish were excessively negative or hostile, they could conceivably have inspired the Cornish to hide their ethnicity to reduce external prejudice and ill-treatment. This was not the case. Instead, the Cornish accepted the appellation 'Cousin Jacks', a term that many have sought to explain. It has been suggested that the universal response of the Cornish to news of an employment vacancy was that 'I have a Cousin Jack' in Cornwall willing to immigrate for the position.[46] This is a reasonable explanation, but it fails to explain why the name stuck. The name 'Cousin Jack' may, in fact, have functioned on at least two levels. For the non-Cornish, the term 'cousin' is reminiscent of 'country cousin', or country bumpkin. In addition, 'Jack' was a common British name for a farmer or labourer, thus supporting this interpretation. Indeed, the Cornish were sometimes characterised as simple rural fools, and the name Cousin Jack may have served to make gentle mockery of the immigrants. On the other hand, the Cornish may have preferred a name that reinforced the idea of kinship while subtly reminding the mining community that although the Cornish often shunned multi-ethnic labour organisations, they possessed a type of union in the form of their ethnicity. As Payton has pointed out, the myth of 'Cousin Jack' reflected a wider Cornish identity based on industrial prowess, confirming the Cornish miners as a 'labour aristocracy' and attributing to them unmatched expertise in the extractive industries. To be a Cousin Jack was to be a member of an envied exclusive club.[47]

ETHNICITY AS AN ECONOMIC STRATEGY

Thus far, the discussion has focussed on how Cornish ethnicity manifested itself. It is, as the myth of Cousin Jack suggests, equally appropriate to examine why the Cornish maintained their ethnicity. Above all, Cornish immigrants chose to characterise themselves as miners. This was perhaps their most important voluntary marker of ethnicity, but it was also the most economically expedient way to present themselves. The Cornish could have also portrayed themselves as farmers or sailors: both were traditional occupations in Cornwall. Although Edmund Humkin, a Cornish immigrant, managed to find a career as captain of the *Nevada*, *Meteor*, and *Tahoe*,[48] three ships on Lake Tahoe, sailing would not have been a consistently profitable career to market in the intermountain West. Moreover, there were many maritime men from various backgrounds in the New World, so the Cornish could not have commanded a monopoly as they did with mining. The same was true of farming. With mining alone, the Cornish immigrant (whether actually miner, farmer, or sailor) was able to lay claim to unique skills in a market with obvious needs.[49] The Cornish in America were wise to promote the old saying that 'a mine is a hole in the ground with a Cornishman at the bottom'.[50]

One additional aspect of the Cornish immigrant experience may have contributed to their maintaining ethnicity and a sense of group: the Cornish competed with and were antagonistic towards the Irish. Of course, Irish anti-Cornish feelings reinforced Cornish anti-Irish sentiment. There are many examples of clashes between the two Celtic groups that further served to maintain the ethnic identity of both. For example, in an article reporting an Irish-Cornish riot at the Ontonogon copper mines in April 1859, an Ohio newspaper opined that 'The Cornish are a peculiar race of their own, generally strong and hardy, determined in purpose, rather rough, and keeping well together according to the ancient watchword of their native county, "One and All"'.[51] As Payton has suggested, the intensity of this conflict may have reflected not only religious antagonism and a skills differential but also their competing and paradoxical claims to be 'Celtic'. For the nineteenth-century Cornish, to be 'Celtic' was to be an 'Ancient Briton', more British than the English, while for the Irish to be 'Celtic' was to be non-British and indeed anti-British.[52] Certainly, in the Western mining towns, Irish antagonism towards the Cousin Jacks helped create a sense of unity and ethnicity among the Cornish. Prejudice and economics forced Irish immigrants to act as labourers in the New World industrial markets. In the mining West (as with the coal fields of the Appalachians), this typically meant labouring underground. Mining, however, was the very niche that the Cornish wished to occupy and had the expertise to fill. If there were a slack in the mining economy, each ethnic group was likely to feel the danger of being displaced in favour of the other.

The Cornish may have been the experts underground, but the Irish could be proficient politicians on the surface, capable of undermining the superior position that the Cousin Jack won by skill and reputation. Rowse quotes a complaint (in dialect) of a Cornishman of Butte, Montana voiced against Irish voting practices: 'Thee robbing Hirish, they not honly 'ave two votes heach on Helection day, but the buggers vote seven years hafter they 'ave been dead hand buried'.[53] This sums up what must have been a problem: the Cornish could out-compete the Irish in the mines, but above ground Irish political organisation could defeat Cornish ambitions. Confronted with the Cornish assertion that hard work and talent (together with a healthy dose of nepotism) should win the day, the Irish had the potential to manipulate the system to their own advantage. These different, competing skills, promised to accentuate problems between the two ethnic groups.

Virtually every historian who has examined the Cornish immigrant nationally or locally has mentioned Irish-Cornish antagonism. Expressions of the conflict run the gamut from shootings, knifings and other forms of fatal violence to bar fights and street brawls. Often the conflict had labour/ management overtones: in 1864, a group of Comstock Irish miners were unhappy about a new Cornish foreman recently arrived from San Francisco and working in the Uncle Sam mine. They blamed him for an effort to reduce wages and subsequently bound the supervisor, placed him in an ore bucket and had him hauled to the surface with a note saying 'This is Cornwall dirt'. The supervisor resigned and as the *Gold Hill Daily News* observed, 'we have heard of no more rebellion in Uncle Sam's dominions – except the rebellion "down South"'.[54]

A similar incident in 1875 at the Brunswick mill of the Comstock Mining District also pitted a Cornish supervisor against an Irish worker. In this case, an Irishman asked permission to attend his child's funeral. The supervisor said that he could but that he need not return to work 'as Irish funerals were pretty much 4th of July celebrations, anyhow'. The Irishman subsequently sprung into action against the supervisor, 'knocking out a number of teeth, breaking his nose and using him up generally'. The Cornishman denied that he had been insensitive and insisted that the real problem at the mill was Irish labour agitation.[55] In contrast to this, antagonism between the Cornish and Irish was sometimes expressed in more institutional ways with an organised prize fight, pitting the opposing nationalities against one another. Shooting competitions between the Comstock's Irish Emmet Fenians and the Cornish Washington Guard occurred and in at least one occasion in 1878 resulted in a pitched battle using rifles as clubs.[56] In spite of such outbursts, frontier camaraderie could occasionally win the day. Most historians agree, however, that rivalry was the rule, not the exception.[57]

Perhaps competition with the Irish and a wish to secure employment in the mines were critical factors in the formation of the previously-mentioned Washington Guard of Virginia City, Nevada. The Cornish organised the Guard in the midst of two key events. The first was a local mining depression: in early 1873 the prospects of the Comstock mines seemed less promising than in more prosperous bonanza years. The second event was the celebration of Saint Patrick's Day ten days earlier. Alfred Doten, local newspaperman and writer, witnessed the parading of several Fenian military units and noted that it was 'The most celebrated I even have seen – The Emmet, and Montgomery Guards of [Virginia City] and Sarsfield of [Gold Hill] were out in full uniform . . . Also Divisions No 1 & 2 of the Ancient Order of the Hibernians, and the Irish Confederation . . . About 300 of them in all'.[58] The effect of this display of Irish unity and nationalism on the Cornish is difficult to determine. Nevertheless, it is possible that the formation of the Washington Guard was a response to the unified Irish presence just when employment might have been threatened. It was an opportune time to remind the community of the Cornish and to do so in a unified, formidable way.

The nineteenth-century Cornish identification with mining was based on economics and competition, a claim to superior status. Although the near extinction of mining in twentieth-century Cornwall has challenged this identity,[59] in the last century mining and the wider ethnic sense of 'Cornishness' were inextricably entwined. The Cornish immigrants in America identified themselves with mining so that they could be assured jobs in the industry. As one Cornish supervisor is reported to have said to Irishmen applying for work in a Butte, Montana mine, 'Thee are in the wrong line, boy!'[60] His message was clear: in a Cornish-run mine, employment was reserved first for other Cornishmen. They occupied both the role of miner and manager, selected over people of other ethnic groups because of their reputation for expertise in hard rock mining.[61]

The strength of this preferential treatment is underscored by the example of Frank F. Osbiston, the founder of the Washington Guard. Born in 1834 in Cornwall, Osbiston emigrated to a wealth of opportunities in New World mining. He served as the superintendent of a mill in Reno, Nevada, and as an agent for the Bank of California as it explored investment opportunities in the Comstock mines. Later, he held management positions there in several places. Nevada Governor L.R. Bradley (1871-1878) appointed him Chief of Engineering Corps. Osbiston's last position on the Comstock was as superintendent of the Savage mine under John Mackay.[62] Mackay was an immigrant from Ireland who associated himself with nationalist movements and regularly attended the Catholic Church.[63] His sense of Irishness was strong, and yet when it came to hiring a superintendent for his mine, he overlooked his fellow countrymen and found a Cornishman. The strength of the Cornish reputation must have been powerful indeed.

As an epilogue to Osbiston's career, he left Nevada when the Comstock played out and travelled to Colorado where he worked in the industry and ran for public office.[64] Later, he pursued his mining career in Australia, where he died in 1902 at the age of sixty-eight. Forever the miner, an exemplar of the Cousin Jack experience, he needed to follow the path of the industry in order to market his skills and ethnicity successfully.

CONCLUSION

In the arid, windy cemetery of Virginia City, Nevada, stands a tombstone with the following verse:

> Perfect health I left my home:
> Thinking that my race was run
> as flowers grow so they decay;
> and so death snatched me away

Dated 1880, it provides an epitaph for one of the many occupants of that rocky hill who were born in Cornwall only to leave for foreign riches and yet find death. Although this was one aspect of the New World Cornish experience, the story of those immigrants is much more complex than that, and certainly, many lived long, prosperous lives. Clearly, the Cornish could profit by encouraging others to regard them as the best in their field. A superb reputation, albeit reinforced by exemplary work in New World ore fields, would be nothing without the members of this elite group being easily recognised. This is probably the most important reason why the Cornish sought to maintain their ethnicity.

In the case of Cornish immigrants to the nineteenth-century mining West, maintenance of ethnic identity was a matter of choice, encouraged by an economic environment. Of all the immigrants who came to North America the Cornish were perhaps the most extreme example of this: white Protestant native speakers of English could have blended in without notice. Instead they found it expedient to project themselves as ethnically distinct, and in so doing, they provide keys to understanding broader issues concerning the immigrant experience. The Cornish expressed ethnicity as an economic strategy, not as a buttress against the stress of immigration. Although each group reacted to the process differently and faced unique issues, this example demonstrates how ethnicity and immigration functioned in one instance.

NOTES AND REFERENCES

1. There is a well-developed body of literature dealing with ethnicity and immigration; for example, see Fredrik Barth (ed.), *Ethnic Groups and Boundaries: The Social Organisation of Cultural Difference*, Boston, 1969, pp.9-38, and G. Carter Bentley, 'Ethnicity and Practice', *Comparative Studies in Society and History*, 29:1, January, 1987.
2. Samuel Clemens (Mark Twain) and Charles Dudley Warner, *The Gilded Age: A Tale of Today*, New York, reprint 1970, pp.248-252.
3. John Rowe, *The Hard-rock Men: Cornish Immigrants and the North American Mining Frontier*, Liverpool, 1984; A.L. Rowse, *The Cornish in America*, London, 1969, reprinted Redruth 1990; A.C. Todd, *The Cornish Miner in America*, Truro, 1967.
4. John Rowe, 'The Cornish', in Stephen Thernstrom (ed.), *Harvard Encyclopedia of American Ethnic Groups*, Cambridge: Mass, 1980, p.243.
5. A.K. Hamilton Jenkin, *The Cornish Miner*, 1927, reprinted Newton Abbot, 1972, p.322. Lynn I. Perrigo, 'The Cornish Miners of Early Gilpin County', *Colorado Magazine*, 14:3, May 1937, discusses the issue of demography and the difficulty of identifying the Cornish.
6. See, for example, John Rowe, *Cornwall in the Age of the Industrial Revolution*, Liverpool, 1953, new ed. St Austell, 1993.
7. See, for example, Bernard Bailyn's discussion of this phenomenon in *The Peopling of British North America: An Introduction*, New York, 1986, p.20ff.

8. John Rowe, 'Cornish Emigrants in America', *Folklife: Journal of the Society for Folklife Studies*, 3, 1965.
9. The Manx, perhaps, are also contenders for this distinction. Both Cornish and Manx have been revived, but Welsh, Breton, and Irish and Scots Gaelic have survived as indigenous vernaculars.
10. Martyn F. Wakelin, *Language and History in Cornwall*, Leicester, 1975.
11. Rowe, 1953 & 1993; Philip Payton, *The Making of Modern Cornwall: Historical Experience and the Persistence of 'Difference'*, Redruth, 1992, pp.73-94.
12. See, for example, Stanford M. Lyman and William A. Douglas, 'Ethnicity: Strategies of Collective and Individual Impression Management', *Social Research*, 40:2, Summer 1973, and Erving Goffman, *The Presentation of Self in Everyday Life*, Edinburgh, 1958. Lyman and Douglas refer to two types of ethnic characteristics – the innate and the voluntary – as 'cues and clues'.
13. Dress, tools and material culture (including traditional garments in a few locations) could set the Cornish apart; see, Perrigo, 1937.
14. Robert M. Neal, 'Pendarvis, Trelawny, and Polperro: Shake Rag's Cornish Houses', *Wisconsin Magazine of History*, 29, June 1946, provides a version of this poem.
15. Although outdated, Oscar Handlin deals with these issues in, *The Uprooted*, New York, 1951, new ed. 1973.
16. See Oscar Handlin. *Race and Nationality in American Life*, New York, 1957, p.72, and John J. Appel, 'From Shanties to Lace Curtains: The Irish Image in Puck, 1876-1910', *Comparative Studies in Society and History*, 3:4, October 1971, p.374.
17. Rowse, 1969 & 1990, p.22.
18. North Americans appear to have taken less notice of the Irish dialects; see, Kerby A. Miller, *Emigrants and Exiles: Ireland and the Irish Exodus to North America*, New York, 1985.
19. See, for example, Rowse, 1969 & 1990, p.186 and p.222; Rowe, 1974, p.83, pp.280-281 and p.293.
20. *Gold Hill Daily News* (Nevada), 26 April 1876. Simon Ogg, an immigrant from Switzerland, was locally popular and had served in the state legislature. His name lent itself to Cornish dialect humour because a misplaced aspiration turned it into the word for a male pig.
21. Richard M. Dorson, 'Dialect Stories of the Upper Peninsula: A New Form of American Folklore', *Journal of American Folklore*, 61:240, April-June 1948.
22. Samuel Clemens (Mark Twain), *Roughing It*, New York, 1871, reprint 1913, Vol.II, p.43. For the international character of the mining West in the nineteenth century see also Wilbur S. Shepperson, *Restless Strangers: Nevada's Immigrants and their Interpreters*, Reno, 1970.
23. Rowe, 1974, p.275.
24. For example, see Rowe, 1965, p.28, and Rowse, 1969 & 1990, p.186.
25. The definition of folklore is, of course, disputed; see, for example, Francis Lee Utley, 'Folk Literature: An Operational Definition', and William Thoms, 'Folklore', in Alan Dundes (ed.), *The Study of Folklore*, Englwood Cliffs, 1965.
26. Jenkin, 1927 & 1972, p.339.
27. Todd, 1967, p.16.

28. R.W. Raymond, *A Glossary of Mining and Metallurgical Terms*, Easton, 1881; see also, Caroline Bancroft, 'Folklore of the Central City District', *California Folklore Quarterly*, 4, 1945.
29. Ronald M. James, 'Knockers, Knackers, and Ghosts: Immigrant Folklore in the Western Mines', *Western Folklore*, 51:2, 1992; James C. Baker, 'Echoes of Tommy Knockers in Bohemia, Oregon, Mines', *Western Folklore*, 30, 1971.
30. Wayland D. Hand, 'Folklore from Utah's Silver Mining Camps', *Journal of American Folklore*, 54, 1941; Wayland D. Hand, 'California Miners' Folklore: Above Ground', *California Folklore Quarterly*, 1, January 1942; Wayland D. Hand, 'California Miners' Folklore: Below Ground', *California Folklore Quarterly*, 1, April 1942; Wayland D. Hand, 'The Folklore, Customs and Traditions of the Butte Miner', *California Folklore Quarterly*, 5, 1946; Lydia Fish, 'The European Background to American Miners' Beliefs', in Kenneth S. Goldstein and Neil V. Rosenberg, (eds.), *Folklore Studies in Honour of Herbert Halpert*, St Johns, Newfoundland, 1980, pp.157-186; Mary E.Rowe, 'Little Bit of Cornwall Lives on Shake Rag Street', *Milwaukee Journal*, 9 October 1948.
31. See, for example, Rowe, 1865, pp.36-37.
32. Todd, 1967, p.70.
33. See Myron Angel, *History of Nevada with Illustrations and Biographical Sketches of its Prominent Men and Pioneers*, Oakland, 1881, reprint. Berkeley, 1958, p.657.
34. See Rowland Tappan Berthoff, *British Immigrants in Industrial America: 1790-1950*, Cambridge, Mass, 1953, pp.58-61 and pp.93-94.
35. Thomas Wren, *A History of the State of Nevada: Its Resources and People*, New York, 1904, pp.79-80; see also *Territorial Enterprise* (Virginia City, Nevada), 6 April 1876, 6 June 1876, 7 June 1876, for references to an Irish anti-Chinese organisation in Nevada.
36. Rowse, 1969 & 1990, p.17 and p.185; Todd, 1967, pp.97-98.
37. *Nevada State Journal* (Reno, Nevada), 7 September 1925; Shirley Ewart, *Cornish Mining Families of Grass Valley, California*, New York, 1989.
38. See William d'Arcy, *The Fenian Movement in the United States: 1858-1886*, Washington DC, 1947.
39. Joseph Wickenden, 'History of the Nevada Militia, 1862-1912', unpub. MS, 1941, Getchell Library, University of Nevada, Reno.
40. *Territorial Enterprise*, 27 March 1873, 4 April 1873, 7 September 1880, 24 November 1880.
41. See, for example, Rowe, 1974, p.117 and pp.272-273.
42. Census data was provided courtesy of Richard Hartigan of the Nevada State Historic Preservation Office and Kenneth Fliess and his students at the University of Nevada.
43. Moira Tangye and the Murdoch House/Institute of Cornish Studies 'Cornish American Connection' project provided extensive assistance in identifying names of Cornish origin.
44. For a discussion of this Census data in relation to women and ethnicity, see Ronald M. James, 'Women of the Mining West: Virginia City Revisited', *Nevada Historical Society Quarterly*, 36:3, Fall 1993.
45. For a map and a discussion of the Irish neighbourhoods, see Ronald M.James, Richard D. Adkins, and Rachel J. Hartigan, 'Competition and Coexistence in the

Laundry: A View of the Comstock', *Western Historical Quarterly*, 25:2, May 1994.

46. The explanation from Michigan, cited by Rowe, 1974, p.280, that Cousin Jacks is a corruption of 'cussing' Jacks, is almost certainly a folk etymology with little basis in fact.
47. See Archie Green, 'Single Jacket: Doublejacket: Craft and Celebration', in Roger D. Abrahams, Kenneth S. Goldstein, and Wayland Hand (eds.), *By Land and By Sea: Studies in the Folklore of Work and Leisure Honoring Horace P. Beck*, Hatboro, 1985, pp.97-100; Philip Payton, 'From Cousin Jack to Map Kernow: Re-defining Cornish Ethnicity', *Australian Studies*, forthcoming, 1995.
48. Edward B. Scott, *The Saga of Lake Trahoe*, Lake Trahoe, 1957, p.209, p.405, p.406, p.423, p.432.
49. See, for example, Rowe, 1965, p.25.
50. Wells Drury, *An Editor on the Comstock Lode*, Palo Alto, 1936, p.70, provides a common variation: 'Wherever a hole is sunk in the ground today – no matter what part of the globe – you'll be sure to find a Cornishman at the bottom of it, searching for metal'.
51. *Daily Herald* (Cleveland, Ohio), reprinted in *Royal Cornwall Gazette*: see Michael Tangye, 'Murder in Mexico and America', *Cornwall Today*, July 1994.
52. Philip Payton, 'Historical Experience and Ethnic Identity: The Quest for a Celtic-Australian Heritage', in R. Snedden (ed.), *Celtic Studies: The Australian Contribution – The Proceedings of a Conference at Monash University*, Melbourne, forthcoming, 1994.
53. Rowse, 1969 & 1990, p.359.
54. *Gold Hill Daily News*, 21 March 1864; compare Eliot Lord, *Comstock Mining and Miners*, Washington, 1883, reprint. San Diego, 1959, and the *Territorial Enterprise*, 22 March 1864.
55. *Nevada Appeal* (Carson City, Nevada), 3 April 1875, 7 April 1875; *Territorial Enterprise*, 4 August 1870.
56. *Territorial Enterprise*, 6 August 1878.
57. Todd, 1967; Rowe, 1965; Rowe, 1974; and Rowse, 1969 & 1990, all elaborate this theme. Perrigo, 1937, describes the ethnic conflict between the Cornish and the several groups which competed for their jobs, and an Australian comparison of Cornish-Irish conflict is provided in Philip Payton, *The Cornish Miner in Australia: Cousin Jack Down Under*, Redruth, 1984, pp.70-71.
58. Alfred Doten, *The Journal of Alfred Doten: 1848-1903*, Reno, 1973, p.1193.
59. The issue of mining, the Cornish identity and culture change is addressed by Payton, 1992, and Bernard Deacon and Philip Payton, 'Re-inventing Cornwall: Culture Change on the European Periphery', *Cornish Studies: One*, second series, 1993.
60. Rowse, 1969 & 1990, p.354.
61. Rowe, 1974, p.204; Rowse, 1969 & 1990, pp.170-176.
62. See Angel, 1958, p.238 and p.637; Doten, 1973, p.1128, p.1303, p.1581, p.2007, p.2131.
63. Angel, pp.56-57; *Territorial Enterprise*, 30 September 1880.
64. *Rocky Mountain News*, 1 February 1880.

CONSTANTINE STONEMASONS IN SEARCH OF WORK ABROAD, 1870-1900

Hörst Rossler

INTRODUCTION

The 'Great Emigration' from Cornwall assumed its mass character during the 'hungry 40s' when increasingly large numbers of farmers, agricultural labourers, miners, building tradesmen and other skilled mechanics left for abroad, particularly for the British colonies and the Americas. Thereafter, Cornwall became a principal emigration region, ranking fourth in 1841 among all English and Welsh counties. From 1860 to 1900 Cornish emigration was exceptionally high and Cornwall lost some 118,500 people. Assuming a general return migration rate of about 40% the gross emigration rate from Cornwall was about 20% of the male and about 10% of the female Cornish-born population in each of the decades between those years.[1] Agriculture and mining dominated the Cornish economy, and thus the emigration of small farmers[2] and hard-rock miners was persistent throughout the nineteenth century. Miners, especially, were sought after across the world and they began leaving Cornwall for Central and South America as early as the 1820s. By the 1840s Cornish miners were leaving in large numbers for the United States and Australia, and later South Africa emerged as an important destination for emigrant Cornish people – especially during the 1880s and 1890s.

However, despite the large number of miners (and the attention that they have received from historians), even in the years of mass exodus after the crash of Cornish copper in 1866 only about one half of Cornish emigration was directly connected with hard-rock mining.[3] As Baines observes, even if there had been no depression in mining there would have been a high emigration rate, such was the socio-economic climate of nineteenth-century Cornwall.[4] Additionally, many skilled workers employed in trades ancillary to or serving the mining industry, such as blacksmiths, carpenters or stonemasons, formed a part of the mining emigration. Thus, for example, Cornish stonemasons built cottages for the miners at the Real del Monte silver mine in Mexico and constructed the chimneys and engine houses of the copper mines at Okiep in

Namaqualand (South Africa) and Burra Burra in South Australia.[5] Indeed, from the late 1860s onwards Cornish stonemasons became a significant emigration category in their own right. These stonemasons left for overseas in slack as well as in good times, and their movement added considerably to the volume and importance of Cornish emigration. Although they sometimes found work overseas as miners,[6] their emigration patterns were distinct from those of tin and copper miners, and their experience deserves greater attention than it has received hitherto.

This article, therefore, is concerned with the overseas emigration of Cornish granite stonemasons in the last third of the nineteenth century. It focuses specifically on the parish of Constantine. Not only was Constantine an important centre of granite quarrying in nineteenth-century Cornwall (so that it might safely be treated as an exemplar) but also recent work has confirmed the value of location-specific micro-research in emigration history. As Morawska puts it, 'Social-historical analysis at the lowest, community/individual level can significantly contribute to our knowledge of the directions and mechanisms of labour migration movement'.[7]

QUARRIES & MASONS IN CONSTANTINE

Building and construction was one of the fastest growing branches of the British economy in mid-Victorian times. Intense urban growth prompted a steady rise of the stone quarrying and manufacturing industry, producing a mass of artifacts from decorative facades for public buildings to major public works such as lighthouses or harbour piers.[8] Granite played a major role in stone quarrying and manufacturing, with significant centres in the Aberdeen area of Scotland and in south-west Britain, particularly Cornwall, where modern granite quarrying started in the late 1820s.[9] The Penryn area, of which Constantine parish was a major part, was the principal centre of the Cornish industry. In the first half of the century population growth in Constantine (from 1,229 inhabitants in 1801 to 2,004 in 1831) was due mainly to the emergence of hard-rock mining. But with the decline of mining in the parish in the 1850s and 1860s, granite quarrying and manufacturing became the most important occupation in an area which was otherwise overwhelmingly agricultural.[10] In 1871 the population was still 2,077, although emigration thereafter reduced it to 1,765 by 1891.

The principal Cornish quarrying firm was John Freeman & Sons of Penryn, which employed around 500 workers in the mid-1870s and 1500 men in 1900. In the late 1880s it owned upwards of 60 quarries in the large Penryn district embracing the parishes of Mabe, Stithians, Constantine and Wendron, and also worked quarries in Penzance, Luxulyan and the Liskeard area. The other important granite manufacturers in the Penryn area were Richard Hosken and the West of England Granite Company. All quarries in the district were no more than four miles distant from ports such as Gweek, Port Navas and Penryn itself. Freeman was the largest employer in Constantine parish, where by the mid-1880s Mean Pearne, Tresahor, Bosahan (all worked by Freeman) and Mean Toll (worked by Hosken) had become established as the principal quarries. Altogether there were around 30 quarries in the parish at that time, development characterised by the simultaneous growth of large works and small, the latter dominating numerically. In all, Constantine quarries employed around 150 stonemasons in the 1880s.[11]

One of the small quarries, employing between two and eight men, was at Tresahor Praze. This family business, run by James Richard Grigg, was established around 1877/1878 and continued working until 1965. It started its operation with two men (one of whom was Grigg) and a boy (Grigg's son Richard Henry) and very probably produced only for the local market: stone for local house building, tombstones, and many farm items such as troughs, gate posts and rollers. Farmers, like William H. Jenkin of Trewardreva Mill Farm, owning horses and various vehicles, sometimes worked as carriers and delivered the masoned stone.[12]

However, the main activity in the Constantine quarries was the cutting and dressing of large granite blocks for civil engineering projects such as bridges, dockyards, and breakwaters, as well as the production of architectural and monumental work for the London market.[13] Most stonemasons were on piecework, an echo of the tribute and tutwork system of employment which prevailed in Cornwall's mines. While this made them relatively independent workers, it also made their employment uncertain, a finely executed work attracting high reward but a small mistake bringing disaster.[14] Working conditions were hard and dangerous. Dressing and cutting was often outdoor labour and even the sheds where the men worked provided little shelter against bad weather.

Like the miners, masons suffered from the long term danger of phthisis (silicosis) due to the inhalation of dust. In the quarries they were often subject to accidents from blasting. Thus, for example, Constantine masons John Pascoe and John Veale were blown to pieces in Maen and Bosahan granite quarries in 1874 and 1883 respectively. Others died in rock falls, such as Francis Williams, another Constantine mason, who was killed at the Tressoir (Tresahor?) Granite Quarry in 1883.[15] Granite manufacturing was labour-intensive. The stonemason's work was hand-tooled (each man kept his own tools) and it was not until the end of the century that parts of the industry became mechanised. But even then the industry continued to rest to a considerable degree on the handicraft skill of the granite masons, on workers whose knowledge of the nature of the rock and whose skill in its manipulation were remarkable.[16]

Constantine masons were skilled craftsmen who handed down their trade from father to son. Thus in the 1881 Census 18 households were headed by stonemasons; of the 32 sons in these households 30 were also described as masons (apprentices and journeymen); of 81 Constantine-born stonemasons 38 had a father whose occupation was also given as mason, seven stonemasons were recruited from other crafts (miner, wheelwright etc.), eight from among unskilled workers (agricultural and quarry labourers) and two were from farming families. To be acknowledged as a Constantine stonemason was not only to be duly recognised as a qualified craftsman but was to be confirmed within a family's heritage, something which defined a family's status within the parish. As Mulligan has pointed out, the transfer of trade and skill was an important aspect of the life of the community of artisans, a process that insured the survival of the group, its values, customs and traditions. Thus the stonemason apprentice did not only acquire the skills necessary to work as journeyman, he also learned to identify himself as a practitioner of the craft, part of the transition to adulthood and a preparation for full participation in the community.[17]

The long-held view that nineteenth-century Cornwall was temperamentally unsuited to trade unionism has been challenged successfully of late, and a clearer picture of union activities amongst Cornish miners at home and abroad has emerged.[18] Certainly, in 1878 branches of the Operative Stonemasons Society (OSM), one of the most important British unions of the time, were present in all the Cornish granite quarrying districts: there were three branches in Penryn, one at Constantine (founded by 1838) and others at Cheesewring, De Lank, Gunnislake, Lamorna, Liskeard, Penzance, St Blazey, and Wadebridge.[19] Indeed, the union lodge was the most important institution of the stonemason's community. In 1880 the local OSM branch at Constantine had 67 members. In 1890 74 masons were on the membership roll, while the 1881 and 1891 Censuses for Constantine reported 93 and 89 journeymen masons respectively. That the jurisdiction of the Constantine lodge did not coincide with the parish boundary makes comparison of membership and Census statistics a little difficult; in 1878, for example, the secretary of the Penryn (Longdowns) lodge, William Francis, resided in Constantine.[20] It appears, however, that the rate of unionisation was high.

CONSTANTINE TRADE UNION MASONS LEAVE FOR OVERSEAS

In the last third of the nineteenth century hundreds of members of the Operative Stonemasons Society were reported to have emigrated in search of work to North America, Australia and South Africa. As Table 1 below indicates, in years of both high and low emigration stonemasons from the Cornish granite quarrying districts contributed significantly to this movement. And as Table 2 below shows, Penryn was the major source of emigrants, while Constantine had a relatively average emigration rate.

TABLE 1:
OSM members leaving for abroad in selected years

year	all members	Cornish members	% Cornish
1870	192	61	31.8
1878	94	26	27.7
1880	112	26	23.2
1883	153	18	11.8
1885	68	14	20.6
1887	154	51	33.1
1900	53	9	17.0

N.B. Statistics in Tables 1-7 are compiled from: OSM Returns, 1870-1900; Constantine Lodge Contribution Books, November 1847-September 1921; and Constantine Lodge Minute Book, March 1866-February 1888; held in the Modern Records Centre at the University of Warwick.

TABLE 2:
Number of OSM members emigrating from selected places in Cornwall in selected years

year	Penryn	Constantine	Cheesewring	Gunnislake	Liskeard	Penzance	De Lank
1870	23	2	5	5	4	6	8
1878	5	3	5	1	-	6	1
1880	7	5	-	4	2	1	1
1883	2	4	1	2	1	-	1
1885	6	1	1	7	-	1	-
1887	20	6	2	-	1	7	3
1900	2	1	1	-	-	7	-

TABLE 3:
Number of migrations of OSM members from Constantine, 1870 - 1900

years	number of migrations
1870-1879	46
1880-1889	59
1890-1900	26
1870-1900	131

As Table 3 above indicates, in the three decades before the turn of the century in about 130 cases union masons left Constantine for overseas. This figure records the number of movements (migrations) which is not the same thing as the actual number of emigrants. The figure may be compared with the number of 'registered emigrants' in the Constantine lodge (Table 4) which indicates that in the 1880s, the decade with the highest emigration rates amongst Constatntine union masons, up to 20% and more of the lodge members in a given year did not work in the quarries of Constantine but toiled in distant areas overseas. Interestingly, 28 out of 74 union members in 1890, and 28 out of 93 in 1900, had been overseas at least once in their working lives, so that a third and more of all unionists in those years had worked abroad once or several times.

TABLE 4:
OSM lodge members and 'registered emigrants' in Constantine

year	number of lodge members	registered as emigrants	%
1880	64	7	11.0
1882	70	14	20.0
1885	75	13	17.3
1887	73	16	21.9

Although the emigrants were not a majority of the lodge members, they were nevertheless a significant element of the stonemasons' community. Departing for abroad was not regarded as deviant behaviour but was part of their work culture, with emigration seen as merely an extension of internal travellings in a region from which emigration was already widespread.[21] Scattered evidence of people from Constantine who went abroad shows that emigration from that parish was in no way confined to stonemasons, an indicator of the strength of the emigration culture within that parish.[22]

According to the lodge's contribution book, William Tresidder was the first Constantine union mason to leave for abroad (for Australia) in 1861. He was accompanied by his younger brother Richard, also a stonemason but not a union member when he left Cornwall. According to the emigrant ship's passenger list the brothers described themselves as 'labourers'. They seemed to have been aware that the Australian governments at that time were more interested in the immigration of agricultural workers than stonemasons.[23] Another three masons left for the United States and Australia in 1869 but the real movement did not begin until the early 1870s. However, it soon became evident that for Constantine masons two destinations were of prime interest, South Africa (the Cape of Good Hope) and the United States.

MOTIVES FOR GOING ABROAD

There were various (and often complementary) motives for emigration. However, attractive labour market conditions abroad was probably the most important reason. As will be shown later, throughout the three decades before the turn of the century the fortunes of the granite trade in Constantine and in the Penryn area in general were fluctuating wildly. Thus the threats of under-employment and unemployment were ever-present. Finding employment abroad was one way of coping with slack times at home. But it was also attractive during good times when trade prospects abroad seemed to be even better than in Cornwall. Certainly, wages in the United States were considerably higher than at home. In 1883, for example, the general average weekly wage for stone workers (quarrymen and granite masons – or 'cutters' as they were known in America) in Massachusetts, one of the centres of granite manufacturing in the United States, was more than 40% higher than for the same categories of workers in Great Britain. Although we do not have similar detailed information for the wages of immigrant masons in South Africa, in times when their skills were needed rates must have been higher than at home. As one mason who had just returned from the Cape reported to the union journal in 1892, 'a steady man must save money, and a great deal faster than he can in England'.[24] Since Cornwall was a low wage area, with granite masons earning less than their colleagues in other parts of Britain,[25] wage differentials between labour markets at home and overseas were correspondingly high.

In general, the United States was not only attractive to skilled building tradesmen intending to settle permanently in the New World but also to temporary migrants. These were anxious to keep the cost of living as low as possible during their sojourns abroad in order take optimum advantage of the wage differentials between the British and American labour markets. Their thrifty behaviour was noticed (and often criticised) by native workers and American labour unions. Thus New York City stone cutters asserted that Scottish stonemasons came to work in the city during the season without spending anything for clothing. The Brooklyn secretary of the bricklayers' and masons' union stated that English masons would 'work during the summer here, live poorly, bank all they get . . . and take all they earn back to England'. At Westerly, Rhode Island, a granite cutter remarked that transient immigrants picked up 'the best work, spending nothing more than is absolutely necessary'.[26] Additionally, temporary migrants sometimes worked as unpaid cattlemen on board ship to get a free passage home.[27]

While the expectation of a comparatively higher living standard and better wages must have played a decisive role in the emigrant's decision to leave for abroad, other motives must not be overlooked. Like Fred Bower, the 'rolling stonemason', who all his life 'shifted about, up and down the country, picking up experience all the while', granite masons may have travelled overseas in order to acquire new skills. With regard to mechanisation and the application of technological innovations, the American granite manufacturing industry had surpassed the British industry by the 1880s and 1890s. In that period, most of the Constantine masons who returned from America were reported to have found work in their former quarries or under their former employers.[28] While granite manufacturers could expect the temporary migrants to come back with extra skills of benefit to their operations, so the returning workers could hope to more easily find a job or better wages.

In discussing the nature of 'labour aristocracy' in Britain, Hobsbawm has asserted that the bulk of the better-off skilled workers and artisans did not want to give up working for wages and accepted their proletarian status as a lifetime destiny. By contrast, workers in America saw wage work only as a temporary stage in their life-cycle.[29] Cornish granite masons, however, saw in emigrating to the States an opportunity to set up their own small businesses. Time and again the journal of the American granite cutters union reported 'brothers' who had gone into business for themselves, and wished them good luck. For the workers this was often a quest for independence, an effort to be free from the arbitrariness of the capitalist employer and to achieve a greater control over their working lives. The union encouraged these moves not only during strikes (favouring the establishment of co-operatives) but also hoped that unionists-turned-manufacturers would make better employers.[30] A considerable number of Cornish stonemasons became highly successful granite manufacturers.[31]

The desire to establish a small granite yard or quarry was by no means confined to those masons who settled permanently in America. A number of Aberdeen stonemasons used the savings and experiences acquired in the States to set up a business of their own at home after their return from abroad. There is also some evidence that a few Cornish granite masons who had been to America did likewise. James Richards, for example, a stonemason from Stithians, worked for several years in the United States and set up his own business after his return.[32] Similarly, Richard Henry Grigg, who had been to the States three times, invested his American experiences and savings into his father's small business which he took over in 1916. Probably, most of the mason emigrants had more limited ambitions. Single travellers had to support their parents in the old country, while most of the money earned abroad by married men had to be more or less regularly sent back to Cornwall to support the family. However, there is some evidence that many migrants dreamed of earning enough money abroad to be able to build a house or buy a piece of land after their return. Thus after his return one Will Gill, a St Breward stonemason who had worked in America, bought a piece of land, called it 'Little America' and built a house on it.[33]

INTERNAL TRAVELLINGS & OVERSEAS EMIGRATION

In the nineteenth century, Cornish people were deeply rooted in their native parishes and fiercely attached to Cornwall. Paradoxically, however, 'America to many Cornish people has never been a foreign land but, rather, the next parish to St Just or Sennen, just across the water'.[34] Constantine stonemasons exhibited similar contrasting sentiments, an intimate connection with their place of birth but a willingness to travel abroad. An examination of the Census returns for 1861 and 1871 shows that a majority of Constantine masons were born in the parish while the rest had in-migrated from villages in the immediate neighbourhood, from Wendron, Mabe, Stithians, Mawnan. In 1861, 34 masons were natives of Constantine, 26 were born in other Cornish places, only one was born in Devon and another one was Irish; in 1871, 64 masons were born in Constantine, 42 in other Cornish places, two in Devon, one in Wales. Taking the birth places of children as an indicator of geographical mobility, the 1881 Census returns confirm that the stonemasons were very much rooted in their native district: of a total of 135 children born in families headed by masons 122 were born in Constantine, 13 in neighbouring villages and none in other Cornish parishes or British counties. In addition, the OSM lodge records show that masons from elsewhere moving to Constantine had usually joined the union somewhere else in Cornwall – at Penryn, De Lank, Penzance, Hayle, and Redruth, with only one or two from Devon.

On the other hand, OSM material also shows that until the 1880s Constantine masons who had taken to the road (not including those who had gone overseas) rarely left Cornwall but worked in Penryn, Penzance, De Lank or Hayle. This changed, however, in the 1890s when a considerable number of masons left Constantine to work in stone quarrying areas in Devon, while others went as far as Wales where they were very probably employed at dock work in Barry or Cardiff, dressing the granite which had been supplied by John Freeman & Sons.[35]

In 1891 we find the following entry in the Constantine OSM branch's contribution book: 'the following members have paid all demands and left the lodge in search of employment, Albert Winn, James H. Thomas – emigrated to Africa, William Tremayne, Edward Symonds, William Bishop, E.G. Rowe'. While Thomas returned from Africa in 1894, Tremayne, Symonds and Bishop returned from Ivybridge (Devon) in 1891 and 1892 respectively, Winn from Exeter (Devon) in 1892, and Rowe from Hope (Wales) in 1893. A more detailed examination of the migrations of Constantine masons in 1891 and 1892 shows that in these years as many stonemasons, that is 12 workers, took to the road or migrated abroad. Furthermore, from 1887 to 1893, 29 masons participated in internal migrations within the United Kingdom to and from Constantine, while 33 emigrated from the parish or returned to it from overseas. This indicates that tramping in Britain and travelling abroad were of equal importance for stonemasons in search of work.

In this context it is interesting to note that all those (33) stonemasons who had returned from places in Devon, Wales or Cornwall to Constantine in the years from 1891 to 1895 were reported as residents of Constantine parish in the 1891 Census. However, it is also true that of 63 masons (including apprentices) in the 1861 Census only 26 were also recorded in the 1871 Census. Similarly, of the recorded 104 masons in 1871 only 41 appeared in the 1881 Census. Among union masons the persistence rate seems to have been higher: of 49 members in 1871, 27 were still members of Constantine lodge in 1885 (12 had died and five had emigrated permanently). Of those who took to the road to tramp in Britain, several decided to move on overseas, so that of the 29 Constantine masons involved in internal travellings between 1887 and 1893 eight had also left for abroad during the same time.[36] It appears that to some of these travelling Constantine stonemasons it made little difference whether they went to De Lank (Cornwall), Cardiff (Wales), or some place in South Africa or North America – they moved between internal and international labour markets.

ALTERNATIVES TO OVERSEAS EMIGRATION

Even taken together, internal travellers and overseas emigrants were only a minority (albeit substantial) among the union masons. Migration research has indicated that, generally, older, settled and married workers stayed at home, preferring to work for lower wages and under worse working conditions during slack times than taking the risk of emigrating in search of a better job elsewhere.[37] Thus, instead of moving around, Constantine masons could if needs be turn to making street kerbs and channels when the manufacturers were able to secure such contracts in default of other orders. This was called 'working for poverty' by the stonemasons since this kind of work was less skilled and therefore lower paid than building or monumental work.[38]

Moreover, a few entries in the Census records and union material suggest that in bad times some stonemasons were even forced to work as quarry labourers. For example, Edward G. Rowe was described as stonemason in 1871, as quarry labourer in 1881, and again as granite mason in the 1891 Census. The same was true for older workers who were no longer strong enough to perform mason's work. Thus former stonemason Sampson Jenkin, nearly 60 years old, had had to work as a quarry labourer since losing an eye.[39] However, unions at home and abroad were generally resistant to such behaviour since working for lower wages or taking unskilled work was seen as a serious affront to the rules and traditions of the craft.[40] Similarly, 'dovetailing' (as it was known), quite common in Cornwall among small farmers, clay workers and agricultural labourers who would work seasonally in the quarries while quarrymen would go out harvesting in summer,[41] was usually resisted in the craftsmen's community.[42]

In times of recession and/or when the children were still too young to contribute to the family income, the work of the women could be of great importance. But, again, craft custom was resistant to this and there is evidence that skilled workers did not allow their wives to work (outside the family) because this was regarded as below the status of the respected craftsman.[43] However, in the Censuses for Constantine the women described as stonemasons' wives are often recorded as taking in boarders, while other ways were also found to help support the family. Emily Grigg, for example, wife of the granite mason Richard Henry Grigg, was a farmer's daughter and kept hens from which she expected to make a profit of around 30 pounds a year.[44] Coping with slack times and unemployment was to a great degree a private affair. Institutional relief provided by the Poor Law was despised by the independent, proud craftsmen and the union paid only travelling benefits. Thus unemployment was a burden shared with kin, friends and neighbours within the stonemasons' community, with the wives negotiating as necessary for credit with grocers or delays of rent.[45]

Whether tramping in search of a job, 'working for poverty' or as quarry labourers, or relying on the ingenuity of their wives, there were various ways in which Constantine stonemasons could attempt to cope with slack times. However, they were not always successful and sometimes the option of seeking work abroad was seen as unavoidable.

DESTINATIONS

Although William Tresidder, the first union mason to leave for abroad, went to Australia, few OSM members from Constantine followed him. Francis Williams (2nd) migrated to that continent in 1869 (returning in 1871) and James Symons went to Queensland in 1877, but most had heard that New South Wales was 'the only colony in Australia that has a good building stone'.[46] Certainly, Australia provided only a small labour market for stonemasons and, compared with conditions in Cornwall or the United States, trade was far more fluctuating and irregular. With few exceptions, throughout the 1870s and 1880s there were constant warnings in the union press not to emigrate to Australia since trade was bad and the labour market overstocked.[47] Exceptionally, 1883 was reported as a good year for the building trade in New South Wales and a full third of all OSM overseas migrants were reported to have sailed for Australia, but no stonemason from Constantine was among them.[48] Australia, apparently, was not a traditional destination for Constantine granite workers.[49] Similarly, Canada provided few job opportunities for granite masons. Warnings not to emigrate to Canada abounded in the union press and among those Constantine unionists who went abroad none headed for Canada.[50] As the Ontario Stonecutters' Union observed in 1872,[51] Canada was better suited to those who wished to take up farming, although at the turn of the century it did attract some Scottish granite workers.

In contrast, Table 5 below shows that South Africa and the United States were the most important destinations for emigrant Constantine granite masons.

TABLE 5:
Number of migrations of Constantine masons

years	South Africa	United States
1870-1879	9	30
1880-1889	12	38
1890-1900	6	19

In the 1860s Cornish stonemasons began granite quarrying in South Africa, manufacturing stone for banks and finance houses for expanding Johannesburg.[52] Later, Cornish stonemasons helped construct the infrastructure serving the expanding diamond and gold mining industries: they worked under government contracts in civil engineering projects such as bridge building, railroad construction or harbour and dockworks.[53] These contracts brought regular work and reasonable wages, although conditions (such as the necessity of living in tents) were sometimes criticised by the immigrants.[54] Constantine and other skilled Cornish masons were especially sought after.[55] For Constantine men South Africa was often a welcome alternative to America. In North America most quarries shut down during the winter because frost and snow made work impossible but at the same time it was mid-summer in South Africa. South African winters were also mild. Additionally, when times were hard in the States, South Africa was seen as an especially attractive destination, as in 1876-78 when seven Constantine stonemasons left Cornwall for the Cape. By the late 1890s, however, the South Africa became less popular as its labour market had become overstocked with stonemasons.[56]

As the statistics indicate, most Constantine masons left for the United States. After the Civil War there was a growing demand for memorials and monuments, while the growing cities of burgeoning industrial America needed skilled building tradesmen. As Berthoff observes, American industry drew heavily on the large pool of British workmen specialised in quarrying and cutting stone: slate workers and quarrymen came from Wales, masons or stone cutters immigrated from Cornwall and Scotland.[57] The American granite manufacturing industry expanded rapidly.[58] From 1865 the rich granite deposits in Ohio, Indiana, New York State and, above all, New England were increasingly exploited, employing the skill and experience of Scottish, Cornish, English, and later Italian and Scandinavian, granite masons. By 1890 the native American industry, largely due to the transfer of skill from immigrant workers, had reached a level of craftsmanship equal to that of the British.[59] The Cornish were especially successful, some making enough dollars to enable them to spend the idle winter months back home in Cornwall. Thus in 1885 the local union branch in Richmond, Virginia, reported that:

> our genial friend Bro. Thomas Tressider has returned from his trip in England and is once more well and hearty and would at present pass more readily for a gentleman of leisure than a stone cutter, but a few weeks at the banker (the workplace) will rub some of the polish off which he acquired during his travels.[60]

In the 1870s and 1880s Cornish stone cutters in America were probably second only in numerical importance to Scottish masons from the Aberdeen granite area. Alongside Scots names (Duncan, Scott, McDonald, and so on) Cornish names (such as Spargo, Veal, and Williams) abound in the lists of (travelling) members of the American granite masons' union journal. This considerable influx led to the establishment of a close transatlantic communication network between Cornwall and America based on trade, kin and ethnic/regional background. The existence of a great number of Cornish immigrant masons in the United States made the latter even more attractive as a destination for others in Cornwall wishing to leave for abroad. The granite manufacturing centres in the New England states of Massachusetts, Connecticut and Rhode Island were the favoured destinations for Constantine union stonemasons. Between 1885 and 1900, 39 migrations to America were recorded in the contribution books of the Constantine lodge and in the OSM Fortnightly Returns. In 29 of these cases the emigrating members were reported to have joined branches of the Granite Cutters National Union (GCNU) in America.[61]

CONSTANTINE STONEMASONS IN NEW ENGLAND

In the 1870s and, especially, the 1880s, Clark's Island in Knox County, Maine acted as a principal reception area for Constantine granite masons. In the history of the GCNU this place played a special role. Although the union was officially established as a national labour organisation in March 1877 in Rockland, Maine, it was the Clark's Island workers who had initiated the foundation of a national union in January of that year. Cornishman William T. Spargo was the first president of the Clark's Island branch and the vice-president was Thomas Venner, father-in-law of the Constantine mason Richard Grigg who died in South Africa in 1885. In July 1877 the GCNU had already 17 branches in seven different States and in one of the British provinces, with a total of 1,300 members.[62]

Between 1880 and 1885 ten Constantine masons turned up at Clark's Island; five others made their ways to places such as Quincy, Massachusetts. In Clark's Island one firm specialising in building work employed between around 30 and 90 granite cutters, depending on the local state of trade. Almost all workers seem to have been GCNU members. Among them were two emigrants who had left Constantine as early as 1872, William John Caddy and Thomas H. Hocking, who, along with a few other Constantine masons (Robert Hocking, John Richards, Walter Williams) settled with their families in Clark's Island for good or, at least, for a long period of time. In 1902 W.J. Caddy was appointed high sheriff of Knox County. Fellow Cornishman, Harry Julian, corresponding secretary of the Stony Creek, Connecticut branch of the GCNU, where Caddy had worked for some time, congratulated him 'on laying down the handhammer for the more important duties to which he has been called'.[63]

In late 1885 the Clark's Island quarries fell into swift decline, and production was suspended from 1886 until 1900. Constantine masons began to look elsewhere for work, and between 1888 and 1898 Hallowell, Maine attracted eight Constantine men, although none seems to have settled permanently. Hallowell was prominent for its building and tombstone work, two companies employing together between 80 and 225 granite cutters in the late 1880s and as many as 285 in December 1897. In search of employment nine Constantine masons travelled to Hurricane, Maine, between the late 1880s and the turn of the century, one Simon L. Drew settling there in the 1890s. In the late 1880s between 70 and 125 stone cutters were employed by the Hurricane Granite Co. As in Hallowell, most of the workers were GCNU members. From 1889 onwards more and more Constantine union masons turned up at Stony

Creek, Connecticut where three large firms, mainly engaged in building work, employed several hundred workers. Thus membership figures for the local GCNU branch rose from 155 in the summer of 1891 to around 500 only one year later. Amongst the fifteen Constantine migrants who worked in Stony Creek, only Peter Francis Caddy, brother of the W.J. Caddy noted above, settled there in the 1890s.

However, from 1886 the destination most favoured by Constantine emigrants became Westerly, centre of the Rhode Island granite industry and known for its building as well as monumental work. By the late 1880s around 400 workers, most of whom were unionised, were employed by C.P. Chapman, the Rhode Island Granite Works and the Smith Granite Co., the largest manufacturers in town. Between 1882 and 1900 altogether 21 granite masons from Constantine parish worked at Westerly, a considerable number of them settling there: Peter F. Caddy (who moved to Stony Creek in the 1890s), Richard J. Greenway (who had emigrated from Constantine in the early 1870s), William John Veal, Charles J. Rowling, William J. Symonds, Alfred Jenkin, William John Drew (brother to S.L. Drew) and Nicholas Dower whose brothers Richard, James B., Alfred, Benjamin and John B. also turned up at Westerly.

With the expansion of the American industry membership figures of the GCNU also increased, as did the number of its branches (there were 88 in 1888). The majority of the Constantine OSM members joined the GCNU, and Cornish members played a considerable role in its development. The best known is Josiah B. Dyer who was born at Cross in the parish of Luxulyan in 1843. He joined the OSM at the age of 18 and had worked in the Penryn district for eight years before coming to the United States in 1871. He was National Union Secretary of the GCNU from 1878 to 1895 while his brother James Edward was General Secretary of the OSM from 1872 to 1883. John Spargo was another prominent Cornish stonemason who played a major role in the American workers' movement. He was born in Stithians, worked as a granite mason in Penryn, joined the OSM and became an early member of the Social Democratic Federation before he left for the United States in 1901, becoming a leading figure in the American Socialist Party.[64]

Like Dyer and Spargo, Constantine migrants were experienced unionists. The OSM's quarterly system of election of officers[65] resulted in many Constantine unionists having acquired experience as local union officials during their working lives in Cornwall. Thus many of them knew how to run a union branch, how to organise a lodge meeting, to collect and manage members fees, or to negotiate wage questions and working conditions with employers. Sometimes a local union officer left for abroad before his period of office had expired. Thus the Constantine lodges minute book for March 1886 records: 'Lodge opened in due form at 7 o'clock Henry Jenkin 2nd (then vice president of the branch) left for America 25th March and still continued membership'.[66] In the United States a number of Constantine masons were active union officials at the local level: William John Caddy at Clark's Island and his brother Peter Francis at Stony Creek were shop stewards, while William John Veal at Westerly, Simon L. Drew at Round Pond and Hurricane, Maine, Thomas H. Hocking, at North Jay, Maine, and P.F. Caddy, at Stony Creek, were reported to have been elected as (vice) presidents or into other positions of union leadership in their respective branches. As a rule, it seems that it was primarily the older members (Drew was the exception) or those who were settled semi-permanently (rather than continually on the road) who were chosen for union offices.[67]

A great number of employment opportunities in many places awaited Constantine masons in the United States. Why, then, did they favour a few, particular places? For example, relatively few ever went to Quincy, Massachusetts or Barre, Vermont, the largest centres for granite manufacturing in the United States at the time. Wage levels and piece rates, regularity of work and other labour market conditions may have been significant considerations in determining destinations. But another factor of great importance was the emigrants' ethnicity, their regional and local background. Given similar labour market conditions in a great number of places, Constantine masons tended to move to those areas where the Cornish element was already well-established. These were also places about which they were already well informed: places where other members of the Constantine lodge had gone, where relatives, friends or workmates had worked or were working, places where Constantine people were settled and could provide lodging facilities. For example, Richard Henry Grigg spent some time living with his sister Rosina (who had married one of the Dower brothers) in Westerly. Thus community knowledge and personal contact (as well as a network based on trade union connections) shaped destinations and created a system of chain migration, maintained by letters and word sent by kin and compatriots abroad as well as through the information of returning and travelling migrants.[68]

A dynamic sense of Cornish ethnic identity was fuelled by the frequent travellings between the New World and the Old, cementing the links between those in the United States and those who had stayed behind. In the winter of 1888, the Cornish stonemason and secretary of the Westerly GCNU branch, George H. Spargo, reported in the union journal:

> A great number of boys have left within a few days for a trip across the ocean to see their friends, the old home, and spend the winter. We are sorry to miss them at the banker, in the different organizations they may be identified with, and also, but not at least, in our churches . . . I suppose some of them will be taking a wife.[69]

Most of the travellers were labour migrants who returned on completion of their working sojourn in America or those who used the slack winter season to visit and relatives at home. But there were other reasons to travel to Cornwall, too. Edward Kessel, Cornish secretary of the Stony Creek union branch, reported in 1892 that 'Brother James Pellow has left us for a visit to Penryn, Cornwall . . . it being the advice of his medical attendant'.[70]

As Spargo had intimated, some went back to Cornwall and then returned with a wife. Additionally, there is considerable evidence that first or second-generation Cornish granite cutters in America tended to marry first or second-generation Cornish women, an important factor in the consolidation of the Cornish ethnic identity. To give only a few examples: in 1887 Edward Warmington was married to Miss I. Tregaskis, both of Penryn, Cornwall, at Chicago, Illinois, while in 1890, at Milford, Massachusetts, Thomas Winn of Penzance was married to Miss Selina Thompson of Truro. In June 1901 'brother' John Spargo married Miss Jennie Caddy and a few months later Alex Caddy married Edith Opie at Stony Creek. The latter was the daughter of a Cornish-born stonemason and the Caddys were most probably the children of Constantine mason, P.F. Caddy. Thus ethnic and trade identity were often consolidated simultaneously.

Similarly, funerals were events that concerned the whole union branch, often with distinctive features such as the singing of Cornish funeral hymns. When William John Parry died at Stony Creek in 1903, Cornishman Harry Julian, then corresponding secretary of the local union branch, reported that 'a choir of Cornishmen sang funeral hymns in their well known quaint and impressive manner'. The funeral of Cornish granite mason Robert Kessel (brother of Edward Kessel), however, indicates that skilled craftsmen of differing ethnic backgrounds could unite on the basis of common craft traditions. Kessel, who was born in the parish of Mabe, in the immediate neighbourhood of Constantine, and had emigrated to New England in 1886, died at Stony Creek in 1892. As one contemporary report remarked, 'At his grave (were) men from Italy's sunny climes, from the green hills of Ireland, from Scotland's bonnie vales, from the home of the swarthy Swede and from his own loved native land, all testifying by their presence their sympathy and brotherly love'.[71]

TRAVELLING PATTERNS IN THE UNITED STATES

Typically, Constantine stonemasons did not remain in one place during their sojourn in North America but engaged in tramping. In the following, short sketches of the travellings of a number of granite cutters from Constantine, several migration patterns emerge.[72] There were various reasons why Constantine masons took to the road while in America but two stand out: seasonal unemployment and industrial disputes. But because their aim was often to maximise their income (often with the hope of returning to Constantine with savings) the masons sometimes travelled when trade was good in order to find the best piece rates.

In April 1881, at the age of 20, Henry Hill Roberts left Constantine for the first time for America, along with Robert Hocking, John Richards, Henry Williams, Francis Williams (2nd) and John Roberts. He returned in December 1882, only to again migrate to the States in April 1883, together with Henry Jenkins (lst), Henry Jenkins (2nd) and Walter Williams, returning in December of the same year. In April 1892 he went to the United States for the third and last time but almost immediately returned to Constantine in July when the New England granite manufacturers' association locked out all its workers on May Day. He remained a member of the OSM Constantine lodge until his death in November 1918. Roberts was the first of four brothers (Thomas John, John Hill, William James were the others) who all went to the United States in search of employment but returned eventually to their native village.

To judge from the scattered evidence we have (the union journal is particularly incomplete for 1881/1882) Henry Hill Roberts did little tramping in New England but worked in Clark's Island most of the time. But in the spring of 1883 business there was reported dull, which induced him to travel to Quincy. Here, however, trade was also on the decline and a large exodus of workers from that place was reported in the union journal. Roberts immediately joined this exodus and returned to Clark's Island where he was lucky to find business improving and very probably got a job at a time when many other workmates from Constantine – W.J. Caddy, Henry Jenkins (lst), Walter Williams, John Pearce, John Richards; very probably also Thomas H. and Robert Hocking – were also working there. During his brief visit to Cornwall in 1882/83 he married Bessie Burton, sister of Constantine mason Alfred Burton (who had joined the Constantine lodge in 1875 and died in 1890 at Johannesburg, South Africa, aged 35), using the occasion as an opportunity to try to persuade his brothers to join him in America.

William James Roberts eventually left Constantine with his brother John Hill and William H.J. Williams in April 1887, when he was 21 years old. His Constantine-born wife Louisa must have joined him at some time during his sojourn in America since, according to the Census, their first son was born in the United States in 1890. The birth was perhaps the reason why the family returned to Constantine in December of that year, although Roberts went again to America in the spring of 1891, returning to Cornwall in October of that year. He remained a union member until he died of phthisis in Constantine in April 1898. In America Roberts was a most active traveller. During his first sojourn he worked in Milford and Quincy, Massachusetts, in Millstone Point and Stony Creek, Connecticut, in Westerly, Rhode Island and Vinal Haven, Maine; he went to Hallowell twice and to Hurricane four times, in almost every place meeting other Constantine masons. In 1891, in his second sojourn, he again worked in Hallowell as well as in Concord, New Hampshire and Monson, Massachusetts. From November 1888 until the summer of 1889 he travelled with his brother John Hill, working together successively in Hurricane,

Hallowell and Vinal Haven. Roberts was lucky to sojourn in New England States during a period prosperity in the granite manufacturing industry, and he looked for every opportunity to earn as high a wage as possible, reading carefully reports in the union journal on the relative fortunes of the various districts.[73]

William Henry James Williams was 23 years old when he and the Roberts brothers left for the United States in 1887. After six years, in 1893 he returned to Constantine where in May 1896 he drew his travelling card and left the parish, not returning until the outbreak of the First World War. While William James Roberts represents the type of the granite mason who was always on the move, Williams travelled very little during his long sojourn in New England. In search of optimum conditions and wages, he shuttled several times between Hurricane and Hallowell between 1887 and 1890. In the latter year he participated in a successful strike for higher wages and shorter hours in Hallowell. In the spring of 1892 he left Maine and tramped via Stony Creek to Concord, New Hampshire where he was affected by the large scale lock out of all New England granite cutters by the employers' association.

The employers wanted yearly bills of prices (i.e. union-negotiated contract rates) to expire on 1 January instead of the traditional May Day. This was rejected by the GCNU, which argued that the employers were attempting to take advantage of the seasonal oversupply of workers in the winter months to force down wages and dilute union influence. 'It seems', the Concord branch secretary wrote, 'that they manufacturers want the bill to expire in the winter, when the snowbirds (itinerant stone cutters) who move to places where winter employment seems possible are flying around; then they think that the granite cutters will be solely under their control'.[74] Although the contest was protracted, the employers were unsuccessful. Indeed one Concord firm, that of Cornish-born W.H. Perry, which employed 40 workers, signed a union bill of prices and did not participate in the lock out. However, business was nearly at stand-still for several months with 400 workers idle. Nothing is known about the activities of Williams during the dispute, but in September 1893 he was reported as having returned to Constantine.

In 1881, at the age of 23, Walter Williams went to America for the first time, spending most of his time in Clark's Island before returning to Constantine in late 1882. In April 1883 he returned to Clark's Island, settling there with his family (a daughter was born in March 1885). But in the mid-1880s the granite trade in Clark's Island declined disastrously. In September 1885 he and others made an abortive trip to Milford only to find that men were being laid off there too. As one unionist remarked, 'It is a very hard blow to some as it is too late in the season to get work somewhere else, and on the other it is too early to quit for the winter as it makes the winter too long'. Williams made his way back to Clark's Island in February 1886 but in early 1887 he was on his travels again, in search of work. He was last heard of at Barre, Vermont where his tracks end in March of that year, and there is no evidence that he ever returned to Constantine. Interestingly, Walter Williams was not the only member of the family who went abroad. His brother Thomas left for Africa in November 1882, and remained registered as an emigrant member of Constantine lodge until May 1889 but was never reported to have returned home.

Robert Hocking was 19 when he went to the United States for the first time in 1873; the next year he went there again and in 1880 he travelled abroad for a third time before emigrating permanently to New England with his family in 1881. Taking this step, he followed his brother Thomas H. who had already left Constantine in 1872. Nothing is known about Hocking's whereabouts in the early 1880s but from later information it can be inferred that he settled at Clark's Island, where his brother Thomas and family lived and where in 1892 his 14 year old son drowned in an accident. His daughter was born in Clark's Island in 1896. Like many others, Hocking was forced to leave Clark's Island in the mid-1880s, tramping in search of employment time and again. His travelling activities were characterised by short sojourns and short distance moves, with periodic returns to his family at Clark's Island. Between 1885 and 1900 he worked at various locations within Maine (Belfast, North Jay, Hurricane and Spruce Head); only twice did he leave the State for short working sojourns in Vermont (Barre, South Ryegate).

In April 1889, 19 year old William J. Symonds left Constantine parish for America, along with his brother John (and their workmates William Charles Emmett and Charles John Rowling). Another brother, George, went to the States two years later. As far as is known, none of the brothers returned to Constantine. In North America W.J. Symonds was among the most active travellers of all Constantine granite cutters. Via Stony Creek, Quincy and Millstone Point he came to Westerly in the early summer of 1891, where he settled. From that time on this place became the hub of his travelling activities: until 1900 he took to the road from Westerly altogether nine times, working twice each in Hallowell, Concord and Milford. Although he had emigrated with his brother, in the United States they never tramped together in search of work.

Peter Francis Caddy left Constantine in March 1874 at the age of 19, following his brothers William John, who had left in 1872, and Alexander, who had gone to America in 1873, the latter being the only one who ever returned to Cornwall. Nothing is known about Peter Caddy's whereabouts in the United States in the 1870s. However, he appears to have lived at Westerly from at least the early 1880s to the mid-1890s (his daughter, who died at the age of six, was born there in 1883), while his brother went to Clark's Island. By September 1897 Caddy was at Stony Creek where he was reported to have joined the local GCNU branch. He was elected officer of the local union leadership twice (in 1901 and 1902); he seems to have settled at Stony Creek.

TRADE CYCLES, INDUSTRIAL DISPUTES & EMIGRATION

'Several Constantine stonemasons are emigrating to America, work being slack in the granite quarries at home',[76] so ran a short notice in the *West Briton* newspaper in mid-April 1886. Reporting on the Constantine quarries a week later, the paper stated that the parish's stonemasons 'have become migratory of late years, younger ones especially go to and from America as the work fluctuates in either country. They come and go almost as frequently as Irishmen come to England to work during the harvest months'.[77] Clearly, then, there was a close relationship between the trade cycle and the emigration of masons, but there was also a specific relationship between the emigration of Constantine stonemasons and the relative fortunes of the Cornish and American granite industries.

The 1870s were a case in point. Although trade was reported as good in Penryn in autumn 1871, other evidence shows that in the early 1870s the granite trade was rather dull in the area (for example, trade was reported as very slack in Constantine in spring 1871) but seems to have revived from 1874 onwards. Conversely, from mid-1873 onwards a decline in stone manufacturing was reported from various places in the United States. For the whole decade the granite trade cycle closely resembled the British and American building cycles. While the British building cycle reached a trough in 1871, peaked during the years 1876-1878 and declined thereafter, in the United States building activities peaked in 1871, declined after 1872 and reached a trough in 1878.

Given this relative state of trade on both sides of the Atlantic, it is no surprise that in 22 cases Constantine masons left for America in 1870-1873. And in 1874 another eleven migrants headed abroad, among whom were eight who certainly went to America. A break occurred in 1875, when the recession in the States had become general and when knowledge of the bad state of the trade had reached Cornwall: only one stonemason left for America, while for the first time a Constantine mason travelled to South Africa. For rest of the 1870s no further granite stonemasons went from Constantine to the States, although between 1876 and 1878 seven went to South Africa and one to Australia. It is interesting to note that although trade was good at home (work at various Constantine quarries were reported as very brisk in the summer of 1876) masons still left for abroad. Perhaps they had been informed of well-paid jobs in South Africa by John Matthews, the Constantine union mason who had gone to the Cape in December 1875.

There is no detailed information about the state of the trade in the Constantine/Penryn district in the early 1880s, although from 1882 onwards John Freeman & Sons was engaged in producing stone for Truro Cathedral. In November 1883 trade prospects were said to be very good at granite quarries in Cornwall. In the second half of the decade trade fluctuated violently. In April 1886 trade was slack in Constantine; in 1888 trade in Penryn was reported as good in spring, dull in October and brisk in November; throughout 1889 trade was very good in Penryn and Constantine. In fact, as the OSM Fortnightly Returns reported, granite masons with clear books (that is, union masons who had paid their dues) were much in demand at Constantine. Although American industrial cities were still expanding, there was a building depression in 1885 when some masons were reported as returning home.[78] Similarly, in 1885 only one Constantine mason left for the United States, compared to steady emigration to America in the rest of the decade (there were 20 migrations between 1880 and 1884, and 18 more between 1885 and 1889).

In 1881 and 1882 as many Constantine masons left for South Africa as for the United States. Among those unionists who went to South Africa were two who had already been to the Cape in the late 1870s and who seem to have spread their knowledge of job opportunities among their fellow unionists at home. Scattered evidence from the United States (much of it from emigrant Constantine men already established there) in 1882 showed that trade was not as good there as in the preceding years, a message conveyed by those returning to Cornwall from America who were able to report accurately even slight variations in the labour market.[79] In the second half of the 1880s the States became the main destination for overseas emigration and in 1886, when trade was slack in Constantine, 12 masons left for overseas. In 1889, despite an improvement in trade at home, another five masons travelled abroad.

By the 1890s building activity in Britain was increasing, with a peak in 1899. Conversely, building in the United States declined, reaching a trough in 1900. This is a decade for which detailed information about the state of the trade in both Constantine and New England is available. It shows that, although there was a general rise in building activity, trade in Constantine was wildly fluctuating: from 1891 to 1893 trade was very dull, in 1894 and 1895 good, from 1896 until the autumn of 1897 trade was very dull again (with the exception of March 1897), but it began to revive in September 1897 and was reported as very good until the end of 1900. In America trade declined from 1892 onwards, and between 1893 and 1895 the general business depression had a major impact on the granite industry. Trade slowly recovered from 1896 and although general house building activities had reached a trough by 1900, the granite trade was again booming from 1899 onwards.[80]

Again, the emigration of union masons from Constantine reflects this state of trade on both sides of the Atlantic. 1890 is a particularly interesting year. Trade in the States was good and stone cutters were reported to be in demand but not one from Constantine went there. This cannot be explained alone by the fact that trade in the Penryn area in that year was also good. In fact, in early 1890 the GCNU was preparing a struggle for shorter working hours in America and, therefore, Josiah B. Dyer, the Cornish Secretary of the GCNU, sent an address to the OSM hoping that any granite cutter of Great Britain:

> who may contemplate coming to this country will not do so until assured by us that everything has been satisfactorily adjusted, and

> by not coming to this country before May 1st, encourage the employers in their unreasonable attempt to stop the short hour movement, and cause a surplus of unemployed granite cutters ready to take the places of men who are endeavouring to elevate and improve the trade.[81]

A strike broke out and Constantine masons had been wise enough not to travel to America in that year.

In 1891 and 1892 trade was very dull in Constantine and altogether eleven stonemasons left for America in search of employment. However, as noted above, in an attempt to destroy the GCNU's influence the New England granite manufacturers' association provoked a large scale industrial dispute by notifying the union that unless they were willing to sign a bill of prices expiring on the first of January (instead of the first of May, as was the custom) all workers would be locked out. The union, which rejected the employers' unreasonable demand, had been given only ten days notice to submit to the manufacturers dictate. There was, therefore, no time to warn potential granite cutter immigrants. Seven stonemasons had already left Constantine, two of whom immediately returned when the struggle broke out on the first of May. The lock-out lasted for many months but in the end the workers were victorious.

After 1892 trade began to decline, and so did emigration from Constantine to America. The number of individual migrations dropped dramatically after 1893 (1890-1893 = fifteen; 1894-1900 = five) and after 1897 no more masons left for the United States. Only in 1901, when the granite trade had fully recovered, did another two Constantine stonemasons go to America. Trade was very good in Constantine from autumn 1897 till the end of 1900, and between 1898 and 1900 only one mason went abroad at all. John Sampson Jenkin went to South Africa twice, and died there in 1901. In that year South Africa was the alternative to America for most OSM members desiring to leave for overseas, but few left from Cornwall (in 1900 of a total of 53 OSM emigrants, 37 left for South Africa, including nine from Cornwall, and only six went to the States). In general, South Africa featured as a destination when trade was dull in both Cornwall and America; the emigration cycle between Constantine and the States was determined largely by the relative ebb and flow of the building trades.

LIFE-CYCLE, THE FAMILY & EMIGRATION

The great majority of Constantine stonemasons left for abroad shortly after completing their apprenticeships and joining the union, the marks of their initiation into the community of union and journeymen stonemasons. Of 16 first-time emigrants who left Constantine for abroad in the 1870s and who had joined the OSM Constantine lodge in 1868 or later, 13 left within two years of becoming union members; on average these emigrants were between 18 and 25 years old (see Table 6 below). Of course, for some young men the act of emigration was itself a symbol of adult independence, while others may have wished to taste life abroad before settling down to family life in Cornwall.[82] And, as noted already, one of the motives for emigration abroad was to acquire new skills, with temporary migration to the United States for short periods seen as part of a mason's general education in the industry.[83]

TABLE 6:
Age of migrants when travelling abroad for the first time

years	18-25	26-35	36+	unknown
1870-1879	17	4	4	8
1870-1879	24	5	-	8

Certainly, overseas emigration became a custom in a number of Constantine stonemason families in the years after 1870. For example, the four sons of Robert Roberts, quarry labourer, all emigrated to the United States in the 1880s and later returned; the six sons of stonemason John Dower all emigrated to America where they settled for good; the five sons of granite mason William Jenkin all emigrated to either America or to South Africa – some returned, some remained abroad. Similarly, much as the craft was handed down from father to son, so the propensity to travel abroad was transmitted from generation to generation. Between 1901 and 1914 eleven union granite masons left Constantine for the United States; their fathers had already been abroad in the 1870s and 1880s. For example, the two sons of T.J. Roberts, Robert J. and Alphonso, left for the States in 1907 and 1909 respectively, while Alfred Watters (2nd) and his brother Edwin T., sons of Edwin Watters, went there in 1908 and 1911 respectively. John Henry, son of Edwin's brother Alfred Watters, one of the most active Constantine overseas migrants, went to America in 1911. Thus in many a Constantine family, travelling abroad had become an integral part of family life, especially for the young whose strength and health gave them the competitive edge in the demanding environment of the American or South African quarrying industries.[84]

Although marital status played a role in determining emigration decisions (single, young masons were most prominent among the overseas emigrants) there is evidence that marriage did not necessarily restrict the propensity to travel abroad. There was a considerable number of Constantine masons who emigrated to America or South Africa only once they were married; for example, Alexander Caddy (2nd), William Jenkin (2nd), Robert Hocking and Henry Jenkin (1st), to name but a few. Similarly, as has been shown already, emigrants who had settled in the United States with their families carried on travelling a good deal. The migrations of these married stonemasons were, no doubt, to a large degree necessitated by the need to travel in search of employment, but other motives were probably also at work. For some masons going abroad might have been a way to escape the duties, monotony and constraints of family life. For some it may have even been a way to leave their wives for good.[85]

TEMPORARY & PERMANENT EMIGRANTS

From what has been discussed thus far, it is clear that there were principally two types of overseas emigrants among union masons: those who left for abroad once or several times and returned to Constantine after shorter or longer sojourns abroad, and those who emigrated and never returned to Cornwall. Table 7 shows the relative share of temporary migrants and permanent emigrants among all union masons who went abroad from Constantine.

TABLE 7:
Numbers of total emigrants, temporary migrants and permanent emigrants

years	total emigrants	temporary migrants	permanent emigrants
1870-1879	46	30	8
1880-1889	59	46	16
1890-1900	26	21	4
total:			
1870-1900	131	78	28

The figures show that there were more overseas migrations than there were emigrants, quite simply because multiple and return migrations were very common among Constantine stonemasons who travelled abroad. Of those who went overseas, around 50% returned to Constantine while the other half eventually stayed abroad. Stonemasons who returned to Constantine after having worked abroad once or several times usually seem to have been 'single' migrants in the sense that they were either unmarried or had left their families at home. This is indicated by the 1871-1891 Census returns which show that (with one exception) no children of overseas travellers were born abroad. It appears that most masons who went overseas intended to return to Cornwall eventually. This is evidenced by the fact that the great majority of emigrants retained their union membership while abroad; that is, they continued paying dues and remained members of the Constantine lodge. However, there were many who planned to come home but never did. For example, William Murphy left Constantine for Africa for the second time in December 1881 and continued his membership until January 1886 when he left the society. James Medlyn travelled to America in 1892 and was registered as an emigrant member on the roll of the Constantine lodge until April 1908 when he was reported to have left the trade. John Greenway was one of the first Constantine union masons to leave for abroad, in March 1870. He payed his dues to the Constantine OSM lodge until his death in July 1892, in Milford, Massachusetts.

The figures also show that the share of permanent emigrants among all Constantine union migrants rose in the 1880s when compared with the 1870s. This development in the 1880s reflects the general rise in emigration from Constantine in that decade. Throughout the 1870s temporary migrations predominated and the migrants of that decade were pioneers who moved to relatively unknown destinations and into an industry which, even in North America, was in its infancy. Migration abroad at that time was not without risks. For example, in June 1873 the *West Briton* reported that 'a few masons from Penryn who went to America some short time since, have returned, not being able to obtain employment after travelling hundreds of miles in search of it'.[86] By the 1880s, however, the American industry had developed and a Cornish emigration network had been established.

Between 1870 and 1879 the majority of sojourns abroad did not last longer than one year. Twenty migrations were of one year duration, one of two years, two of three years, one of four years, and two of five years or more duration, with nine unrecorded. In other words, the majority of overseas travellings were annual/seasonal migrations. The main reason for this cycle was the seasonal employment patterns prevailing in the New England granite industry, not least the paradox of high wages but winter inactivity.[87] The number of working days in America lost per year due to bad weather varied enormously. For example, in 1894 the percentage of working days declared idle in eight Connecticut stone cutting establishments varied between 8% and 49%. Also, the percentage of hours worked full time varied enormously throughout the year, according to the season: in 1893/1894, again taking Connecticut as an example, the percentage was high from May to November, peaking in June and July, but low in winter, particularly from January to March. The American granite industry was still in its infancy, and although some of the pioneer Constantine men stayed abroad most returned home.

Nevertheless, despite the early emergence of this short-term seasonal cycle, some Constantine men did settle abroad, and in the 1880s emigrants were inclined to stay overseas for longer periods. Thus, between 1880 and 1889 in 13 cases migrants stayed abroad for one year while in 16 cases they stayed two years or longer. The figures for the 1890s are similar, although in that decade the number of migrations declined as a result of worsening trade in the States, with two migrations lasting for one year and eleven for two years or more, with a further six unrecorded. The reasons for the increasing extensions of sojourns abroad are the same as those for the increasing propensity to emigrate: the expansion of the industry and the granite cutters' union, as well as the establishment of a social network based on Cornish kinsfolk in which it became easier for the migrants to bridge the winter months. In addition, some New England quarries, such as at Quincy or Westerly, began to extend their operations into the winter, albeit with a reduced labour force and at reduced wages.[88]

Significantly, some migrants not only increasingly extended their sojourns but eventually became permanent emigrants. Moreover, of a sample of 17 stonemasons who had joined the union in Constantine and remained members of that lodge for 30 years and more, six had been abroad only once, four had been abroad twice and three had gone overseas three times during their working lives. Only four masons had migrated overseas four times and more: Francis Williams (2nd) went to Australia in 1869, and to America in 1874, 1881 and 1887; Alfred Waters left for the Cape in 1882 and for America in 1892, 1894 or 1895 and 1897; John Sampson Jenkin went to South Africa in 1886, 1895 (?), 1898 and 1900; his older brother Henry Jenkin (1st) migrated to South Africa in 1881, 1886 and 1889 and to the States in 1883 and 1884. The Constantine migrant, therefore, was not the fleeting 'bird of passage' of popular fancy, continually moving to and fro between two continents. An increasing number of temporary migrants stayed abroad for periods of longer than one year. A majority of the migrants moved across the Atlantic only once or twice during their working lives, and 50% eventually became permanent emigrants.

THE IMPORTANCE OF UNION MEMBERSHIP

The great majority of the Constantine OSM members who left for abroad intended to continue their membership, thus indicating that they wanted to return to Cornwall. In places where the union was very strong, as in Constantine and in the larger Penryn area, labour was to a certain extent able to control the labour market and to prevent unorganised workers from finding employment. Thus union membership was of vital importance for returning migrants.[89] Additionally, the unions also functioned as mutual benefit societies. The OSM provided its members with accident and superannuation benefits and had a death fund of which the wives and children of masons could also become members. Overseas migrants who intended to return were concerned not to forfeit these benefits. Unlike many other British unions, the OSM had no emigration fund but its constitution had special emigration rules for those who left for overseas which permitted migrants to retain their membership while abroad. Thus, after their return, migrants were still entitled to the union's superannuation, accident and funeral provisions.[90]

Through the union journal and as a result of information volunteered by returning migrants or visiting 'brothers' from the States or the Cape, prospective union migrants were much better informed about labour market conditions abroad than other emigrants. At times, the union press also helped find a relative lost abroad: thus in 1892 Constantine mason Charles Winn, then at Hallowell, Maine inquired about the whereabouts of Penzance-born Thomas Winn (not to be confused with the Constantine mason of the same name) through the *Granite Cutters' Journal*.[91] Moreover, as noted already, in addition to this union-based communication network was an informal network based on kin, friends and workmates. These two transatlantic information flows became highly intertwined and complementary so that union masons had considerable advantages over the unorganised. Through the *Granite Cutters' Journal* and by word of mouth at union meetings, Constantine migrants were provided with detailed information about the local labour markets; local branches could assist in finding employment and could explain differences in local practices. The migrations of its members were strictly controlled by the union and through travelling loans the GCNU helped the workers in their search for work (between 1880 and 1896 branches could advance as much as ten dollars for travelling 'brothers'; the loan had to be repaid in instalments of not less than 10%).[92] Of course, union members were nearly always more skilled than their non-organised competitors, another inherent advantage in the overseas labour markets.[93] The skilled unionist was paid more than his unskilled/non-organised counterpart, and his job was usually steadier, a reflection of the power of the GCNU in New England (like its counterparts in Cornwall and South Africa) in protecting its members' interests.

During industrial disputes union members could also rely on the solidarity of their organisation. The GCNU not only provided travelling money for those who took to the road but also strike pay for those who remained. Also, militants who lost their jobs because of their union activities received acompensation and the union committed itself to finding new work for them.[94] At the same time, strikebreakers were ostracised and attacked through the *Granite Cutters' Journal*. For example, in 1885 the Westerly branch compared Cornish stone cutter Samuel Richards with Esau who sold his birthright, stigmatising him as 'a degenerate son of Cornwall who scabs himself in a republic for a few dollars', one who had *not* been inspired by the ballad 'ancient Cornishmen sang in resisting tyranny:

'There's Tre, Pol and Pen
And shall Trelawney die,
There's thirty thousand Cornishmen
Will know the reason why.'[95]

While strikebreakers were excluded from the trade union community, union meeting places offered a familiar social focus for the stonemasons and their relatives. For example, in 1885 the Milford, Massachusetts branch organised picnics and sports competitions, while in 1881 the Westerly branch announced the commencement of a series of entertainments for the winter months, consisting of singing, recitations and other amusements. These social gatherings, it was hoped, would have a good effect on the branch and would also induce those few who had not joined the GCNU yet to cast their lot with organised labour. Indeed, the branch considered that 'the attractions are numerous and above all may be mentioned the exhibition of beauty which our lady friends will lend to the occasion and any enterprising bachelor from abroad will do well to take advantage of opportunities which are so seldom offered and which deserve appreciation'.[96]

During the period of proletarian mass immigration (from about 1880 onwards) American labour unions became critical, even hostile towards newly-arrived workers. Although, as Collomp argues, the American working classes were in fact suffering the effects of rapid technological transformations, the unions claimed that there was a direct, negative effect of mass immigration on wages and employment. Between 1881 and 1897 there was hardly a year in which American labour did not demand legislative measures to restrict immigration. Most unions were craft organisations of skilled workers seeking to promote the interests of their members by aiming to limit the numbers of those who were to be admitted to the craft. Thus unions of skilled workers tried to protect themselves against a massive inflow of 'cheap' labour immigrants which was thought to embody a permanent danger to the union movement and the standard of living of its members.[97]

Although the restrictionist and exclusionary policy of American unions was directed mainly against unskilled Southern and Eastern European peasant labourers, skilled workers in the building trades, including the stone cutting trades, were not exempt from criticism. Moreover, this criticism was not confined to the new immigrant groups (such as the Italians) but was also directed against members of the 'old immigration' from which the American building trades were to a large extent recruited: the Germans, the Irish, the Scottish, the English and the Cornish, that is, those men, (the New York Journeymen Stone Cutters Association complained in 1895):

> who come here in the busy season, undercut us in wages, and leave in the fall to spend their savings on the other side of the ocean in porridge, bloaters, macaroni and sauerkraut. They return in the spring, enriched in experience, but impoverished in pocket, their appetites sharpened for American beef, and incidentally the American dollar.[98]

Despite the high proportion of foreign-born amongst its membership, the GCNU also harboured restrictionist attitudes. Like the New York stone cutters' association, granite cutters accused immigrant stonemasons of flooding the labour market and cutting down wages, although the inter-ethnic solidarity of the craft remained strong. As the secretary of the Concord branch put it: 'brethren let us drop calling one another foreigners and say we are members of the GCNU'. Craft was therefore increasingly more important than ethnicity, although there was a recognition that the GCNU owed much to the efforts of certain immigrant nationalities. As one Rhode Island granite cutter put it: 'Foreigners hurt the trade in some respects, owing to working for small pay . . . but Workmen belonging to trades unions are the best, Scotch, Irish, and English workmen are the best in the trade, and assimilate with the native workmen better than any other nationality'.[99] Thus craft tradition, union membership, and ethnic background combined to earn the Constantine and other Cornish granite stonemasons a privileged position in an atmosphere in which immigrant labour was often viewed with hostility.

CONCLUSION

After 1900 Constantine stonemasons continued to travel and work abroad. Although British emigrants increasingly turned to the Dominions and Colonies, most Constantine workers, following an emigration tradition by then well-established, left for the United States. The increasing competition of high quality Norwegian granite led to a severe depression in Cornish granite manufacturing in the years 1904-1910. Quarries were forced to close and workers lost their jobs or had to work at reduced wages. Under these circumstances, as Stanier notes, workers went abroad to seek employment, notably in the granite quarries of Vermont.[100] From Constantine, of a total of 41 stonemasons who emigrated abroad between 1901 and 1910, 31 left for America during the years 1904-1907 alone, when the crisis was at its peak. In this period, probably more than ever before, economic conditions forced granite masons to travel abroad.

The classic era of Constantine emigration, however, was the period 1870-1900, and it was due to the courage of these travelling Cornish stonemasons that Constantine and similar places in Cornwall became connected with the wider world, with places like Westerly, Rhode Island, Johannesburg or Golden Square, Victoria. By working in the New Worlds these ordinary working men with their skill and persistent diligence helped build Australia, South Africa and, particularly, the United States of America. By sending back remittances or returning enriched with money and new experiences, Cornish stonemasons also helped their families to live secure and decent lives, and assisted the development of the granite trade at home. The high rate of return shows that Cornwall was very dear to those who took part in these international labour migrations. Like Cornish emigrants generally, Constantine stonemasons abroad were proud of their Cornish descent.

ACKNOWLEDGEMENTS

The author is indebted to Peter H. Stanier, Dirk Hoerder, Franco Ramella, and especially Geraldine L. Gove of the Constantine Local History Group, for their assistance. Research for this article was made possible through a grant of the *Deutsche Forschungsgemeinschaft.*

NOTES AND REFERENCES.

1. Dudley Baines, *Migration in a Mature Economy: Emigration and Internal Migration in England and Wales 1860-1900*, Cambridge, 1985, p.73, p.157.
2. Philip Payton, *The Cornish Farmer in Australia*, Redruth, 1987.
3. For an assessment of the impact of emigrant Cornish miners, see: John Rowe, *The Hard-rock Men: Cornish Immigrants and the North American Mining Frontier*, Liverpool, 1974; Philip Payton, *The Cornish Miner in Australia*, Redruth, 1984; A.C. Todd, *The Cornish Miner in America*, Truro, 1967; A.C. Todd, *The Search For Silver: Cornish Miners in Mexico*, Padstow, 1977; G.B. Dickason, *Cornish Immigrants to South Africa*, Cape Town, 1978; Gill Burke, 'The Cornish Diaspora of the Nineteenth Century', in Shula Marks & Peter Richardson (eds.) *International Labour Migrations: Historical Perspectives*, London, 1984, pp.57-75; see also A. L. Rowse, *The Cornish in America*, London, 1969, republished Redruth 1991.
4. Baines, 1985.
5. Todd, 1977, p.59; Dickason, 1978, p.39; Payton, 1984, p.36.
6. As detailed in the volumes noted at reference 3.
7. Ewa Morawska, 'Labour Migrations of Poles in the Atlantic World Economy, 1880-1914', *Comparative Studies in Society and History*, 31, 1989.
8. Raphael Samuel, 'Mineral Workers', in Raphael Samuel (ed.), *Miners, Quarrymen and Saltworkers*, London, 1977, pp.14-16.
9. Peter Stanier, 'The Granite Quarrying Industry in Devon and Cornwall', *Industrial Archaeology Review*, VII, 1985, and XI, 1986; Philip Payton, 'Quarrying: Slate and Granite', in *Cornish Studies for Schools*, Truro, 1992.
10. Charles Henderson, *A History of the Parish of Constantine in Cornwall*, Truro, 1937, p.213, pp.227-28; set firmly in the antiquarian tradition, this history fails even to mention the existence of the granite industry.
11. *West Briton*, 31 August 1876, 22 April 1886; George F. Harris, *Granites and Our Granite Industry*, London, 1888, pp.34-37, pp.48-49; Joyce and Basil Green, 'The Granite Industry - Stithians' in Alison M. Penaluna (ed.), *Still More Aspects of History in Stithians*, Stithians, 1986, p.7; 'Operative Stone Masons Society, Constantine Lodge Minute Book', March 1866, February 1888.
12. For this information the author indebted to Mrs Geraldine L. Gove, great-granddaughter of James Richard Grigg.
13. Stanier, 1985.
14. *West Briton*, 22 April 1886.

15. *West Briton*, 19 February 1874; 15 February 1883, 15 March 1883; for the death of Constantine masons due to phthisis see 'Operative Stone Masons Society, Constantine Lodge Contribution Books', November 1847 – September 1921.
16. Harris, 1888, p.48.
17. William H. Mulligan, 'From Artisan to Proletarian: The Family and the Vocational Education of Shoemakers in the Handicraft Era', in Charles Stephenson and Robert Asher (eds.), *Life and Labour: Dimensions of American Working-Class History*, New York, 1986, pp.23-24; David Methven and Donald Bousfield, 'The De Lank Granite Quarries', in *A History of St Breward: The Life of A Moorland Village*, Padstow, nd, p.103.
18. Bernard Deacon, 'Attempts at Unionism by Cornish Metal Miners in 1866', *Cornish Studies*, 10, 1982; Bernard Deacon, 'Heroic Individualists? The Cornish Miners and the Five-Week Month 1972-74', *Cornish Studies*, 14, 1986; Philip Payton, *The Making of Modern Cornwall: Historical Experience and the Persistence of 'Difference'*, Redruth, 1992, pp.139-150.
19. See 'OSM Returns', 12 December 1878 – by comparison, in the same year there were only two branches of the Amalgamated Society of Carpenters and Joiners with a handful of members in Cornwall, one at Penzance and another at Falmouth/ Penryn, see 19th Annual Report of the ASCJ; for the history of the OSM see Raymond W. Postgate, *The Builders' History*, New York, 1984; W.S. Hilton, *Foes to Tyranny: A History of the Amalgamated Building Trades Workers*, London, 1963; the first contribution book of the Constantine lodge, held at the Modern Records Centre, University of Warwick, starts with entries in November 1847; for the early history of unionism among Cornish masons see Alfred Jenkin, 'The Operative Masons of Luxulyan', *Journal of the Cornwall Association of Local Historians*, No.8, 1984.
20. See 'OSM Returns', 12 December 1878, which shows that Constantine masons may have worked in Penryn and joined the union lodge there; according to the 'Contribution Books' membership rose from 33 in 1848 through 49 in 1871 and 67 in 1881 to 93 in 1900, while according to the Census the number of masons including apprentices (who were not allowed to join the OSM) rose from 63 in 1861 to 127 in 1881, but dropped to 104 in 1891; only very few of them (seven in 1861, eight in 1881 and eight in 1891) were house-building masons, the rest were described as stonemasons/cutters or granite masons/cutters.
21. Robert A. Leeson, *Travelling Brothers: The Six Centuries Road from Craft Fellowship to Trade Unionism*, London, 1979, p.242; Eric Hobsbawm, 'The Tramping Artisan', in Eric Hobsbawm (ed.), *Labouring Men: Studies in the History of Labour*, London, 1976, p.42, p.52.
22. Payton, 1987, p.28; Payton, 1984, p.36; Dickason, 1978, p.91.
23. The Tresidders were great-uncles of the father of Mrs Geraldine L. Gové, to whom the author is indebted for this information.
24. 'OSM Returns', 21 January 1892; for reports of higher money wages for stone cutters in South Africa see also Anon, *Reminiscences of a Stonemason*, London, 1908, p.233; see also '15th Annual Report of the Massachusetts Bureau of Statistics of Labour, 1883', Boston, 1884, pp.255-256; Peter Shergold, 'Reefs of Roast Beef: The American Workers Standard of Living in Comparative Perspective', in Dirk Hoerder (ed.), *American Labour and Immigration History 1877-1920s: Recent European Research*, Urbana, 1983, pp.81-82.

25. Stanier, 1986.
26. 'Third Annual Report of the New York Bureau of Statistics of Labour, 1885,' Abany 1886; 'Thirteenth Annual Report of the New York Bureau . . . 1896', p.387; 'Sixth Annual Report of the Rhode Island Bureau of Industrial Statistics, 1892', Providence, 1893.
27. *Granite Cutters' Journal*, November 1893, see also November 1894 and Fred Bower, *Rolling Stonemason*, London, 1936, p.75, p.83.
28. Bower, 1936, p.43; *West Briton*, 22 April 1886.
29. Eric Hobsbawm, 'The Aristocracy of Labour Reconsidered', in Eric Hobsbawm (ed.), *Worlds of Labour: Further Studies in the History of Labour*, London, 1984, p.242.
30. *Granite Cutters' Journal*, April 1885, July 1887, September 1887, August 1888, October 1892.
31. Arthur W. Brayley, *History of the Granite Industry in New England*, Boston, 1913, vol. 1, p.99, pp.104-5, p.107, pp.150-51; vol.2, pp.43-44, p.85, p.120; Rowse, 1969/1991, p.401.
32. Marjorie Harper, *Emigration from North-East Scotland: Volume 1: Willing Exiles*, Aberdeen, 1988, p.256.
33. A.L.Rowse, *A Cornish Childhood*, London, 1942, p.34, p.87; the author is indebted to Mrs Pamela Bousfield of the St Breward Local History Group for providing information regarding W. Gill.
34. Rowe, 1974, p.17.
35. OSM Constantine Lodge, 'Contribution Books'; the author is indebted to Dr Peter Stanier for information on the Freemans contracts for Barry and Cardiff docks.
36. OSM Constantine Lodge, 'Contribution Books'.
37. David Crew, 'Regionale Mobilitat und Arbeiterklasse: Das Beispiel Bochum 1880-1901', in Dieter Langewiesche and Klaus Schonhoven (eds.), *Arbeiter in Deutschland: Studien zur Lebensweise der Arbeiterschaft im Zeitalter der Industrialisierung*, Paderborn, 1981, p.85.
38. Methven and Bousfield, nd, p.101; *West Briton*, 16 June 1887; Stanier, 1985, p.177.
39. 'OSM Returns', 27 November 1890.
40. See 'Thirteenth Annual Report of the New York Bureau of Statistics of Labour', 1895, pp.317-318; ASCJ, 'Monthly Reports', August 1897.
41. Paddy Powell, 'Farming', in *A History of St Breward*, nd, pp.38-40; see also Samuel, 1977, pp.62-63.
42. Hobsbawm, 1984, pp.231-232; it seems, however, that in some (non-unionised) rural villages artisans did turn to unskilled out-door work when necessary without losing their superior craftsman's status, see Raphael Samuel, 'Quarry Roughs: Life and Labour in Headington Quarry, 1860-1920: An Essay in Oral History', in Raphael Samuel (ed.), *Village Life and Labour*, London, 1975, pp.165-167, p.195.
43. Hobsbawm, 1984, pp.238-239.
44. The author is indebted to Mrs Geraldine L. Gove for this information.
45. Alexander Keyssar, *Out of Work: The First Century of Unemployment in Massachusetts*, Cambridge, 1986, pp.143-176.
46. 'OSM Returns', 3 February 1870; 8 October 1885; see also 8 December 1870; 16 August 1883.

47. 'OSM Returns', 15 April 1880; see also, for example, 12 September 1872, 18 April 1878, 23 June 1881 and *Granite Cutters' Journal*, December 1889.
48. 'OSM Returns', 11 October 1883; 51 of the 153 OSM members who were reported as emigrants in the Returns for 1883 gave Australia as their destination.
49. For the importance of such traditions in the migration process see Reino Kero, 'Migration Traditions from Finland to North America', in Rudolph J. Vecoli and Suzanne M. Sinke, *A Century of European Migrations, 1830-1930*, Urbana, 1991, pp.111-133.
50. See, for example, 'OSM Returns', 3 July 1873, 6 April 1876, 17 August 1882.
51. 'OSM Returns', 4 July 1872.
52. Dickason, 1978, pp.22-23.
53. 'OSM Returns', 20 September 1900.
54. See letter of five Penzance stonemasons, Bloemfontein and Vaal River Railway, Orange Free State, 7 November 1891, in 'OSM Returns' 7 January 1892; see also 9 March 1876, 5 April 1877, 28 September 1882, 21 January 1892, 20 September 1900.
55. The author is indebted to Peter Stanier for this information.
56. 'OSM Returns', 14 September 1871, 12 February 1874, 16 October 1879, 26 December 1889, 20 September 1900; ASCJ 'Monthly Report', December 1893; in the period 1901-1914 only three stonemasons left from Constantine for South Africa.
57. Rowland T. Berthoff, *British Immigrants in Industrial America1790-1950*, New York, 1953, pp.78-81.
58. Brayley, 1913, p.134; 'Twentieth Annual Report of the Massachusetts Bureau of Statistics of Labour', 1889, p.305.
59. Thomas Donnelly, 'The Development of the Aberdeen Granite Industry, 1750-1939, unpubl. PhD, Aberdeen University, 1975, p.195.
60. *Granite Cutters' Journal*, March 1885; this worker was not identical with the Constantine mason Thomas Tresidder who had gone to the United States in 1871 and 1873.
61. For a short sketch of this union see Gary M. Fink (ed), *Labour Unions*, Westport, 1977, pp.136-137.
62. See OSM Returns, 23 August 1877; *Granite Cutters' Journal*, October 1892, February 1897, March 1897.
63. *Granite Cutters' Journal*, February 1902.
64. See *Granite Cutters' Journal*, April 1900.
65. 'Rules of the Operative Stone Masons Friendly Society', Manchester, 1871, pp.7-8.
66. OSM Constantine Lodge, Minute Book; in 1887 or 1888 James H. Jenkin himself also went to the United States where he lived and worked in Westerly, Quincy and Vinal Haven,. Maine; he seems to have never returned.
67. 'Constitution and Bye-Laws of the Granite Cutters' International Union', Rockland, Maine, 1877, p.36.
68. For comparative references to Cornish chain migration see Patricia Lay, 'One and All: The Cornish in Colonial New South Wales', unpubl. MA thesis, Australian National University, 1992.
69. *Granite Cutters' Journal*, December 1988.
70. *Granite Cutters' Journal*, May 1892.

71. *Granite Cutters' Journal*, November 1892.
72. Based on information in the OSM Constantine Lodge, Contribution Books, the *Granite Cutters' Journal*, and the Census returns for Constantine parish.
73. *Granite Cutters' Journal*, January 1890.
74. *Granite Cutters' Journal*, May 1892.
75. *Granite Cutters' Journal*, December 1885.
76. *West Briton*, 15 April 1886.
77. *West Briton*, 22 April 1886.
78. *The Times*, 14 February 1885.
79. *Granite Cutters' Journal*, August 1883.
80. For the 1890s see Brayley, 1913, p.134.
81. OSM Returns, 20 February 1890.
82. James H. Jackson, 'Migration in Duisburg, 1821-1914', unpubl. paper 1991.
83. Donnelly, 1975, p.269.
84. Anon, 1908, pp.119-120.
85. Gill Burke, 'The Decline of the Independent Bal Maiden: The Impact of Change in the Cornish Mining Industry, in Angela V. John (ed.), *Unequal Opportunities:Women's Employment in England 1800-1918*, Oxford, 1986, p.199.
86. *West Briton*, 9 June 1873.
87. 'Second Annual Report of the Massachusetts Bureau of Statistics of Labour', 1871, pp.307-308; 'Tenth Massachusetts Report', 1879, p.154.
88. *Granite Cutters' Journal*, March 1888.
89. OSM Returns, 16 May 1889; 17 October 1889; 27 January 1898; 11 January 1900.
90. 'Rules of the Friendly Society of Operative Stone Masons of England, Ireland and Wales', Sheffield, 1881; for example, when Alfred Walters and Henry Hill Roberts, two active Constantine overseas migrants, died in 1917/1918 they were both entitled to the ten pounds funeral benefit, OSM Constantine Lodge, Contribution Book; see also Humphrey Southall, 'British Artisan Unions in the New World', *Journal of Historical Geography*, 15, 1989.
91. *Granite Cutters' Journal*, January 1892.
92. 'Constitution and Bye-Laws', Maplewood, Massachusetts, 1880, p.17; generally, the GCNU constitution was to modelled on the OSM rules; the British union, however, provided for more insurance benefits.
93. 'Third Annual Report of the New York Bureau of Statistics of Labour', pp.519-521.
94. 'Constitution and Bye-Laws of the Granite Cutters International Union', Rockland, Maine, 1877, p.15.
95. *Granite Cutters' Journal*, September 1885.
96. *Granite Cutters' Journal*, December 1881; see also August and September 1885.
97. Catherine Collomp, 'Unions, Civics, and National Identity: Organized Labours' Reaction to Immigration, 1881-1897', *Labour History*, 29, 1988; see also Robert Asher, 'Union Nativism and the Immigrant Response', *Labour History*, 23, 1982; A.T. Lane, *Solidarity or Survival? American Labour and European Immigrants,* Westport, 1987.
98. 'Thirteenth Annual Report of the New York Bureau of Statistics of Labour', p.392.
99. 'Sixth Annual Report of the Rhode Island Bureau of Industrial Statistics', p.148.
100. Stanier, 1985.

LABOUR FAILURE AND LIBERAL TENACITY: RADICAL POLITICS AND CORNISH POLITICAL CULTURE, 1880-1939

Philip Payton

INTRODUCTION

Considerable attention has been focussed recently on the issues of continuity and change in Cornish politics in both the nineteenth and twentieth centuries,[1] with varying emphases placed on the durability of Liberalism, the fluctuating fortunes of the Conservatives, and the relative inability of Labour to make sustained headway. The purpose of this article is to draw these elements together, to present a concise synthesis of current perspectives, but also to argue that despite (or rather, because of) the rapid socio-economic changes that confronted Cornwall in the late nineteenth century, a remarkable strand of continuity in the Cornish radical tradition perpetuated the issues of 'classical Cornish Liberalism' to the eve of the Second World War. This not only helps to explain the fortunes of the Conservatives and, more particularly, of Labour but also suggests an intimate relationship between a distinctive Cornish political culture and the wider Cornish identity in the period under review. And, although it is not the place of this article to pursue discussion of Cornish politics into the post-War era, it can be argued that the Liberal Party's ability in the years before 1939 to project itself as both the plausible radical alternative to the Conservatives and as the 'Cornish party' meant that it was well-placed to assume the mantle of anti-metropolitanism in the period after 1945, co-opting where electorally appropriate the rhetoric and even policies of Cornish nationalism.[2]

THE POST-1832 LEGACY

The election year of 1885 has often been portrayed as a turning-point in British political history, with the widespread extension of the franchise leading to a more democratic and certainly more popular style of politics.[3] However, this view has been contested of late, at least in its Cornish context, with Jaggard arguing that many of the supposedly 'new' characteristics observable in 1885 could be detected at an earlier period in nineteenth-century Cornish political history, while many of the features of the election in Cornwall represented a considerable degree of continuity rather than change. Certainly, an identifiably Cornish style of politics had emerged in the years after 1832, one whose characteristics were deeply entrenched and familiar by the 1880s.

Gash has commented that politically 'The Denbighshires and the Cornwalls were counties on the fringe of England and hardly representative of the mass of the country'[4] in the period after 1832 but Jaggard notes that Cornwall, although isolated from the 'centre', was in fact not immune to influences from elsewhere.[5] Rather, the particular characteristics of Cornish politics were not the result of any peripheral marginalisation from contemporary political debate but represented both the enduring strength of the Liberal-Nonconformist nexus and the failure of the local Tories to grasp the nature of post-1832 electoral realities.

As Jaggard remarks, even in the late 1850s the Conservatives still 'revealed a preference for the interventions of wealthy and supposedly powerful parties like the Tremaynes, Bassets, Carews, Vyvyans, Edgcumbes and Bullers whose heyday was more than half a century in the past...'.[6] Many of the notable families had in any case found a home in the Liberal camp,[7] while the Liberals proved adept at organising registrations and other local activity.[8] Although, for example, the Tories were able to hold St Ives between 1832 and 1868, and Helston between 1832 and 1857 and again between 1859 and 1865, they did not contest the West Cornwall seat on a single occasion between 1832 and 1884.[9] This Tory ineptitude was against the background of prevailing socio-economic conditions not conducive to Conservative vitality: 'the strength of Nonconformity, the weakness of the large landowners, the generally small scale of farming, and the paucity of nucleated villages . . .'.[10] The latter, the legacy of a scattered Celtic settlement pattern, physically isolated families from the influence of squire and parson and, it has been argued, bred a sense of independence.

To this climate was added a tradition of large-scale, sophisticated and often devious electioneering (such as that which marked the successful Liberal campaigns in the East Cornwall constituency in 1860 and in 1868), a phenomenon which is often claimed as a 'new' feature of 1885 election activity but which in Cornwall at least was already familiar behaviour. Indeed, this level of electioneering may help to explain both the attempts by local Tories in the 1880s to improve their organisation and the increasing resentment felt by radical Liberals towards the stifling hegemony of Liberal Party managers in Cornwall.[11] The former led in 1884 to a Tory threat to field a candidate in West Cornwall, a proposition which did much to galvanise political debate locally. The latter was felt most acutely in the mining districts of West Cornwall, and the extension of the franchise coupled with the creation of the new 'Mining Division' constituency (based on Camborne-Redruth) for the 1885 election was an opportunity for the radicals to vent their frustrations. Arthur Pendarves Vivian had been Liberal MP for West Cornwall since 1868, on each occasion returned unopposed, and his claim to continue as the district's MP rested on his reputation as a good constituency man who had supported local interests. He had managed, however, to upset some local opinion leaders, such as the well-known architect Silvanus Trevail who threatened 'I'll have my knife into him'[12] and threw in his lot with the radical agitators.

THE LEADING EDGE OF BRITISH POLITICS?

The 1885 election in the 'Mining Division' became not, therefore, the anticipated clash between Liberal and Tory but, as L.L.Price put it in 1895, an 'intense and bitter . . . contest between Whig and Radical . . .'.[13] For the radical Liberals had found as their candidate to oppose the offical Liberal (Vivian) one Charles Conybeare, an Essex man with Cornish family connections. In the language of the time, the election was seen as a struggle between 'count house' and 'dry', with Conybeare condemned by his opponents as a 'Red-Hot Radical Agitator'[14] and accused of setting class against class. Conybeare demanded better conditions for the miners and adopted popular radical themes such as anti-landlordism, abolition of game laws, abolition of the House of Lords, disestablishment of the Church of England, graduated income tax, the local option (for pubs to be closed on Sundays), votes for women, and triennial elections – a portfolio of policies built on the traditional Liberal-Nonconformist nexus but also designed to appeal to the newly-enfranchised voters, especially the miners.[15] Interestingly, he advocated a form of 'Home Rule All Round', with the devolution of power to Cornwall and other democratically elected County Parliaments – remarkably, an interpretation of the then forthcoming Local Government Act of 1888 still echoed by Mebyon Kernow in the mid-1960s![16]

Such was the excitement of the election campaign that special constables and even a detachment of troops were deployed in Redruth. The result itself was close but conclusive; Vivian with 2,577 votes had lost to Conybeare's 2,926. Opinion at the time, echoed recently in Deacon's discussion of the election, held that Conybeare owed his success to the Division's miners.[17] Commenting on the radical disposition of the Cornish miners, one observer explained that:

> the political creed of the overwhelming majority . . . is neatly, precisely and completely Democratic . . . .It is as Cornish as the Cornish pilchard and Cornish humour . . . .We may find the explanation in the daily lives of these people, . . . the miners, between whom and the artizans and small farmers exists . . . a solidarity of political opinion and material interest . . . .These

> solidarity of political opinion and material interest . . . .These men are so downright democratic even in their religion![18]

More than fifteen years before Keir Hardy's famous victory as an Independent Labour candidate in Merthyr, when he took on Wales' Liberal establishment and won, Conybeare's success meant that, as Deacon has put it, 'Redruth and district was at the leading edge of British politics'.[19] However, for reasons to be discussed below, this status was short-lived. But, before proceeding to that discussion, it is important to consider further the background to this radicalising impulse in the Mining Division. Conybeare's careful manipulation of the Liberal-Nonconformist nexus and the newly-enfranchised miners was significant but is best understood in the light of the radical behaviour that had come to typify the Cornish miners at home and abroad in the twenty years before 1885.

Although A.K. Hamilton Jenkin and others have characterised the Cornish miner as resistant to collective action, an 'innate' individualism combining with the competitive effects of the tribute and tutwork system of employment to inhibit co-operative behaviour,[20] recent research has done much to focus on what Deacon has termed the 'lost history' of the Cornish working class.[21] Sporadic strike action at certain Cornish mines in the 1830s and 1840s had turned to more concerted action by the 1850s, and in 1866 the first determined attempt at organised trade unionism occurred at the East Cornwall and Tamar Valley mines where miners from St Cleer, Menheniot and Gunnislake flocked to join the Miners' Mutual Benefit Association. In the early and mid-1870s there was another upsurge of collectivist activity amongst the Cornish miners, exhibited throughout Cornwall in places as disparate as St Cleer, St Blazey, Helston and St Just-in-Penwith, with its epicentre in the Camborne-Redruth district – particularly the tin mines of Illogan parish. Overseas, the Cornish miners were similarly active, especially in the copper mines of South Australia (run on Cornish principles, including tribute and tutwork) where during the 1860s and 1870s they forged an effective trade union structure.

It is clear that the unrest in the Cornish mines in the 1870s had had a radicalising effect in what was to become the Mining Division constituency, and Conybeare benefited from this. He also received encouragement from emigrant Cornish miners, with telegrams of support from 'Cousin Jacks' in North America arriving during the campaign.[22] However, Conybeare had caught not the highpoint of radical activity amongst the miners but rather its tail-end, for by 1885 the heady days of 1866 and the 1870s were already passed long since. The Association in East Cornwall had fallen victim to the calamitous crash of copper in 1866, when many of the mines were forced to close and the aspirant trade unionists had been compelled to emigrate, taking their newly-formed collectivist notions to destinations such as South Australia. Similarly, the shortlived tin boom that accompanied the wave of collectivist action in the

1870s was over by 1874, with emigration again depriving the community of many of its natural leaders. This situation was of crucial significance because not only did it leave Conybeare dangerously exposed in the period after 1885 but also it nipped in the bud these early attempts to form a labour movement. As Burke has remarked, 'The diminution of the Cornish industry during these years was most certainly one important factor in the delayed advent of Trade Union organization on any scale in Cornwall . . .'.[23] More generally, this served to retard the development of the Labour Party in Cornwall and ensured that the Liberals would remain heirs to the Cornish radical tradition. In that sense, the cataclysmic socio-economic catastrophe that had overtaken Cornwall – the widespread abandonment of mines and the consequent unemployment, emigration, depopulation, de-industrialisation, and general dereliction – actually promoted continuity rather than change in Cornish politics.

LIBERALS & LIBERAL UNIONISTS

This continuity was disguised, however, by the apparent flux of the years after 1885. Conybeare's victory had suggested a move to the left (in an election where every other seat in Cornwall was won by the Liberals) but the subsequent events of the late 1880s and 1890s indicated an apparent swing to the right, to the emergent Liberal Unionists. It is possible to interpret this shift as the collapse of Cornish radicalism (attendant on the collapse of Cornish mining), with the Liberal Unionists becoming swiftly the core of a re-defining Conservative (and Unionist) Party in Cornwall.[24] But, while Conybeare's radicalism came to little, the Liberal Party (and its Nonconformist connection) was more enduring and the Cornish electorate more consistently anti-Tory than the fortunes of the Liberal Unionists in Cornwall might at first glance suggest.

The general election of 1886 was a disaster for the Liberal Party throughout Britain, with the loss of scores of seats as Chamberlain's Liberal Unionists deserted the Liberal fold in opposition to Irish Home Rule. Amongst the areas of Liberal Unionist strength was Cornwall ('Chamberlain's Duchy'[25]), the Unionists winning three Cornish seats. Two other seats remained in official Liberal hands, with Conybeare continuing to hold the Mining Division. However, the popularity of Unionism as a cause could not disguise the weakness of Conservatism proper in Cornwall, a weakness reflected in the great difficulty experienced by the Tory grass-roots Primrose League in establishing itself in Cornish constituencies. Despite its impact elsewhere in Britain in the 1880s (including other areas of traditional Liberal support, and even in neighbouring Devon and Somerset), the League found Cornwall almost impenetrable: 'Only in some rural districts such as the Scottish Highlands and parts of Cornwall and Wales did the political culture prove hopelessly hostile to the league's form of Conservatism'.[26] Liberal Unionists in Cornwall, then, were by no means a Tory 'Trojan Horse' but were quite genuiniely Liberals with a Unionist (and Cornish) face.

Certainly, the Liberal Unionists remained a significant force in Cornwall until the 1906 'Liberal Landslide' general election and, indeed, they re-emerged briefly in 1910 in some strength. However, in practice the Liberal Unionists in Cornwall were virtually indistinguishable from their Liberal opponents, save for their hostility to Irish Home Rule, as in St Ives constituency where the Liberal Unionist MP, T.R. Bolitho, (returned unopposed in 1892 and 1895), was a staunch radical. As Pelling has observed, the attraction of Bolitho and others was not at all the Liberal Unionist pact with the Conservatives but rather the fact that *Cornish* Liberal Unionists were opposed to Irish Home Rule while remaining unswervingly Liberal on domestic and Cornish issues. As Pelling concluded, in Cornwall 'representatives of the Unionist cause had fought as Liberal Unionists rather than as Conservatives; their success indicated a body of opinion which, while radical on domestic questions, was conservative on Imperial policy'.[27] Given the size and economic importance of the Cornish communities in South Africa and Australia, the Cornish interest in Imperial policy is understandable. Cornish hostility to Irish Home Rule is more difficult to explain (there were no sizeable Irish communities in Cornwall) but may have reflected a Cornish-Irish antagonism that had emerged overseas, bolstered by domestic religious and strategic issues. Just as Cornish Methodists had earlier opposed Catholic emancipation, so in the 1880s they may have feared for the future of their fellow Nonconformists in a 'Rome Rule' Ireland. Equally, given the geographic proximity of Cornwall to southern Ireland, Cornish fishermen may have expected to be excluded from Irish waters. Thus they were persuaded to vote Liberal Unionist, despite the fact that 'The fishermen . . . were regarded as being strongly Radical'.[28] Paradoxically, support for the Liberal Unionists emphasised the continuing political importance of Cornish Nonconformity while also highlighting the significance of Cornish issues and Cornish perceptions.

A victim of this paradox was Conybeare himself, when in 1895 he was defeated by the plausible A. Strauss, a Liberal Unionist who advocated the notion of 'bimetallism' to raise the price of tin, winning the attention of a disappointed electorate in the Mining Division which after the euphoria of 1885 had had to endure a decade of increasing depression. Many of those miners who had voted so enthusiastically for Conybeare had subsequently lost the vote as a result of dependence on poor relief, while others had emigrated to South Africa or America.[29] But just as Cornish perceptions on Imperial issues (such as Ireland) had allowed the emergence of the Liberal Unionists, so it was that similar perceptions (this time on South Africa) led to an erosion of that support. The Boer War was a political issue of importance throughout Britain, of course, but in Cornwall it had a peculiar immediacy and relevance. Although there were those who feared for the future of emigrant Cornish communities at the hands of the Boers, and argued therefore for a vigorous prosecution of the war, there were also those who feared that the hostilities would threaten the flow of all-important financial support (monies sent home by Cornish miners) from South

Africa to Cornwall. Others were genuinely 'pro-Boer' as a result of their democratic convictions, and in Cornwall the Liberals were successful in marshalling this range of opinion so that in the 1900 election 'Cornwall voted against the national tide when Liberal Unionist lost to the Liberal Radical, who was a pro-Boer'.[30] In the Mining Division, Strauss was defeated by the Liberal 'pro-Boer' W.S. Caine who, in an echo of 1885, received considerable support from emigrant Cousin Jacks, claiming that 'out of 700 Cornish miners home from South Africa, at least 650 had voted for him'.[31]

Liberal Unionist support in Cornwall was further eroded in the early 1900s as a result of Nonconformist hostility to the Conservatives' Education Bill (with which, inevitably, the Unionists were implicated), the Liberal *West Briton* noting that some Liberal Unionists had returned to the Liberal camp: 'Unionist Nonconformists have not sunk all their Nonconformity in their Unionism'.[32] In North Cornwall the Kilkhampton Bible Christian Circuit rallied against the Education Bill, in 1902 exclaiming that 'The members of our churches and congregations prize and stand by the privileges of civil and religious liberty won for them by their forefathers at a great cost and handed down not simply to enjoy, but to establish and extend'.[33] At the same time, South Africa remained a political issue, with the proposal that the Transvaal mines be restored to full scale production through the employment of Chinese labour provoking heated debate in Cornwall. At first Cornwall was equivocal, the *Mining Journal* noting that 'contrary to what might generally have been expected in a county which, taken by and wide, is essentially Liberal not to say Radical . . .'[34] the proposition was receiving support from those who saw the rapid restoration of South Africa's mines as being in Cornish interests. However, the arrival of 'Coolies' in the Transvaal hardened Cornish opinion. Fears that the Chinese would take Cornish jobs (and money destined for Cornwall) was articulated as Radical-Christian opposition to 'Chinese Slavery', the Coolies portrayed as unwitting victims of exploitation. Cornish Methodists had played a major role in the abolition of slavery (this is why, it was said, they did not take sugar in their tea) and were susceptible to persuasion from the likes of the *Cornubian* newspaper: 'Will you vote for Chinese labour? If it be not a kind of slavery, what is it?'[35]

THE AGE OF ALIGNMENT?

In the general election of 1906 the Liberal Unionists (supposed supporters of 'Chinese slavery') were trounced in Cornwall, each Cornish constituency returning a Liberal member. The reassertion of Cornish Liberal Nonconformity was complete, with contemporary observers from Launceston to St Austell to the Penwith peninsula noting both the return of traditional radicals (such as the miners and fishermen) to the Liberal fold and the time-honoured use of Methodist chapels as Liberal recruiting stations.[36] 'Chinese slavery' was indeed stopped by the incoming Liberal government, and in the general election of 1910 – when the Liberal Unionists regained many of their former seats – Cornwall remained solidly Liberal, although in the December marginal Bodmin did fall to the LIberal Unionists. By then Cornwall had become confirmed in its position as part of Britain's 'Liberal heartland', although the potential for the further radicalisation of the electorate (and thus the intrusion of Labour) was clearly limited by the continuing decline of mining, the consequent retardation of trade unionism, and emigration. In Britain as a whole, however, the period between 1910 and the Second World War was marked by a process in which the Liberals were replaced progressively by Labour as the principal radical alternatives to the Conservatives, an 'Age of Alignment' (as Cook has termed it)[37] in which British politics was transformed into a Labour versus Tory contest.

In Britain as a whole, argues Cook, the fatal point of Liberal downfall was reached in 1924, while by 1929 they had slipped too far to be an effective force in British politics, their role as the radical alternatives to the Conservatives inherited by Labour. As Koss has observed, this process of Liberal decline was exacerbated by the changing nature of Nonconformity. Not only were the Nonconformist churches by now increasingly depoliticised but their numerical strength and thus influence was falling, while the Liberal-Nonconformist link was increasingly perceived as anachronistic: 'Radical Nonconformity, once a force to be reckoned with in national life, was not dormant but dead'.[38] There were, however, as Koss admitted, 'isolated areas' where the Liberals continued to enjoy a close relationship with a still vibrant Nonconformity, and one of these was Cornwall. As Kinnear has shown, Cornwall in the inter-War period remained overtly Nonconformist in character, even when compared to neighbouring Devon or other Methodist strongholds such as County Durham.[39] Against the background of a continuing and deep paralysis in Cornish society and economy which Labour found difficult to penetrate, the Nonconformist vote remained, as Tregidga puts it, 'the key factor in the electoral base of Cornish Liberalism'[40] in the 1920s and 1930s. Indeed, in 1929, the point of no return for the Liberals in so many other areas, Cornwall could be described as 'the last refuge of Liberalism'.[41] As Smart has remarked, in Cornwall 'the age of alignment was the age of consolidation'.[42]

In the aftermath of the First World War, Cornwall had participated in the bewildering faction-fighting of British politics, in the 1918 general election returning two 'Lloyd George Liberals' and two Conservatives, and in 1922 returning two 'Lloyd George Liberals', one 'Asquith Liberal', and one Conservative. In 1923, however, the Liberals recaptured all five Cornish seats, although in 1924 (when the Liberals were almost annihalated at Westminster) they held only Camborne – the old Mining Division – and even then with their candidate standing as a 'Constitutionalist'. Five years later, in 1929, there was a very limited Liberal revival in parts of Wales, Scotland and rural England, despite the increasing consolidation of the Conservative-Labour contest, but in

Cornwall the Liberal recovery was spectacular and complete. They took all five seats, presenting Cornwall to puzzled outsiders as a curious anachronism. In the remaining general elections of the inter-War era – 1931 and 1935 – Liberal representation of Cornwall was swifly reduced to two and then one (with the newly-emerged National Liberals additionally taking St Ives), mirroring their even more disastrous performance elsewhere in Britain. Although, as Tregidga says,[43] it must be admitted that the Liberals in Cornwall were generally in decline in this period, their share of the vote falling in each successive election after 1929 and not beginning to rise again until as late as 1955, they had nonetheless secured the consolidation of Cornish politics as principally a Liberal-Conservative contest. Cornwall had not participated in the great 'Alignment'.

This consolidation served to perpetuate the classic concerns of Cornish Liberal Nonconformity such as the local option and Prayer Book revision, with Sir Francis Acland, Liberal MP for North Cornwall, campaigning in the 1930s for the disestablishment of the Church of England.[44] Indeed, Tregidga asserts that the 1929 'election in Cornwall was virtually a referendum on temperence',[45] and in the Parliamentary career of Isaac Foot traditional Cornish Liberalism and its demands had a major voice. Foot represented Bodmin for much of the period, monopolising the radical vote (Labour did not save its deposit until 1945) and benefitting from his status as a popular local preacher in South East Cornwall. It is said that at Looe the local fishermen painted their boats in Liberal colours in honour of 'Our Isaac'; he was 'a radical, uncompromising Liberal, a staunch Methodist of illuminating faith . . .'.[46] To Koss, who stressed the demise of Liberal Nonconformity in the inter-War period, Foot was an inexplicable enigma: 'surely the last of the great Nonconformist parliamentary careers'[47] But in Cornwall he was anything but an enigma. In the by-election campaign which led to his victory in March 1922 Foot caught the imagination of Bodmin constituency. A by-election song, 'And shall our Isaac win?' (sung, inevitably, to the tune of 'Trelawny'), was composed for the occasion, while:

> The scenes on Saturday afternoon at the declaration of the poll beggared description . . . the enthusiasm of Nonconformist farmers, of earnest young preachers, of dark-eyed women and fiery Celtic youth had something religious about it. No such fervour could be seen elsewhere outside Wales.[48]

It was difficult for Labour to make much headway against such vehement championship of Cornish Liberalism. For reasons discussed above, the Labour movement in Cornwall had been handicapped by the disastrous collapse of mining and consequent socio-economic change. In 1906 a socialist candidate had received a paltry 1.5% of the vote in the Mining Division, the non-Tory vote going overwhelmingly to the radical Liberal, A.E. Dunn, the same

Dunn who unsuccessfully contested St Ives as a Labour Party candidate in 1918 (the first Labour contestation in Cornwall). In Camborne constituency Labour was hampered by the dramatic decline in the number of working miners (from 8,700 in 1913 to only 400 by 1920). In Falmouth and Penryn their prospects were firmer, trade unionism having established itself in the local dockyard, but in the St Austell area (where the clay workers had flirted with trade unionism) the Liberals were seen as the traditional supporters of Free Trade and thus the clay industry. Bodmin was difficult country for Labour and North Cornwall was equally hopeless – indeed, in the 1939 by-election (and 1945 general election) Labour and Liberal party members worked together to support T.L. Horabin, the radical Liberal candidate who, ironically, later defected to Labour.

Generally, Labour failed to exploit the potential of a Nonconformist connection, although where it was successful locally at grass roots level it was often when it acted as a surrogate Liberal Party.[49] In this way, for example, Labour had some success in local government in the china clay country in the inter-War period. At the Parliamentary level, Labour targeted the Falmouth and Penryn seat in particular, with A.L. Rowse, the well-known Cornish historian, carefully nurturing the constituency. In Labour's debacle in 1931 he kept his share of the vote steady, in 1935 coming second with 32.1% of the vote, preparing the way for Labour's historic victory there in 1945. Indeed, elsewhere Labour was able to achieve some respectable results, so that in 1929, for example, it obtained 17% of the vote in St Ives and 25% in Camborne. As Smart observed, 'the Liberal victors in the Cornish seats must have reflected on how close Labour came to letting in the Conservatives'.[50] However, as Smart has also noted in his analysis of Labour fortunes in the 1920s, 'Labour's regional performance at the end of the decade in vote share terms is no better than at the beginning'.[51] For A.L. Rowse and other Labour activists this was a source of great frustration, Rowse complaining of 'backward Cornwall, smothered as it was in Nonconformist Liberal humbug . . .'[52] and explaining that 'The prime task for Labour was to bring home the futility of going on being Liberal'.[53]

But if Labour was unable to 'break the mould' of Cornish politics, the Conservatives in the 1920s and 1930s established themselves more securely than had been possible before. Despite the spectacular Liberal triumphs of 1923 and 1929, Liberal-Conservative conflict did become more finally balanced, with the Conservatives doing especially well in the 1930s. In the aftermath of the union between Conservatives and Unionists, there developed an understanding between the Tories and the National Liberal faction, epitomised (as Lee has noted) in St Ives constituency where 'the period since 1918 has seen an unusual relationship between Liberals and Conservatives'.[54] In 1931 and 1935 the National Liberal candidate was returned unopposed, and thereafter the National Liberals continued to hold the seat, the tacit understanding between National Liberals, Liberals, and Conservatives reflecting a common desire to ensure that a Labour candidate was not elected. This, in turn, reflected the tone of Liberal anti-Labour invective in Cornwall, a phenomenon which, paradoxically, played into Conservative hands at a time when Conservatism generally in Britain was being rehabilitated under the guiding hand of Baldwin. The progress of the Conservative Party in Cornwall was to some extent an expression of hostility towards Labour's intervention but contributed to the situation in which Cornish politics was consolidated as a Liberal-Tory contest.

CONCLUSION

On the eve of the Second World War, therefore, Cornish politics was still essentially a battle between Liberals and Conservatives – a consolidation rather than participation in the great 'Alignment' that had occurred elsewhere. This represented a remarkable degree of continuity from the nineteenth century but it was a political continuity dependent upon the socio-economic change that had retarded Labour. This consolidation and continuity also meant that Cornish politics was increasingly differentiated from that of England, evidence of an increasingly distinctive Cornish political culture. This was to become important for although the Cornish Revivalists of the inter-War period generally eschewed the notion of political (as opposed to cultural) nationalism, after 1945 they were less fastidious. They were able to exploit the legacy of political distinctiveness inherited from the inter-War period, while the Liberals themselves moved to absorb elements of Cornish nationalism into their political catechism.

NOTES AND REFERENCES

1. E.K.G. Jaggard, 'Patrons, Principles and Parties: Cornwall Politics 1760-1910', unpubl. PhD, Washington University, 1980; Peter Heyden, 'Culture, Creed and Conflict: Methodism and Politics in Cornwall c1832-1879', unpubl. PhD, University of Liverpool, 1982; Philip Payton, 'Modern Cornwall: The Changing Nature of Peripherality', PhD, CNAA (Plymouth), 1989, especially chapters 7 and 10; Garry Tregidga, 'The Liberal Party in Cornwall, 1918-39', unpubl. MPhil, University of Exeter, 1991; E.K.G. Jaggard, 'The Age of Derby outside Parliament: New Orthodoxy for Old?', *Journal of the Royal Institution of Cornwall*, new series, Vol.10, Pt.1, 1986-87; N. Smart, 'The Age of Consolidation: South West Electoral Change in the Age of Alignment', unpubl. paper, Plymouth Polytechnic, 1988; Bernard Deacon, 'Conybeare for Ever!', in Terry Knight (ed.), *Old Redruth: Original Studies of the Town's History*, Redruth, 1992; E.K.G. Jaggard, 'Political Continuity and Change in Late Nineteenth-Century Cornwall', *Parliamentary History*, Vol.11, Pt.2, 1992; Philip Payton, *The Making of Modern Cornwall: Historical Experience and the 'Persistence' of Difference*, Redruth, 1992; Garry Tregidga, 'The Survival of Cornish Liberalism, 1918-45', *Journal of the Royal Institution of Cornwall*, new series II, Vol.1, Pt.2, 1992; E.K.G. Jaggard, 'Liberals and Conservatives in West Cornwall, 1832-1868', *Cornish Studies: One*, new series, 1993; Adrian Lee, 'Political Parties and Elections', in Philip Payton (ed.), *Cornwall Since the War: The Contemporary History of a European*

Region, Redruth, 1993; Bernard Deacon, 'The Cornish Working Class: A Lost History' in Jenni Thompson (ed.), forthcoming, 1994.

2. Payton, 1992, pp.228-230.
3. For example, W.A.Hayes, *The Background and Passage of the Third Reform Act*, New York, 1982.
4. Norman Gash, 'The Organisation of the Conservative Party 1832-1846: Part II', *Parliamentary History*, Vol.2, 1983.
5. Jaggard, 1986-87.
6. Jaggard, 1986-87.
7. For example, see Alison Adburgham, *A Radical Aristocrat: Sir William Molesworth of Pencarrow*, Padstow, 1990; T.A.Jenkins (ed.), *The Parliamentary Diaries of Sir John Trelawny, 1858-1865*, London, 1990.
8. Jaggard, 1993.
9. Jaggard, 1993.
10. Henry Pelling, *Social Geography of British Elections, 1885-1910*, London, 1962, p.162.
11. Jaggard, 1992.
12. Jaggard, 1992.
13. L.L. Price, 'West Barbary', 1895, reprinted in Roger Burt (ed.), *Cornish Mining: Essays on the Organisation of Cornish Mines and the Cornish Mining Economy*, Newton Abbot, 1969, p.130.
14. *Royal Cornwall Gazette*, 29 May 1885.
15. Deacon, 1992, p.38.
16. Geoffrey Moorhouse, *The Other England*, London, 1964, p.41.
17. Deacon, 1992, p.40.
18. *West Briton*, 24 September 1885.
19. Deacon, 1992, p.37.
20. A.K. Hamilton Jenkin, *The Cornish Miner*, 1927, republished Newton Abbot, 1972; see also D.B.Barton, *Essays in Cornish Mining History, Vol.1*, Truro, 1968, pp.46-47.
21. Deacon, forthcoming, 1994; see also Gillian Burke, 'The Cornish Miner and the Cornish Mining Industry 1870-1921', unpubl. PhD, University of London, 1981; Bernard Deacon, 'Attempts at Unionism by Cornish Metal Miners in 1866', *Cornish Studies*, 10, 1982; Bernard Deacon, 'Heroic Individualists? The Cornish Miners and the Five Week Month 1872-74', *Cornish Studies*, 14, 1986; Philip Payton, *The Cornish Miner in Australia*, Redruth, 1984, chapter 8; Payton, 1992, pp.140-148.
22. *West Briton*, 30 November 1885.
23. Burke, 1981, p.383.
24. Ian Soulsby, *A History of Cornwall*, Chichester, 1986, p.108.
25. Soulsby, 1986, p.108.
26. M.Pugh, *The Tories and the People*, Oxford, 1985, p.136.
27. Pelling, 1962, p.173.
28. Pelling, 1962, p.164.
29. Pelling, 1962, p.165.
30. Richard Dawe, 'The Role and Influence of the Cornish in South Africa 1886-1925', unpubl. MA, CNAA (Middlesex), 1986, p.48.
31. *Cornish Post*, 27 September 1900.

32. *West Briton*, 12 February 1903.
33. Cornwall Record Office, DDX 384.3, 'Kilkhampton Bible Christian Minute Books 1891-1910', 19 June 1902, Resolution 11.
34. *Mining Journal*, 2 April 1904.
35. *Cornubian*, 20 January 1906.
36. *Western Morning News*, 19 January 1906; *West Briton*, 23 April 1906; W.H. Hudson, *The Land's End: A Naturalist's Impression in West Cornwall*, 1908, republished London, 1981, p.102.
37. Christopher Cook, *The Age of Alignment: Electoral Politics in Britain 1922-29*, London, 1975.
38. Stephen Koss, *Nonconformity in Modern British Politics*, London, 1975, p.11.
39. Michael Kinnear, *The British Voter: An Atlas and Survey*, London, 1981, p.127.
40. Tregidga, 1992.
41. Cited in Tregidga, 1992.
42. Smart, 1988, p.28.
43. Tregidga, 1992.
44. Tregidga, 1992.
45. Tregidga, 1992.
46. Sarah Foot, *Isaac Foot: My Grandfather*, Bodmin, 1980, p.6.
47. Koss, 1975, p.161.
48. *Cornish Guardian*, 3 March 1922; see also Tregidga, 1992.
49. Tregidga, 1992.
50. Smart, 1988, p.15.
51. Smart, 1988, p.15.
52. A.L. Rowse, *A Man of the Thirties*, London, 1979, p.55.
53. Rowse, 1979, p.91.
54. Adrian Lee, 'How Cornwall Votes', unpubl. paper, Plymouth Polytechnic, 1977, p.15.

AUTHENTICITY IN THE REVIVAL OF CORNISH

Charles Penglase

INTRODUCTION

Cornish people who are eager to speak the language of their ancestors are confronted by many problems, evident from their first enquiries about the language, for not one but three forms of Cornish are spoken in Modern Cornwall. These different versions of the language are 'Unified' Cornish, 'Phonemic' or 'Common' Cornish, and 'Modern' Cornish. Nance presented Unified Cornish, his reconstruction of Middle Cornish, in the inter-War period, and it is still used by many people (including the Cornish Gorseth in its ceremonies) although it has been abandoned by a significant number of prominent revivalists.[1] Phonemic or Common Cornish and Modern Cornish, both of which appeared in the 1980s, are the two alternative forms of the language now used by the revival movement in Cornwall, and they differ radically. For the confused Cornishman or Cornishwoman who wishes to participate in the revival of the language, the decision must be faced as to which form he or she is to speak.

This article is a response to this problem and it has one basic premise: that authenticity is the most desirable quality of a revived language. It is this quality which gives the revival movement its validity for the Cornish people whose aspirations it represents. Indeed, contravention of the principle of authenticity, the necessity of ensuring that the revived language mirrors traditional Cornish, has caused enormous and continuing problems in the revival movement and provoked scepticism amongst academics in the field of Celtic Studies. In the search for the authentic Cornish language, the recognition of philosophical assumptions, premises, and methods underlying the research which resulted in the current forms of the three versions of the language is vital, since the relative authenticity of each form of the language (and its relevance to the Cornish people) depend on these crucial features.

UNIFIED CORNISH

Despite the recommendation of Henry Jenner, the instigator of the revival, that the Cornish language should be revived from the point where it left off (i.e. 'Late' or Modern Cornish), the language in the period of the sixteenth to the eighteenth centuries, Robert Morton Nance reconstructed his version of the language, Unified Cornish, based on Middle or Mediæval Cornish, the language of the fourteenth to the early sixteenth centuries. Although this version of Cornish has come under sustained fire from both academic observers and popular practitioners, it is important to give a brief description of its composition because Phonemic Cornish or Common Cornish as it was later called,[2] the version promulgated by the Cornish Language Board, is essentially the same language with changes to the phonology and orthography carried out in the 1980s. The sources for Middle Cornish and the nature of the language itself posed inherent difficulties for the accurate reconstruction of the language and these are the factors mainly responsible for the contrived nature of Nance's version.

The Middle Cornish language survived in religious literature, the so-called miracle plays and the Mount Calvary or Passion Poem. Since there were gaps in the language presented in these texts Nance reconstructed aspects of the language employing techniques of internal analogy. He also adopted grammar (together with idiom) from Modern Cornish. Since the extant sources of the language exist in rhymed or scanned verse rather than prose, Nance constructed the syntax by comparison with Middle Breton. The Middle Cornish verb structure is complex and requires many verb parts not all of which naturally exist in the texts. Comparison with other Celtic languages was, therefore, brought to assist in the construction of these parts of the relevant verbs. For gaps in vocabulary, words were borrowed from Welsh or Breton.[3] The whole was spelled according to the orthographical system devised by Nance which was essentially a rationalisation of the Middle Cornish spelling.[4] The pronunciation of the language was based predominantly on Modern Cornish phonology and the traditional West Penwith pronunciation of English.[5]

The problems with this version of the language are self-evident. The grammar is in some important respects invented, the syntax is a combination contrived from different periods and another Celtic language, the vocabulary includes words not of Cornish origin, the orthography (although it looks much like the original) is not exactly as the language was spelled, and the phonology is influenced by that of another period and another language. It is, therefore, like no Cornish spoken at any period in the history of the Cornish language. Academics in the Celtic field rejected Unified because they recognised that it was not 'genuine' but, rather, to an appreciable degree 'invented'. One scholar concluded that Unified was 'to a considerable extent a nineteenth and, more especially, a twentieth-century invention, in its orthography, its pronunciation, its vocabulary, and even its grammar'.[6] Due to such criticism of Unified from without as well as within the language movement, various changes were adopted by the Cornish Language Board, changes that focussed on the phonological and orthographical systems. The basis for the changes was the proposals presented by Ken George in his dissertation 'A Phonological History of Cornish' (1984).[7] As an academic work, specifically a doctoral dissertation presented at the Université de Bretagne Occidentale in Brittany, George's proposals provoked considerable interest and attention.[8] It is important to investigate this study here since the change from Unified Cornish to Phonemic was based on its results.

THE PHONEMIC REVISION

Given the criticism of Unified that had emerged, some sort of improvement in revived Cornish was clearly necessary. The approach followed in George's dissertation was to leave the grammatical and syntactical basis of the language essentially unchanged and to concentrate on the matters of phonology and orthography. These appear to be Ken George's chief concerns with the language; it is entirely understandable in view of the inadequacies of Unified that he should try to do something about these aspects.[9] On the basis of his (not uncontestable) assumption that Nance's preparation of the language was essentially satisfactory in grammatical and syntactical aspects,[10] the only answer to at least some of the major criticisms directed at Unified was to take steps to improve the existing language in its phonology and orthography. Indeed, the phonology and orthography were really the most attractive aspects for reorganisation in view of the fact that they are the easiest parts of the language to change. There is really little that could be done differently from Nance in the approach to the reconstruction of the grammar and syntax of Middle Cornish, in view of the nature of the language and of the extant sources, since they are few and all exist in the form of religious rhymed or scanned verse rather than the relatively normal syntax of prose. A complete reworking would have been a task with no real concrete rewards. To introduce its results would have required a probably unobtainable level of consensus. The proposals of Ken George were in effect the only real solution for the Board to the problems inherent in Unified unless the revivalists were prepared to abandon Nance's version entirely. The only other alternative was the adoption of Modern Cornish but this appeared to be no solution since no thorough study of Modern Cornish was generally available, while the conventional wisdom suggested that Modern Cornish represented an impure and corrupt form of the language greatly influenced by English, naturally an unattractive feature for revivalists.[11] The course adopted by the Board may have been different had it been generally known that Modern Cornish was in reality a flexible, varied and distinctly Cornish vernacular, far less influenced by English borrowings than Middle Cornish.[12]

In the absence of a clear picture of Modern Cornish, revision of the phonology and orthography of Nance's system was seen as the best solution, and an academic study appeared to be the most effective instrument for the purpose. The result was Ken George's dissertation and the new Phonemic or Common Cornish soon to be adopted by the Cornish Language Board. Unfortunately, however, there are serious objections to George's work, and these help to explain the uncertainty and confusion that has overtaken the revivalist movement in recent years. For those accustomed to a traditional humanities approach to language studies, George's dissertation is unconventional. For instance, there is no critical review of relevant literature, no general discussion of the many controversial issues involved, and a considerable reliance on assertion. Another unusual feature is the lack of a thesis statement. It was certainly a good idea to try to make use of computer power for the analysis of large quantities of data, and this is to be commended. However, the use of a computer does not actually enhance the credibility of the results since examination of the research methods soon reveals that the computer serves only to give technical assistance in the processing of the data. In any case, even if an advanced programme had been devised, it would only have been as good as its initial assumptions. In addition, instead of using *Fortran*, which brought the unnecessary complication of mathematical coding into the study, it might have been much better to use one of the other systems available at the time, such as the *Datatrieve* programme used regularly in the humanities and social sciences. Numerical coding assigned according to the programmer's premises actually precludes comprehensive analysis of verbal data.

Certain assumptions underlie important aspects of George's argument. Unaddressed assumptions are, of course, undesirable in any discussion, and if they are sufficiently central to the argument (as these are) then their effect is to disqualify or at least seriously question the conclusions of the discussion. One unwarranted assumption which affects the analysis of the phonology (and thus George's proposals with regard to phonology) is that the orthography and hence the presumed phonology of Middle Cornish is adequate and accurate for all the periods in which the Cornish vocabulary is extant.[13] On the contrary, it would have been a far better idea to devise a method of studying the phonology of the different periods in their own terms. Likewise, the effect that variations in spelling have in the study of the phonology is also an important issue, but it seems that it is merely assumed that variations in spelling reflect alterations in the pronunciation. A difficulty the impact of which it is hard to estimate is the assumption that Cornish spelling follows contemporary English spelling, which in fact was itself variable in every period of relevance to Cornish.[14] This aspect needs discussion at the very least. These assumptions are all central to the discussion of the phonology and their presence seriously compromises the validity of the proposed system. In addition, there should be examination of the proposition which assumes certain precise sounds for the reconstructed Middle Cornish phonology. In fact, the proposition is untestable which means that the sounds remain merely hypothetical. A further point not answered is the question of the relationship of early Breton phonology to early Cornish. For example, the lack of discussion of the derivation of the hypothetical sounds of early Breton raises the fear that Breton phonology is being arbitrarily imposed on Cornish phonological history, an impression strengthened by references elsewhere.[15]

The use of appropriate research methodology is essential in an academic work. There is a number of unusual methodological features in George's dissertation, but there is no point in listing them all. However, one crucial omission which deserves mention is the lack of a critical investigation of the validity of the Middle Cornish phonology; this is assumed. Whether one thinks a feature is valid or not, it has to be critically examined and supported by firm evidence. In fact, the absence of these requirements makes the application of this phonological system to Cornish an arbitrary imposition on the language. In this context the critical analysis of sources, which is entirely missing in the dissertation, is essential. The phonology of Middle Cornish is, after all, an inherently controversial subject on which it is possible for widely different stands to be taken. As there is no critical examination of the issue, George's phonology can be viewed at most only as one opinion. For instance, the work of A.R. Thomas in his section on Cornish in *Language in the British Isles*[16] presents a quite different account of Middle Cornish phonology but the only reference by George to this work is the comment 'His (Thomas') account of MidC phonology bears little resemblance to the results of my own researches, and one can have little confidence in it'.[17] Another methodological criticism which may be levelled at the study is that there appears to be some influence of French phonology via Breton on the precise definition of certain sounds, and if this is so it is surely an ineligible connection. For instance, the precise definition of (*oe*) as in French seems to indicate this influence, as do the conclusions on the Cornish vowel system in George's *Pronunciation and Spelling of Revived Cornish.*[18]

The second proposal of the dissertation is the replacement of the Unified orthography with a new orthography. The new orthography incorporates the phonological system for Middle Cornish presented earlier in the dissertation. Since nowhere in the dissertation was the new system critically examined for validity this tends automatically to place the spelling system on a somewhat insecure footing. However, some justification for the adjustment of the spelling system is attempted in the one section of the dissertation which exhibits sustained argument[19] but unfortunately there are a number of unacceptable assumptions. For example, it is immediately apparent that the question of historical authenticity was overlooked in the discussion of orthography, despite the concern earlier in the dissertation to establish an 'authentic' Middle Cornish phonology. Perhaps it was assumed that the issue of authenticity was irrelevant or inappropriate to orthography. Indeed, where Nance's Unified system was basically a rationalisation of the Middle Cornish spelling, George's modification was in many ways an invention.[20] George's justification for this, as he says elsewhere, is that 'invention is not of itself a bad thing' if the reasons given for it are sufficiently persuasive.[21] As he explained, in inventing his new orthography he was guided by four main principles.[22] First of all, the new orthography should be as phonemic as possible since most people learn Cornish from books. Secondly, the etymology of words, and (strangely) their relation to Welsh and Breton cognates, should still be recognisable. Thirdly, the new spelling system should try to reconcile the desires of different groups in their attempts to pronounce Cornish in approximately Middle Cornish and Modern Cornish fashions. Lastly, the system should retain enough similarity to the Unified so that the contemporary Cornish speakers would not reject it.

There is, therefore, no discussion of the central issue of trying to remain true to traditional Cornish. And yet the underlying assumption involved in a revival movement is the need to restore a traditional language, something which once existed, and it is this which gives a revival movement its cultural and historical validity. This was overlooked with the invention of a new twentieth-century system in which, as the guiding principles reveal, the real concern was language planning rather than language revival. It is not surprising that the decision by the Cornish Language Board in 1987 to accept George's system should have led to a series of objections, expressed in the words of one leading Cornish scholar who warned that 'the Language Board has taken an unjustifiably wrong turn . . .'.[23] Oddly enough, in criticising Richard Gendall's attempts at Modern Cornish innovation in the Unified *Kernewek Bew*[24] with the observation that 'this automatically introduced a 300 year difference between the spelling and pronunciation',[25] George seemed unaware that in his new system there was a 500 year gap between the presumed Middle Cornish pronunciation and the invented orthography of the 1980s.

Although it is understandable that the Cornish Language Board should desire to improve Unified Cornish, one must conclude that no especial reliance can be put on the authenticity of the new phonology, while the new orthography is clearly not authentic. At the practical and popular level, potential learners are being offered a language which is not traditional Cornish, while at an academic level Phonemic Cornish is no more appropriate for university studies than is Unified, which was never accepted by the academic world because of the contrived aspects of grammar, syntax and some vocabulary. Phonemic Cornish is essentially the same language as Unified Cornish, with a new phonology and a new orthography, neither of which advance it to a new academic plane. Indeed, the original Cornish texts of all periods cannot be studied without transliteration, and the translation of texts from the Modern period into Phonemic Cornish would be particularly undesirable.

MODERN CORNISH

As a response to the perceived difficulties in Unified Cornish and the problems inherent in trying to reform it, some concerned revivalists decided to abandon this version of the language and return to Henry Jenner's suggestion of taking the language up where it had left off in about 1800. The intention was to revive Modern Cornish, which is the name now given to the form of the language which spans the ('Late') period from the sixteenth to the eighteenth centuries. Since the early 1980s when serious research was begun, Richard Gendall (currently an Honorary Research Fellow at the University of Exeter) has carried out the majority of the work on this form of the language, and the result of his efforts is the revival of Modern Cornish, presented in a complete form in several publications.[26] The high quality of the research into the Modern form deserves commendation, especially for its detail, precision, and accuracy in analysing Modern Cornish as it exists in the texts. These characteristics have ensured the authenticity of the language and have resulted in increasing academic interest, with several academics wishing to include Modern Cornish in their studies and courses.[27] The basic premise which is evident in all of the research into Modern Cornish is that authenticity should be the ruling factor in the language, that the language should be as it was spoken and written by the Cornish people of the seventeenth and eighteenth centuries.[28] This premise accords with the assumption which commonly underlies the activities of a revival movement. Gendall shows that he is aware that a revival movement depends on authenticity for its validity and argues that the construction of an artificial form of a language 'that has no historical precedent, severely limits the credibility . . . and does much harm'.[29]

Gendall's research stresses authenticity in all aspects of the language – grammar, syntax, phonology, and orthography. The success in achieving authenticity in these aspects was, of course, aided considerably by certain characteristics of the language and its extant remains. Modern Cornish grammar is relatively simple in comparison with the complexity of aspects of Middle Cornish. For instance, the tense formation in Modern Cornish follows a simple system involving the use of five auxiliary verbs, *boaze*, *gweele*, *gallus*, *guthvaz*, and *menna*, whereas Mediæval Cornish inflects virtually all available verbs. The simplicity of the tense formation in Modern Cornish verbs means that the parts of the irregular auxiliary verbs are extant in the texts, and the few other verb parts necessary, such as the verbal root, can be directly derived with considerable accuracy from any extant forms. The advantage that Modern Cornish has in the authenticity of its syntax is due to the fact that the extant sources of Modern Cornish exist predominantly in the form of prose which generally follows everyday speech patterns, in contrast to the artificial patterns which occur in verse. The sources for Middle Cornish exist, of course, in the form of rhymed or scanned verse and as a result Nance had no alternative but to reconstruct the syntax by comparison with Middle Breton. The enormous strength of Modern Cornish with regard to the authenticity of its phonology is the fact that it was documented shortly after 1700 when it was still a living language. In 1707 Dr Edward Lhuyd, an Oxford scholar, published in *Archaeologia Britannica* his study on Modern Cornish, including a detailed account of the pronunciation system.[30] Regarding the orthography, the same orthography as found in the texts of the Modern period has been adhered to in the recent presentation of the language, so that the spelling of words follows that in the texts of the Cornish writers of that period.[31]

Despite the general high quality of research that has led to the revival of Modern Cornish both as a spoken language and as a subject of academic study, there are some problems, particularly with regard to aspects of the phonology and grammar. With regard to the phonology, it is important to remember that the only sources relevant to the establishment of the sounds of Modern Cornish and the pronunciation of individual words are the contemporary phonological study of Lhuyd and the original texts themselves; the latter often supply alternative spellings for words thus helping to define their pronunciation. Gendall has argued, however, that the sounds of Modern Cornish as last spoken may be detected in the speech of elderly people in West Penwith today, insisting that their sounds match those recorded by Lhuyd, while Séamus Ó' Coileáin has attempted a reconstruction of the sounds of Modern Cornish.[32] Ó'Coileáin agrees with Gendall's assessment, and notes that just as in bilingual areas of Wales and Ireland people use the sounds of their first language in their pronunciation of English, so in West Penwith the same may have been true. However, such arguments do need to be treated with caution, not least because there is no method for defining the relationship between the sounds of Cornish and English in *eighteenth-century* West Penwith. Similarily, the relationship between the sounds of English in eighteenth-century West Penwith and West Penwith of the present day is also undefinable. In the absence of clear and precise contemporary documentation these definitions cannot be made, and despite all the tantalising apparent evidences the view that the English dialect sounds of the 'old people' of West Penwith should reflect the sounds of eighteenth-century Cornish is ultimately an untestable hypothesis.

An example of this problem is the definition of the pronunciation of the Cornish word *gwave*, 'winter'. The pronunciation of the word *gwavas*, 'winter farm', in the twentieth-century Cornish dialect of English has no logical bearing on the pronunciation of *gwave* in Modern Cornish two centuries earlier.[33] The word *gwavas* is, in addition, only cognate, not actually the same word, a point which presents further problems of definition. The situation is similar with the words *have* and *clave* and the pronunciation of the related words '*hewas*' and '*claw*' in the Cornish dialect of English in present-day Cornwall. Another point regarding pronunciation is that, after an examination of Lhuyd's explanations concerning the pronunciation of short and long '*a*' and his use of his orthography in the Cornish extracts which he presents, it can be seen that the '*a*' termination of infinitives and the letter '*a*' in many other words at present given an '*au*' pronunciation (approximately as in the Standard English pronunciation of the word '*cause*') should be pronounced as a short '*a*', most probably as in the Standard English pronunciation of the word '*but*'. Similarly, the '*shwa*' sound does not seem to apply in the light of the absence of its documentation in Lhuyd's study of Cornish, despite the variations which exist in the spellings of many words in the extant Modern Cornish authors.

Of course, regarding the precise sounds indicated by Lhuyd, the pronunciation of English in any historical period is a controversial issue, and the study of the seventeenth and eighteenth century pronunciation of English demands initially a thorough survey of the research on the topic before any definite and reliable conclusions as to the precise sounds indicated by Lhuyd in his study can be determined with any accuracy. In the revival of Modern Cornish, this has clearly been undertaken to a considerable extent and it can be seen that the pronunciation of revived Modern Cornish is, in the vast majority of cases, remarkably consistent with Lhuyd's study and the sounds which are represented there. The definition of the Cornish '*ll*' sound is a commendable example of the care and precision which has been taken over the pronunciation.[34]

A further point relates to grammar. An assumption is made that if Modern Cornish had lived on past its eighteenth-century demise, the language would have lost its second person singular, *che* and its forms, in the same way as English lost its own second person singular '*thou*'. Accordingly, the view taken is that *che* could be used for religious purposes, but that *why* (the second person plural) should always be used for singular and plural in all other, normal, situations.[35] Similarly, another view seems to be that *why* was eventually used for everything in the extant texts with the exception of special circumstances, such as the whim of the speaker to indicate a close relationship or, conversely, to show contempt.[36] However, a close and careful analysis of all the extant Cornish texts of the full-blown Modern period reveals that *che* and its verbal forms were very much alive and well in the language, so that the view that it either did or would have faded from usage seems to be an assumption with little to recommend it. It is also clear that *che* was often simply used in the Modern period in all kinds of situations, including everyday situations, simply to indicate one person, with no clearly demonstrable examples in the texts to show that it had associations and connotations attached to it.[37] That *che* played an important part in the language can be seen by the fact that it exists for all the paradigms of the verbs and prepositions. It seems logical then that in an authentic rendering of the language *che* should be present in everyday use. In the Modern period, the usage of *che* and *why* for one person is quite confused and some resolution of the situation is obviously necessary, but the answer is not to discard this important part of speech. It is important rather to keep it, and in the normal, everyday usage, but since there is no sense in continuing the confusion which often reigns in the texts, it seems better to use *che* for one person and *why* always for plural. Since Cornish still does have this facility for *che*, it is especially attractive to keep using it in view of the fact that it makes Cornish a much more intimate language, something which is very lacking in English now that it has lost '*thou*'. Indeed, being able to make the distinction between '*you*' singular and '*you*' plural is something to be treasured. In short, in the existing texts of the language in the full Modern period the Cornish people did use *che*, frequently, and simply for one person in all sorts of situations including everyday use, and there is then no good reason why the Cornish person of today should not do so when speaking Modern Cornish. At the same time it seems best that *why* should be limited to plural as the only reasonable solution to the confusion in the extant texts.

One final point of discussion concerns the vocabulary of Modern Cornish. The language has at a rough calculation 15,000 words remaining for use, and although this is more than in the other versions of the language (in view of the additional 'traditional' vocabulary which lived on into the English dialect of Cornwall) it is clearly not adequate for the language to become a complete living vernacular in Cornwall, in use by all sorts of people in everyday as well as more demanding situations. The language must therefore acquire more vocabulary and this brings into consideration the underlying assumption of authenticity in the language. The adoption of English words is not the solution because this would soon make the language little more than a dialect of English, which has over a million words.[38] Cornish did in the past adopt many English words, but this was when it was a complete living language like Welsh, and the adoption of English did not essentially change the general character of Cornish. The situation is different now.

In the interests of authenticity the only viable method of expanding the vocabulary may be to recreate Cornish words according to Cornish principles from the Celtic vocabulary of the cognate languages Breton and Welsh since, of course, these languages were once close dialects of the same early British language with essentially the same vocabulary base. An examination of Welsh and Breton immediately reveals the close similarities which exist in the extant vocabulary of Modern Cornish. The best approach seems to be to compare the forms of extant Modern Cornish words with the cognate words of Breton and Welsh to determine the relative Cornish characteristics and then, after carrying out a careful study of the principles of Cornish word and idiom construction, to form Cornish words and expressions from the existing Welsh and Breton vocabulary of Celtic origin. By this means it may be possible to reach the probable form of lost Cornish vocabulary. This is not a perfect solution because it does involve reconstruction, but it is the closest that can be achieved to 'revival' in a situation which demands the acquisition of more vocabulary. At the same time, it is authentic in the sense that the restoration of words would follow Cornish principles, using word roots which Cornish in most cases certainly once possessed and furnishing a typically Cornish character. Thus extended, Modern Cornish would be satisfactory for both the revival movement and also for higher study (since the restoration of the vocabulary would not affect the ability to read the extant texts, which is the primary requirement of higher study) because the grammar, syntax, phonology, orthography and the necessary vocabulary will be identical. At the same time, those learning the language for higher education purposes at university have but to extend their knowledge of the vocabulary and they have a living language at their disposal.

CONCLUSION

Modern Cornish appears, therefore, to be overwhelmingly the most acceptable version of the language for the revival, not least because of its strict adherence to the principle of authenticity. It is important that in the future development of Modern Cornish this should continue to be a primary concern. Indeed, it must be said that the major problems which have arisen in the history of the revival movement have been as a result of departure from this principle.

NOTES AND REFERENCES

1. A spirited defence of Unified and robust critique of Phonemic is contained in P.A.S. Pool, *The Second Death of Cornish*, Redruth, 1994.
2. Wella Brown, *A Grammar of Modern Cornish*, 2nd ed., Cornwall, 1993, pp.v-vi; confusingly, 'Modern' in this context means contemporary rather than the version of the language now generally described as Modern.
3. Philip Payton and Bernard Deacon, 'The Ideology of Language Revival', in Philip Payton (ed.), *Cornwall Since the War: The Contemporary History of a European Region*, Redruth, 1993, p.272; Wella Brown, *A Grammar of Modern Cornish*, 1st ed., Cornwall, 1984, pp.v-vii.
4. Kenneth J. George, 'A Phonological History of Cornish', unpublished these de troisieme cycle, Université de Bretagne Occidentale, 1984, p.478.
5. Robert Morton Nance, *A New Cornish-English Dictionary*, St Ives, 1931, p.v; Ken George, *The Pronunciation and Spelling of Revived Cornish*, Cornwall, 1986, p.17.
6. Glanville Price, *The Languages of Britain*, London, 1984, p.142.
7. George, 1984; the results of this study were published in an abridged version in George, 1986.
8. For example, N.J.A. Williams wrote approvingly of George's work in his 'A Problem of Cornish Phonology', in Martin J. Ball, James Fife, Erich Poppe, and Jenny Rowlands (eds.), *Celtic Linguistics: Readings in the Brythonic Languages*, Philadelphia, 1990, pp.241-242; Williams has subsequently revised his opinion.
9. George, 1984, pp.478-494.
10. George, 1984, p.470; George, 1986, pp.12, 17, 36, 39; Payton and Deacon, 1993, p.281. Of course, this assumption is itself not uncontested; see Charles Thomas, 'An Dasserghyans Kernewek – The Revival of the Cornish Language,' *Old Cornwall*, Vol.vi, No.5, and Peter Berresford Ellis, *The Cornish Language and Its Literature*, London, 1974, p.199.

11. For instance, George, 1986, p.59.
12. Richard Gendall, *1000 Years of Cornish*, Menheniot, 1993, pp.1-2.
13. George, 1984, p.45.
14. George, 1984, p.18.
15. A.R. Thomas, 'Cornish', in P. Trudgill (ed.), *Language in the British Isles*, Cambridge, 1984.
16. George, 1986, p.36.
17. George, 1986, p.67.
18. George, 1986, pp.203-206; Brown, 1993, p.2.
19. George, 1984, pp.478ff.
20. George, 1984, p.478.
21. George, 1986, p.37.
22. George, 1984, p.502.
23. Professor Charles Thomas in *Associates' Newsletter: Institute of Cornish Studies*, Spring 1990; see also Payton and Deacon, 1993, p.284.
24. Richard M.M. Gendall, *Kernewek Bew*, St Ives, 1972; see also George, 1986, p.21, and Payton and Deacon, 1993, p.282.
25. George, 1986, p.21.
26. Richard M.M. Gendall, *A Student's Grammar of Modern Cornish*, Menheniot, 1991; Richard M.M. Gendall, *A Student's Dictionary of Modern Cornish: Part 1: English-Cornish*, 3rd ed., Menheniot, 1991; Richard M.M. Gendall, *The Pronunciation of Cornish*, 2nd ed., Menheniot, 1991; Richard M.M. Gendall, *An Curnoak Hethow*, 2nd ed., Menheniot, 1993.
27. Payton and Deacon, p.486; additionally, the University of Sydney in New South Wales, Australia, now also teaches Modern Cornish.
28. See Gendall, *1000 Years*, 1993, and Gendall, *Curnoak*, 1993, pp.i-ii.
29. Gendall, *1000 years*, 1993, p.11.
30. Edward Lluyd, *Archaeologia Britannica*, Oxford, 1707.
31. Gendall, *Curnoak*, 1993, pp.i-ii.
32. Payton and Deacon, 1993, p.285; Séamus Ó'Coileán, *Late Cornish: An Accurate Reconstruction of the Sound System*, BA (Hons) by Independent Study dissertation, Polytechnic of East London, 1990.
33. Gendall, *1000 Years*, 1993, p.8.
34. Gendall, *1000 Years*, 1993, p.7.
35. Gendall, *Curnoak*, 1993, p.13.
36. Rod Lyon, *Let's Learn Cornish: Gero Nye Deske Curnoack*, Nancegollan, 1993, p.43.
37. On Mediæval usage, see for instance, Gendall, *Grammar*, 1991, p.135.
38. Gendall, *1000 Years*, 1993, p.12.

TOURISM IN CORNWALL: RECENT RESEARCH AND CURRENT TRENDS

Paul Thornton

INTRODUCTION

So often has the view been repeated that the traditional mass tourism industry in the UK is in permanent decline that it has almost become accepted as a truism. Cornwall's mass tourism industry is perceived as having a similar fate. Perry, for example, argued that mass tourism in Cornwall 'has had a good run for its money, but like all mass consumer products, its commercial life was limited and for more than a decade the writing has been on the wall'.[1]

Those who perceive the social costs of mass tourism as out-weighing any economic benefits that it might derive are happy to celebrate its decline. However, others see any deterioration as a cause for concern, since tourism makes a considerable economic impact. For example, in 1993 visitors to Cornwall spent an average of £195 each on their holiday, which, assuming three million visitors in total, means they spent over £585 million.[2] Any threat to this economic input must clearly be of concern to policy makers.

Assuming that policy makers require good information on which to base their decisions, it is of little surprise that the late 1980s and early 1990s have seen a considerable improvement in the statistical knowledge of the tourism industry in Cornwall. The purpose of this article is to assess some of this new information, and to indicate some of the areas where further research is still required. It is not a full analysis of the tourist industry in Cornwall. The article itself considers several related subjects in turn. Tourism should be viewed as an industry, so the analysis first examines both demand and supply aspects. Attention is then turned to the relationship between tourism and the water industry, before some conclusions are drawn on the potential future course of the industry.

THE TOURISM INDUSTRY: DEMAND ASPECTS

The decline of the traditional British seaside holiday has been visualised as the result of two factors. One is the development of new competitors, particularly in the Mediterranean and other overseas destinations. These offer guaranteed sun, but also produce more competitively priced holidays than the UK industry. The second factor is social change. There is not the space available here to discuss all the theories of change in demand brought about by transformations in society, and for a fuller description readers should examine the works of Urry, amongst others. Suffice it to say many tourists have now come to see the spending of a week or a fortnight's holiday in a traditional UK resort as a much less attractive tourism experience. According to Urry the reason is that broadly speaking mass holiday making was the quintessential form of tourism in an industrial society, since by its very nature it reflected regulated and organised work. With the development of a post-industrial society it is no surprise that new forms of tourism should develop in response. Urry described this new form of tourism as 'post-tourism'.[3]

However, it is easy to over-stress the decline in domestic UK tourism. British residents spent an estimated £7,350 million on domestic holiday tourism in 1990.[4] Since traditional resort areas are losing some of their importance as destinations (in terms of visitor numbers), the implication is that UK tourism is not simply declining but going through a period of restructuring. One explanation may lie in the increasing number of holidays that certain social groups are taking, and the development of 'travel portfolios' where main foreign holidays are being supplemented by shorter additional domestic holidays.[5] The question is, can these trends be identified in Cornwall?

Cornwall is relatively well served in terms of visitor surveys, principally by the Cornwall Tourist Visitor Surveys 1987-1992 and the renamed (but otherwise similar) Cornwall Holiday Survey 1993. These provide a database of 37,868 questionnaires conducted over seven consecutive years. Each year offers a high degree of comparability with the previous one. Very few tourist destination areas can boast such a detailed and complete database. Unfortunately, and despite this valuable source of data, the exact situation is still ambiguous.

The visitor surveys reported that between 1987 and 1989 the proportion of main holidays to additional holidays did not decline, with 73% of respondents in 1989 on their principal vacation.[6] This figure can be interpreted in several ways.

Optimistically it appears that Cornwall's traditional market has remained intact. Pessimistically the argument is that Cornwall has failed to break into new tourism markets. In addition, the survey has been conducted only during the summer season, which might exclude some respondents on additional holidays (which are normally taken outside this period). The survey also suggests that Cornwall has a very loyal market, with 34% of tourists repeating a visit from the previous season.[7] Again this appears to be a positive sign, but there is a downward long term trend in the number of first time visitors (falling from 21% in 1987 to 14% in 1992), while average visitor age is continuing to increase and the proportion of children to decline.[8] The worst case scenario is that Cornwall's traditional market is ageing and declining, while it has failed to break into new tourism markets on a large scale.

Tourists have shown one definite change in demand – a move away from the serviced sector to the self-catering holiday. Here we are lucky enough to have two sources of information – the visitor surveys and the recording of visitor numbers. The visitor survey suggests a persistent decline in the number of guests staying in serviced accommodation from nearly 40% in 1987 to only 19% in 1992.[9] Visitor number records, for all their sampling problems, show a similar trend, as demonstrated in Graph 1. If this is the case the situation may be serious – serviced accommodation potentially offers greater multiplier effects within the local economy than the self-catering sector.

GRAPH 1:

Number of holiday visitors staying in serviced and self-catering accommodation

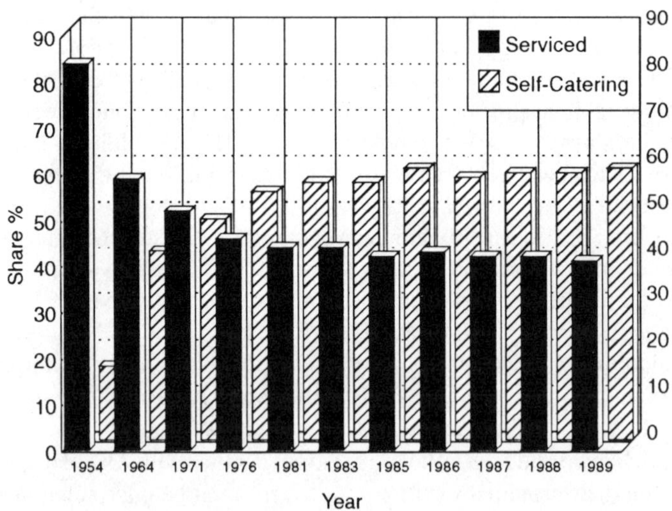

One proposed solution to declining visitor numbers is the improvement of marketing strategies. To enable this visitor surveys normally collect information on which activities tourists consider important, so that marketing strategies may be better tailored to them. These are listed in Tables 1 and 2 below.

Tables 1 and 2 show the activities that tourists considered to be the most or least important to them on their holidays, as revealed over the six years of the survey. Most important were sightseeing by car or coach, strolling, going to the beach, walking around towns and visiting historic buildings. Taken together they indicate the range of activities participated in, including both traditional forms of tourism, and apparently some of the new forms as identified by Urry. However, the surveys fail to indicate whether these are distributed across all sub-markets or vary among sub-markets. The data also does not indicate the actual distribution of time amongst these activities, as opposed to stated preferences.

TABLE 1:

Activities considered 'very important' or 'fairly important' by percentage of tourists[10]

Most Popular Activities	1987	1988	1989	1990	1991	1992
Sightseeing by car or coach	87	86	77	77	72	86
Strolling in the countryside	86	85	66	65	56	80
Going to the beach	83	83	80	77	76	77
Walking around town	80	80	76	81	74	76
Visiting historic buildings	78	78	49	47	39	78

Source: Tourism Research Group (1983)

While opinion seems to be divided on some activities, such as visiting pubs/bars or museums and art galleries, there seems to be little differences in opinion on other subjects, like visiting theme parks. While in 1993 45.8% and 46.5% of tourists considered visiting pubs and art galleries, respectively, as important, 54.2% and 53.5% looked at them as unimportant. However, in 1993 67% thought of visiting theme-parks as unimportant, compared to 33% who saw it as important. There is no certain answer to these peculiarities. However, one possible explanation may be found earlier in the surveys, where it was recognised that Cornwall catered to a bi-polarised clientele. Visitors included an above average, and increasing, number of professional or managerial classes, as well as a slowly increasing number of less-skilled manual workers. The reason for this is uncertain, but it does mean that some degree of social polarisation is at work, with a probable divergence in the types of holiday people seek being the result.[12]

The survey also examined the perceptions of tourists. For example, 98.3% agreed that Cornwall has beautiful scenery, 93% saw Cornwall as offering many places of interest, 89.5% believed the beaches were good, but only 47.3% thought Cornwall possessed good weather.[13] Again, the visitors' priorities can be seen in their suggested improvements to Cornwall, with by far the greatest suggestion being to protect natural beauty. The 1991 survey also found that 80.6% of the tourists in Cornwall did not want to see any more theme parks built.[14]

TABLE 2:

Activities considered 'not important' by percentage of tourists[11]

Least Popular Activities	1987	1988	1989	1990	1991	1992
Climbing, hiking	53	53	20	21	17	50
Ride on a scenic railway	44	48	18	15	16	47
Dancing, disco	35	31	12	13	18	33
Visiting a theatre, cinema	35	35	14	12	10	30
Visiting fun fairs, amusements	30	34	15	16	Not avail.	37

Source: Tourism Research Group (1983)

Whilst the data produced by the Cornwall Tourist Visitor Surveys is valuable in many ways, it is tantalising in what it does not tell us. It is still not certain whether Cornwall is experiencing the full blast of change associated with the restructuring of the holiday industry. The explanation for this failing may be in the one area that has been consistently ignored in tourism research: visitor behaviour and their holiday activities. This is surprising since there are four main areas where the use of behavioural data would be advantageous:

a. Planning of the Tourist Industry: Behavioural approaches to the study of tourism could assist in the more effective planning of the holiday industry. Early behavioural researchers argued that it is impossible to plan for the future unless present day behaviour is fully understood. Potential areas for research are the previously identified on-going changes within the United Kingdom's domestic holiday industry. A transformation in the activities of tourists on vacation is seen as one of the traits of this development. The proposal is that as tourists have changed their desired holiday activities the traditional tourist destinations are unable to offer them attractive vacations. Clearly the identification of tourist activities is important to this research.

b. Improved Planning: Pearce identified behavioural information as being of considerable use to planners, in that assuming that resorts are built, at least in part, for the benefit of the tourist (as well as the financial gain of the developer), then an understanding of how tourists actually use coastal areas and other tourist destinations would seem an important input to the planning process. To what extent do resort morphologies influence tourist behaviour and satisfaction? In what ways might new forms correspond better to tourists' wants? So far these are questions which appear not to have received much consideration. Chapin's observation that 'planning analyses have often emphasised the supply side more than the demand side' is no less true of resort development than urban planning'.[15] Others, such as Debbage, have made similar observations to those of Pearce: 'If more detailed information were available about the factors affecting tourist activity patterns, it might be possible to better anticipate development trends and to minimise the many negative impacts commonly associated with the . . . tourist industry'.[16]

c. Improved Marketing: Behavioural approaches offer the possibility of improving consumer research – especially in the area of preferences – which it is argued should 'constitute the basis for marketing strategies'.[17] Behavioural studies hold the distinct advantage of being able to offer a record of actual visitor activities rather than those expressed by the tourist.[18] This means that at its best, behavioural observation represents an accurate and informative approach to the on-site assessment of tourist behaviour, and is worth the added complexity and cost that is entailed. It is crucially important for the future of a destination to ensure that tourists are satisfied by their holidays, since research shows that even if the tourists are able to attain complete redress for their complaints they are still likely to change their holiday in a subsequent year. That Cornwall achieves such a high rate of return visits suggests that it might well be succeeding in this important area.

d. Refining Theoretical Understanding: Information on behaviour is seen as offering the possibility of generating more realistic models. Traditionally models are normative, which use assumptions of how the world should be. Unfortunately these assumption, or axioms, are not always reflected in real life. Behavioural models, on the other hand, work the other way, by observing the world as it is, and not as it should be. As Dann, Nash and Pearce point out: 'Tourism researchers may be sometimes insufficiently aware of the possibility of collecting invalid data . . . Yet cliché replies, while usually masking deeper realities, are often taken to form the basis for the entire marketing of a destination'.[19]

The Cornwall Tourist Visitor Survey has helped the understanding of tourist behaviour in Cornwall, mainly through the identification of priorities and perceptions. Questionnaires are, however, limited by their format and broad ranging questions. For example, they report that both strolling in the countryside and visiting the beach are important activities, but they can give no indication as to how much time the tourist spends on them. Nor can visitor surveys indicate the spatial distribution of the tourist's time use, or the effect of weather or the presence of children on the activities of a tourist group. To understand these influences a more complete behavioural approach is required.

Until recently no behavioural research had been conducted in Cornwall. However, initial research carried out at the University of Exeter by the Tourism Research Group and the Institute of Cornish Studies in the form of the Cornwall Visitor Activity Survey 1993 goes some way towards correcting this. The survey design addressed the information deficit that surrounds the subject of holiday activities, and their organisation in both time and space. The study adopted a space-time survey approach, which requires tourists to complete a diary recording their activities over the period of a week during their holiday. Such an approach is significantly different to the more usual questionnaire format, which gathers data at only one point in time. The result is a more complete record of activities, with less reliance placed on the memories of individual respondents.

At this time a full analysis of all the diaries is unavailable. However, information gathered from tourists staying in Newquay, arguably the main mass tourist destination in Cornwall, has been analysed. While there is insufficient space available to discuss all the results, some points can be made. Tourists staying in serviced accommodation, for example, are likely to spend more time in dining, sports and child care. Tourists in self-catering accommodation spend markedly more time sightseeing by car or coach, surfing, visiting paying attractions and using night-clubs. However, overall patterns of time use are broadly similar. The use of space is somewhat different, as shown in Table 3 below. This reveals that people self-catering spend less time at their holiday base, and markedly more time away from their accommodation (especially over 24 miles). No firm conclusions can be drawn at this stage, but further analysis should produce some interesting results.

The Activity Survey offers the possibility of detailed examination of the programming of events over the time span of the holiday. Preliminary results suggest that tourists are initially very resort orientated, but this tends to decline over time. Over the first two days of their vacations almost 15% of their activity time budgets are devoted to sightseeing on foot. Thereafter, they become more confident or more exploratory and spend an increasing proportion of their time sightseeing by car, so that by the fourth day this has overtaken the time allocated to sightseeing on foot.[20] This is also reflected in the distance away from the accommodation bases they are willing to travel. Time spent away from accommodation tends to increase over the first few days of the holiday before declining over the latter part of the vacation.

The nature of space-time budget data allows the analysis of time use within each day. There are mostly predictable variations in activities and the distance away from the accommodation base, largely dictated by meal times and other biological needs. However, there are still some interesting points to note. For example, 50% of tourists are away from their accommodation only between 11am and 5pm, while the percentage of tourists at their accommodation never falls below 24% at any time of the day.[21]

TABLE 3:
Activity spaces of tourists staying in Newquay

	Distribution of time	
Spatial location	**Serviced**	**Self-catering**
At accommodation	55.0	37.4
1-4 miles away from accommodation	32.5	43.9
5-14 miles away from accommodation	4.3	6.6
15-24 miles away from accommodation	5.5	6.5
25 miles plus away from accommodation	1.6	3.9
Unspecified	1.1	1.8
Total	**100%**	**100%**
Total Responses	**50**	**30**

Source: Cornwall Visitor Activity Survey (1992).

Finally, the Activity Survey offers the potential to investigate the effects of differing types of family groups on the activities of tourists. For example, little is currently known about the influence of children on tourist activities. Further analysis will also indicate the importance of the location of the holiday accommodation on holiday activities. Do different locations produce different kinds of holidays? Clearly any information will be useful in any investigation of the possibility of changes in the nature of tourism in Cornwall.

The Activity Survey is a useful start to the study of tourist behaviour in Cornwall. However, there remains a good deal left to investigate. A larger survey would be useful, as well as an analysis of how tourists actually make their decisions. This would be important, for the first step in learning how to influence decisions must be an understanding of how tourists make their choices. In summary, our knowledge of tourist activities and behaviour in Cornwall is still limited, and requires improvement.

It seems likely that the nature of the demand for holidays in Cornwall is undergoing some change. The question is, how significant a change is taking place?

Cornwall does not seem to have been affected as much as some UK destination areas. However, if it is accepted that there may be a long term decline in the importance of traditional mass-tourism, Cornwall is most fortunate in being well endowed with the features necessary to change the tourist experience it offers.[22]

THE TOURISM INDUSTRY: SUPPLY ASPECTS

The interest of policy makers in the tourist industry is due to its perceived economic potential, and in particular its role in job creation. As a result there has been considerable interest in the health of the industry. Only recently, however, has attention been focussed on the characteristics of holiday industry businesses, both in terms of the nature of their formation and their operating characteristics. This research has again been conducted by the Tourism Research Group, with a major research project in 1986-87. The study was based on personal interviews, and divided the industry into two main sectors: businesses offering accommodation, and those operating as attractions. These will be considered in turn.

A. Tourist Accommodation Businesses

The survey confirmed the widely held view that the tourism industry in Cornwall is highly fragmented into small, independent units. Of all businesses surveyed 70% were in the private ownership of a single individual, and only 15% were public limited companies. The majority of public companies were manufacturing firms or inns. Virtually all the firms in the accommodation and catering sectors were in individual ownership.

Almost 48% of the businesses employed no full-time employees other than the owner, while a further 10% had only one full-time employee. As Williams *et al.* noted this has important implications since: 'entry thresholds to business ownership are relatively low, large companies do not dominate business trends, and decision-making, potentially may rest on highly personalised criteria'.[23]

The gender breakdown of ownership is variable: 54% of serviced accommodation and 45% of self-catering businesses were owned by women, contrasting with the ownership of tourism related manufacturing firms (90% male). As already described the mostly small, independent tourism firms can be run on the basis of highly personalised criteria. In addition many entrepreneurs show a surprising lack of previous relevant occupational experience in tourism. Most entrepreneurs went directly from being an employee in a non-tourism business to becoming a tourism business owner. That 54.9% of entrepreneurs followed this route to ownership indicates its dominance. This is in stark contrast to the principal routes to manufacturing firm ownership (outside the tourism sector) established in other surveys. These show that 'the overwhelming majority of founders inevitably set up businesses in activities where they have working experience'.[24] Such a result might be expected – new entrepreneurs would have the skills, capital and local connections to have a better chance of succeeding in running a business. Surprisingly in the self-catering, restaurants, cafes and pub sectors of the industry in Cornwall only 6% had relevant employment experience.

Tourism entrepreneurs in many cases, in addition to a lack of experience, also exhibited no formal training background. A large proportion had no formal training whatsoever in any previous jobs, and 35% had received some training but did not consider this to have been relevant to their present businesses. In most cases entrepreneurs setting up a tourism business in Cornwall are ex-employees moving into their first business-ownership, and lack both relevant previous employment and training experiences.[25] Such a situation, in complete contradiction to the wider case, deserves examination. Thus attention might be turned to the method used by new entrepreneurs to generate the capital required to start their business.

The origin of the capital utilised in starting businesses is again unusual. Personal and family savings were the only form of capital invested by 51.4% of those owners surveyed. If at least partial reliance on personal savings is included over 70% of owners have used at least some of their own money. The result is quite unusual. As noted above many tourism entrepreneurs are individuals moving into their first business ownership, from previously being an employee in an unrelated activity. They rarely possess any previous relevant training, while much of their capital comes from their own savings. Given that these entrepreneurs are so unusual it is worth examining where they came from.

In the sample firms, less than one-third of the entrepreneurs had been born in Cornwall. The regional origins of the owners are diverse, but the primary source region was the South East of England. As stated earlier, outside the tourism industry many small firms are set up by locals, since they can take advantage of local knowledge and personal connections.[26] As a result the creation of small firms is portrayed as a positive endogenous method of reducing local unemployment. Interestingly, there appears to be some similarity between the origins of entrepreneurs and the origins of visitors to Cornwall. It might tentatively be suggested that having decided to establish a business outside their local area, potential entrepreneurs pick a location that they think they know. A previous holiday might well form the basis of this knowledge. Alternatively, the main reason for wishing to become an entrepreneur could be as a means of securing a life in Cornwall, which is perceived as a desirable place to live. To assess these reasons we must investigate the entrepreneurs' motivations (Tables 4 and 5).

TABLE 4:
Reasons for leaving last job

Reasons	% Total	Total responses
Redundancy / last job temporary / economic depression	10.2	34
More money	2.9	7
Enhance career	6.0	20
To be self-employed	22.8	76
Dissatisfied	14.1	47
Get out of the rat-race	3.3	11
Come to Cornwall	9.9	33
Family / personal	18.9	63
Semi / early retirement	7.5	25
Total	**100**	**333**

Source: Shaw, Williams & Greenwood (1987)

The reason given most often for leaving previous employment was the desire to be 'self-employed'. However, this economic motive is also matched by non-economic reasons. Some of these were 'negative', such as dissatisfaction and a desire to get out of the rat-race. Others were positive, like a wish to enter semi/early retirement or a chance to live in Cornwall. Also, the motive of becoming self-employed is one that can be described as social as well as economic, since self-employment is seen as an attractive life-style.

The decision on where to specifically locate their business is also interesting. Three sets of factors govern the choice made: economic, environmental, and chance/being there anyway. Although economics is important, environmental and chance factors have a surprising influence on the decision.

The research indicates that tourism entrepreneurs in Cornwall are not driven by solely economic motives. They are also strongly influenced by social and environmental factors. In fact many entrepreneurs in Cornwall have made their choices through a combination of lifestyle decisions and economic factors. Therefore, for some of these entrepreneurs, involvement in the tourism industry is as much a form of consumption as production. They are consuming the very same product they are producing, that is, tourism. They have been attracted to set up or purchase businesses in Cornwall in order to be able to 'consume' its landscape and life-style. There also seems to be a desire to acquire the life-style mode of self-employment. This is sometimes related to the life-cycle, with many setting up businesses after retiring or as half-way stages to retirement. This process is facilitated by the low entry thresholds to owning these usually very small businesses. Most have relatively little job experience or training and there are few opportunities to acquire the latter anyway. This type of business is especially prevalent in the accommodation sectors, but is also found in other areas of the tourism industry.[27]

TABLE 5:
Reasons for establishing business in particular location

Reasons	% Total	Total respondents
Economic / financial	18.0	68
Close to tourist market / access to market	10.3	39
Environmental / to come to Cornwall	24.7	94
Chance / availability	14.2	54
Here any way	25.1	95
Other	7.7	29
Total	**100**	**379**

Source: Shaw, Williams & Greenwood (1987)

There is, therefore, some explanation for the prevalence of personal savings as start up capital. Many entrepreneurs are approaching the end of their careers, and so will have had time to build up capital. Given that the South East is one of the dominant source regions, regional property price differentials may also play a role. Property prices in Cornwall are still relatively low compared to the South East. It is possible that those arriving from the South East might be able to take advantage of price differentials to such an extent that they can purchase both a home and a business.

There are several important consequences of these identified traits. Firstly the importance of social factors may reduce the drive of some entrepreneurs to achieve maximum profitability, and make them unresponsive to policy initiatives proposed by either the local or regional tourist boards. The creation of new tourism accommodation firms should not necessarily be seen as a positive means of reducing local unemployment, since many opportunities are taken by in-migrants. However, the operation of businesses by individuals in a state of semi-retirement may also mean that many firms can survive by operating at sub-optimal levels or accepting sub-optimal profits. The highly fragmented nature of the industry and the small size of many tourism firms will tend to dictate an emphasis in the mind of the entrepreneur on local issues. The result is the failure of the tourism industry in Cornwall as a whole to project a unified voice, or develop long term strategic thinking. It is this failure that must be the most important lesson to learn. If Cornwall is to thrive as a tourist destination then it must execute a well planned marketing campaign and be able to exert pressure on public bodies. The failure to project a unified front would probably result in the continued loss of visitors to rival destinations, as well as allowing public authorities to turn a blind eye to the problem.

B. Tourist Attractions

This section will examine the characteristics of tourist attractions and some of their linkages with the rest of the economy of Cornwall. Traditionally, both nationally and in Cornwall, tourist attractions have been the subject of less research than tourist accommodation businesses. This is a shame, because although complex interactions exist with other elements of the tourist industry, attractions are in many ways unique.

The main source of survey data on tourist attractions in Cornwall is based on a sample study of 72 attractions, conducted in 1986. The attractions surveyed ran from National Trust historic houses and gardens, through privately run theme and leisure parks, to museums, galleries, railways and small visitor centres. Apart from the main activity of the attraction, many offered additional facilities – principally shops (76.4%), cafes/restaurants (51.4%) and picnic areas (52.8%). In some cases these operations accounted for more than 50% of the business turnover.[28]

With the ever present worries over the ability of the tourist industry to remain competitive in terms of price, and the perceived need to provide reasonably priced wet weather facilities, information on the average level of admission charge is valuable. The modal class of admission price, in 1986, was between £1.01 and £2.00.[29] Obviously such data is of relatively little value, as prices may change from year to year. Of greater use would be time series data, with admission prices recorded at regular intervals, which would allow the identification of any trends. Unfortunately this is not currently available.

In terms of ownership characteristics, tourist attractions show clear differences in comparison to tourist accommodation businesses. Most importantly, they show less of a tendency to be dominated by one individual. Table 6 below illustrates these ownership patterns.

TABLE 6:

Tourist attractions: type of ownership

Type	Number	Percent
Individual	28	38.9
Group	24	33.3
Ltd. Company	17	23.6
Government	2	2.8
Club	1	1.4
Total	**72**	**100**

Source: Shaw, Williams and Greenwood (1987)

Since in many cases investment and operating decisions are being made by a group of people it is logical to assume that individuals have less influence on the development of tourist attractions. As a result the background of individuals is less important than in the accommodation sector. However, the survey did produce data that was broadly similar to the characteristics of accommodation owners. That is that the owners derived from a wide variety of backgrounds, while many of their previous jobs had been based outside Cornwall. However, of greater interest is the nature of the interactions between tourist attractions and the local economy. The benefit of the tourism industry, and tourist attractions in particular, is often proposed as not only coming from their economic activities, but also from the business that is generated locally to service them.

Table 7 produces some interesting results. Within the sample 88.2% use within-firm facilities for publicity and promotion, with a similarly large proportion providing their own cleaning. However, fewer firms provide their own legal or accountancy services, and most of that work goes to Cornish firms. However, in comparison with accommodation businesses, many more attractions provide their own within-firm businesses, and are more likely to use firms from outside Cornwall when they are unable to provide the service themselves.[30] This is partly the function of the organisational and ownership patterns of the firms (with proportionately larger firms, more likely to be controlled from outside Cornwall). Furthermore, there is the influence of nation-wide organisations, such as the National Trust, that are of sufficient size to provide their own services. However, when the firm is unable to provide certain services for itself, Cornish businesses tend to get the work.

TABLE 7:
Tourist attractions: use of by local services

Facility	In Firm		Cornwall		Devon		Elsewhere		Total
	Number	%	Number	%	Number	%	Number	%	Number
Publicity	60	88.2	6	8.8	0	0	2	3	68
Accountancy	26	40.6	27	42.2	2	3.1	9	14.1	64
Legal services	22	36.1	30	49.2	2	3.3	7	11.5	61
Cleaning	62	95.4	2	3.1	0	0	0	0	64
Maintenance & repairs	53	79.1	14	20.9	0	0	0	0	67

Source: Shaw, Williams and Greenwood (1987)

Tourist attractions also exert an influence through their potential to provide employment opportunities. Shaw, Williams and Greenwood found that the 72 attractions in their survey made a significant contribution to employment, creating jobs for just over 500 people.[31] The situation is complicated, however. The largest proportion (41.3%) of attractions employed no one other than the owner. On the other hand four attractions employed over ten people, with the largest providing work for over 120.[32] Also of great significance was the discovery that many of the tourist attractions in Cornwall had continued to expand their employment opportunities.

The ability of the tourism industry to provide employment is rarely disputed. What is a matter of contention is the nature and quality of the work they produce. The survey did indicate that female employees dominate the work generated by tourist attractions, while family labour is also extensively used. The survey also produced limited data on change in employment in ten attractions in the years from 1980-6. This indicated that in ten firms there were 70 new full-time jobs, but 95 part-time jobs were created.[33] This leads to questions over the seasonality of employment, which indeed proved to be a factor. The extremely short season that is the characteristic of much of Cornwall's tourism industry was found to be present, although it was less marked than in other sectors of the holiday industry.

In summary, the tourist attraction sector of the holiday industry in Cornwall can be described as being more dominated by groups, rather than individual ownership, based both in and outside Cornwall. Provision of services tends to come from within the firm, rather than externally. Where external services are sought, Cornish firms are normally used, although the tourist attraction sector makes more use of firms from outside Cornwall than other sectors. Tourist attractions provide significant employment opportunities. The work is female dominated, makes significant use of part-time work, and is affected by the short tourist season in Cornwall. Other sectors of the tourist industry also show these characteristics, but often in a more pronounced fashion.

TOURISM & THE WATER INDUSTRY

While tourism businesses are faced with many growing costs, water charges are increasingly perceived as a major problem. In order to remain competitive the Cornish tourist industry must offer reasonably priced, 'value for money' breaks. Clearly the rapidly increasing charges for water do not assist this. While water bills have increased all over the UK they are at their highest in the South West Water area, averaging more than £300 or doubling in the past five years.[34] This has become something of a *cause célèbre* in Cornwall. In one recent case a guest house owner offered to reduce holiday makers' accommodation bills by up to 50% if they brought their own water with them![35]

The situation is not simple. Cornwall has a population of about 500,000 people. However, at the peak of the summer season up to 250,000 extra visitors are present each day.[36] As a result the water and sewage infrastructure in Cornwall has to be designed and constructed to deal with over 750,000 people, rather than the local population of 500,000. Even given the fact that all sewage may not be treated immediately, it still has to be kept in holding tanks. The previous solution of pumping the sewage untreated into the sea is no longer an option, following European Community regulations. Further regulations over water quality have persuaded South West Water to embark on its epic 'Clean Sweep' programme, with an estimated eventual cost of £900 million. Unfortunately for the local population, the funding of this grand project must come from their water bills. As a result Cornwall is in the unenviable position of having to pay for the sewage infrastructure to cope with a population greater than its own. The irony is that the infrastructure itself is only fully required during the summer months, a fact that was recognised by Cornwall County Council as far back as 1976: 'The seasonal nature of tourism gives rise to abnormally high costs in providing facilities in relation to the short time for which they are used'.[37]

This leads to the classic argument over the sustainability of the tourism industry. While this academic debate has been applied to many other destination areas it has not been fully applied to Cornwall. There are two bases to the argument. Firstly, that tourism, or at least mass tourism, is unsustainable since the result of the arrival of large numbers of visitors is such environmental damage that the original source of attraction is destroyed. Secondly, pronounced seasonal variations in the arrival of visitors produce high infrastructure costs that in turn damage the ability of the industry to compete. In the case of Cornwall, for example, the operation of a highly successful marketing campaign to attract visitors only during the summer months would further increase the water and sewage infrastructure required to deal their needs. This would have to be funded by the local population. As a result the industry would be faced with increased costs, as well as the potential for environmental damage.

The question of how to overcome this situation, that firstly damages the competitiveness of the tourist industry and secondly reduces the industry's contribution to the local economy, is important. This requires some in-depth research, which as yet does not exist. It is, therefore, difficult to make any serious proposals for dealing with the situation. However, four basic options can be visualised:

a. Tourist Tax: The idea of taxing the tourist and then investing the revenue in the industry is an appealing idea. However, it suffers from one fundamental problem: a tourist tax would increase the cost of a holiday in Cornwall, placing Cornwall at a further competitive disadvantage.

b. Centralise Funding for Water: This is perhaps the simplest answer to the problem of reducing the cost of water. Effectively it is another tourist tax: the tourist uses the facilities in the South West, therefore they should be expected to contribute to their upkeep. Unfortunately, in the present political climate centralised funding for water is a fairly remote possibility.

c. Change the Nature of Tourism: This is the most complex option to enact. It would require considerable strategic planning from within the tourism industry, and would doubtless lead to the failure of those businesses least equipped to cope with the change. The principle is to attract tourists over a greater period of the year by offering new and modified touristic experiences. The additional holiday sector would provide the main market, with Cornwall's coastal and inland landscape and – especially – its heritage/cultural features as the main tourist resource. By attracting tourists over a longer period of time infrastructure costs would be relatively less. The reduction of a summer peak would mean there would be fewer tourists in Cornwall at any one time, and the use of infrastructure would be more consistent over the year. Unfortunately, the complexity of even a partial change to new forms of tourism is so great, and the investment required so large, that it is unlikely to happen. In addition, as identified earlier, some tourism entrepreneurs, especially those 'semi-retired', may not be receptive to new policy initiatives.

d. Access to European Funds: Investment by one of the European Union's development funds might be a possibility for either reducing the costs to the local population of water quality improvements, or as a means of encouraging re-investment in the tourism industry. However, even if money is available any application would face stiff competition from other areas, and would require considerable strategic planning and organisation.

THE TOURISM INDUSTRY IN CORNWALL: WHAT FUTURE?

a. Statistical knowledge: It seems logical to assume that the 'information gap' in our knowledge of the tourism industry will continue to shrink, albeit at a steady rate. Questionnaire-derived information is likely to continue its dominance over other sources of data, particularly given the recent initiatives of the West Country Tourist Board (WCTB). This regional board, assuming that the greatest block to more tourism firms conducting their own market research is cost, have developed a series of surveys that can be tailored to individual needs, yet retain a high degree of commonality. The individual nature of the surveys increase their value to tourism businesses, while in an aggregate form provides information on the state of the tourism industry in South West Britain. In addition, since many of the overheads are absorbed by the WCTB, formal market research becomes more affordable to individual firms. The WCTB benefits from an improvement in statistical coverage. Such partnerships may well indicate the future of tourism research in many areas of the UK.

b. The 'health' of the industry: Cornwall's tourism industry might very well find itself in a unique situation. Whereas as many other UK holiday destinations are showing a significant change in their morphology, in particular showing a trend towards converting under-used holiday accommodation into retirement homes, Cornwall may well resist this path. Cornwall continues to be perceived as a desirable place to live, while price differentials and the possibility of running their own businesses in a 'semi-retired' state may continue to attract new entrepreneurs. Thus while there may be a rapid business turnover, and a fall in profitability, the continual demand exerted by in-migrants allows many tourist firms to continue to operate in a sub-optimal or limited profit situation. The result is that the tourism industry in Cornwall may continue to operate, albeit in a state of 'sustained unsustainability'.

The question is, can this be enough? Exactly what does Cornwall want from its tourist industry? If the improvement of local unemployment is seen as one of the main benefits of the tourism industry, how can this be reconciled with the knowledge that many firms are operated by in-migrants? If maximum economic benefit is the driving force, then a unified hard-driving marketing campaign is required, along with a desire amongst entrepreneurs to come closer to maximum profitability. In addition, new markets must be identified and exploited, while entrepreneurs must adapt to policy changes. Perhaps an improvement in the generally woeful state of training might be the key. If the economic fruits of tourism are to be enjoyed then methods of overcoming its costs must be developed. There is no purpose to creating financial benefits if those benefits are lost to the local community by increased burdens in the form of infrastructure costs. Finally, if employment (rather than ownership) in a tourism trade is to be no longer considered 'demeaning' then methods must be identified of ensuring the work is more than seasonal. This requires the development of addititional forms of tourism, and the exploitation of the growing 'post-tourism' market.

The present situation does not preclude some change. The current policy of agricultural diversification, for example, is encouraging many farmers to convert, at least in part, to offering new forms of tourist experiences, many of which are less dominated by the summer season. However, while farm based holidays may show some differences to the traditional Cornish holiday, what will almost certainly remain the same is the small scale, diverse, highly fragmented and robust nature of the tourism industry in Cornwall. The tourism industry in Cornwall might be undergoing change, but it is unlikely that it will face extinction!

NOTES AND REFERENCES

1. R. Perry, 'Cultural Tourism in Cornwall', in Tourism Research Group Paper No. 4, *Tourism and Development: Overviews and Case-Studies of the UK and South-West Regions,* Exeter, 1987.
2. Tourism Research Group, *Cornwall Holiday Survey 1993*, Exeter, 1994.
3. J. Urry, 'The Tourist Gaze Revisited', *American Behavioral Scientist,* vol.36, no. 2, 1993.
4. R. Prentice, *Tourism and Heritage Attractions*, London, 1992.
5. R. Prentice, G. Shaw and A. Williams, 'Tourism Research: A Perspective', *American Behavioral Scientist,* vol. 36, no.2, 1992.

6. A. Griffiths, *The Changing Visitor: The First Six Years of the Cornwall Visitor Survey 1987-1992*, Exeter, 1993.
7. Griffiths, 1993.
8. Griffiths, 1993.
9. Griffiths, 1993.
10. Griffiths, 1993.
11. Griffiths, 1993.
12. Griffiths, 1993.
13. Tourism Research Group, *Cornwall Tourist Visitors Survey 1992*, Exeter, 1993.
14. Tourism Research Group, *Cornwall Tourist Visitors Survey 1991*, Exeter, 1992.
15. D. Pearce, 'Tourist Time-Budgets', *Annals of Tourism Research*, vol. 15, 1988.
16. K. Debbage, 'Spatial Behaviour in a Bahamian Resort', *Annals of Tourism Research*, vol. 15, 1991.
17. W. Van Raaij, 'Consumer Research on Tourism: Mental and Behavioural Constructs.' *Annals of Tourism Research*, vol. 13, 1986.
18. P. Pearce, *The Ulysses Factor: Evaluating Tourists in a Tourist Setting*, New York, 1988.
19. G. Dann, D. Nash and P. Pearce, 'The Methodology of Tourism Research: Priorities, Problems and Possibilities', *Annals of Tourism Research, 1988.*
20. G. Shaw, A. Williams, and P. Thornton, *Tourists, Tourism Time and Tourism Spaces*, Exeter/Redruth, 1994.
21. G. Shaw, A. Williams, and P. Thornton, 1994.
22. P. Thornton, 'Cornwall and Changes in the Tourist Gaze', *Cornish Studies: One*, second series, 1993.
23. G. Shaw, A. Williams, and J. Greenwood, 'From Tourist to Tourism Entrepreneur, from Consumption to Production: Evidence from Cornwall, England'. *Environment and Planning A*, vol. 21, 1989.
24. D. Keeble and E. Wever, 'Introduction', in D. Keeble and E. Wever (eds.), *New Firms and Regional Developments in Europe*, Andover, 1986, pp.1-34.
25. Shaw, Williams and Greenwood, 1989.
26. Keeble and Wever, 1986.
27. Shaw, Williams and Greenwood, 1989.
28. G. Shaw, A. Williams and J. Greenwood, *'Tourism and the Economy of Cornwall'*, Exeter, chapter 8, 1987.
29. Shaw, Williams and Greenwood, 1987.
30. Shaw, Williams and Greenwood, 1987.
31. Shaw, Williams and Greenwood, 1987.
32. Shaw, Williams and Greenwood, 1987.
33. Shaw, Williams and Greenwood, 1987.
34. *Independent on Saturday*, 26 March 1994.
35. *Western Morning News*, 25 March 1994.
36. Cornwall County Council Planning Department, 1994.
37. Cornwall County Council, 1975.

CELTIC TOURISM – SOME RECENT MAGNETS

John Lowerson

INTRODUCTION

For most English enthusiasts the Celtic is essentially an 'Other'. As such it offers a peculiar meld of geographical and temporal remoteness, a partially accessible strangeness, and, for an increasing number of people, a value standard by which their own circumstances are judged and even made tolerable. The purpose of this article is to examine briefly some key elements of this, its growing role in some parts of the British experience and, particularly, its place in the present definition and exploitation of Cornwall.

The idea of the 'Celtic' is a peculiarly complex historical fabrication. It is often place-specific, but singularly vague in chronology, its characteristics both veiled in and formed by a particularly romantic reaction to a dominant industrial and post-industrial materialism. Its greatest value is often portrayed as being a powerful combination of the aesthetic with the holy, deeply rooted in a creation-focussed existence. Its role in sustaining the world-weary modern is stressed increasingly. This is rarely questioned and the refreshingly astringent analysis of Malcolm Chapman's recent book, *The Celts: The Construction of a Myth*, is one that would find little support from many recent popularisers. He writes, 'romanticism created the fringe Celtic minorities as figures of wish-fulfilment, of opposition to the prevailing philosophy and actuality of industrialising England'.[1] The approach here agrees with the substance of his evaluation but is complementary to rather than repetitive of his arguments. The key issue is that of the continued currency and even expansion of this construction, suitably modified for the conditions of the later twentieth century.

This Celticness is essentially regional, peripheral to the mainstream of British political and economic fluctuations since at least the middle ages. It would be fair to say that, where economic change has been experienced in Celtic Britain, it has been largely prompted by the varying requirements of the English. The role played in modern society by tourism, the consumption of place and desired experience, is but the latest example of this. This is not, though, solely a movement from centre to periphery. There is a strong element of local collusion, even of pushing the changes along. From the late Victorian refinement of basic Scottish golf courses to attract English tourists, through the old *Exchange and Mart* advertisements for magic pixie charms, to the stacks of locally-produced mystery pamphlets to be found in virtually any Cornish souvenir shop, the process requires the grasping of entrepreneurial opportunity by those being visited.[2] Indeed, much of the 'Cornish Revival' itself was a rejection of Cornwall's industrial heritage and an appeal to images of pre-modern Celticity.

Lavethan Cross and Well, Blisand, in the Deanery of Bodmin.
Source: Arthur G. Langdon, *Old Cornish Crosses*, 1896.

TOURISM AND THE LURE OF CORNWALL

This exploitation of Wales, Scotland, Ireland and Cornwall grew out of an English middle-class hunger for healthy holidays away from vulgar mass resorts, which was coupled with a very diffused post-Romantic landscape aesthetic, both made realisable by burgeoning transport networks.[3] In the case of Cornwall, the opening of Brunel's Tamar railway bridge in 1859 brought new opportunities for seasonal invasions, although it was not until the early 1900s that this potential was fully realised. Mass tourism, as opposed to middle class 'elite' tourism, came later. Although the railways have largely lost their dominance, the private car has more than consolidated the touristic process, although its road requirements now seem to threaten the desired 'product'. That product offers an experience of temporary simplicity with respectability and low costs, the exploitation of local economic marginality. Its most lyrical expression occurs in the childhood memories of John Betjeman's *Summoned by Bells*, of those 'Safe Cornish holidays'; its latest heir is Posy Simmons'

'Tresoddit', with its polytechnic lecturers and middle-ranking professionals agonising about the impact of mass tourism on 'their' resort.[4] Ironic though her treatment may be she reflects the dilemmas felt by many about Penwith, for instance, with access increased by the 'quite unnecessary motorway' that Professor Charles Thomas so deplored in his inaugural lecture.[5]

The tide of simple holiday-making has always dominated this phenomenon. It has, however, long had an undercurrent which has recently flowed nearer the surface. Cornwall, for instance, has repeatedly been portrayed as a brooding landscape in which geology and position have combined to determine human experience, overriding the basic business of settlement and survival. When local antiquarianism, such as that of Hawker of Morwenstow, passed into print it often found a national market.[6] In one of his Sherlock Holmes stories, 'The Adventure of the Devil's Foot', published in 1910, Conan Doyle had Dr Watson write, of Mount's Bay, 'The glamour and mystery of the place, with its sinister atmosphere of forgotten nations, appealed to the imagination of my friend'.[7]

Arthur Quiller-Couch made much of his reputation as an author of mystery stories, based on local folk tales. Dark legends and powerful place memories also feature in many of the writers who have done so much to create a sense of Cornish place. In this process, legend is a key feature. Although it is a truism that writing down the oral story preserves in aspic and kills continued local refinement, one being contested in such contemporary practice as the work of Mike Dunstan, it is a necessary process if the tale is to attract the wider market that its literary production requires. Betjeman recalled, 'Imagined ghosts on unfrequented roads'.[8] Some have been more place-specific. Much of the constructed appeal of modern Cornwall, for instance, depends on the media exploitation of Daphne du Maurier's works and the Poldark sagas, and the production of such local guides as *Poldark Country*, with its building on 'the romantic imagination of so many viewers' to provide a text for the glove-compartment of the tourist's car.[9]

The process of that particular diffusion has exploited a theme of growing importance as a tourist magnet. Vague underlying strands have been increasingly teased out and then woven into a Celticness which seeks to meet a spiritual unease in late twentieth century Britain. This has both pagan and Christian elements, often treated indiscriminately to produce a synthesis which would have annoyed profoundly most of the original proponents of both.

In the earlier twentieth century this theme appeared repeatedly in general guidebooks aimed at the middle-class holidaymaker, probably to give a mild *frisson* to accompany those hours on the sands. Before the First World War A.G. Folliott-Stokes described Cornwall as 'this land of primeval solitudes and prehistoric monuments'.[10] There was an inevitable irony in such writings being directed at consumers who, with the exception of some few cyclists and ramblers, were most conspicuous in their avoidance of solitude. In the 1930s

Betjeman himself, in one of the first key texts aimed at the incoming motorist, the *Shell Guide*, emphasised Cornwall's spiritual as well as virtual physical detachment from the British mainland with a singular mixture of past monuments and present imaginings which has permeated most guidebooks ever since: 'Cornwall is richer than almost anywhere else in relics of prehistoric civilisation. Forms of old pagan worship survive in some places even today'.[11]

This was reiterated a few years later by Arthur Mee ('It is magic that comes leaping into the mind when we think of Cornwall') but one is left wondering whether the reader was expected to go looking for that magic directly or to feel a slight sense of looking over the shoulder, physically and in time, on holiday.[12] Forty or so years later, Gerald Priestland echoed this at a time when the search for the Celtic as a specific experience was becoming more prominent; extolling the 'metaphysical dimension' of the area he claimed that, 'In Penwith we can come closer not just to history but to tribal pre-history than anywhere else in England'.[13] At the same time as Priestland's book one of the most comprehensive works of this type was published, Denys Val Baker's *The Spirit of Cornwall*. Baker, an expatriate Welshman and the founder of the *Cornish Review*, claimed quite happily that, 'you need be neither a Celt nor an artist to be aware of the strange and compelling powers embodied in Cornwall's granite body'.[14]

Chapman identifies this search for the Celtic as being strongest in times of English industrial confidence, the 1960s and 1970s in particular.[15] To an extent he is right, but he fails to engage with the most important and powerful expression of this, the contemporary New Age movement, which has managed to grow steadily throughout the recent recession. Whereas the sixties in particular fostered an escape from urban residence, something which is still important for new-style 'Traveller' groups, this present emphasis offers an odd compatibility with contemporary urban middle-class lifestyles. Much of it depends on comparative affluence and it fits quite easily into modern tourist patterns. It draws very strongly on neo-antiquarianism, usually stronger on legend than the cautious conclusions of technically-minded current archaeology.

The attractions of this theme, variously described as Celtic 'paganism', 'Celtic Christianity' or 'the occult', literally the possession of secret knowledge, are its distance in time, the liberty of interpretation which the lack of precise primary documentation affords, and its assumed rejection of the materialism which paradoxically makes its consumption possible. It is regarded as creation-centred rather than ecologically threatening and it is often validated by reference to world-views which would have been alien to its early adherents. One major contributor to this trend wrote recently, 'I am sure that if we want to understand the depths of Celtic spirituality we shall find the nearest parallels in the Buddhist teaching of today as well as in the creation spirituality of such Christian teachers as Matthew Fox'.[16] The recruitment of this latter Californian guru disowned by his own Dominican order (he is now an Anglican) to the side of supposed Druids or Welsh-Cornish-Breton saints does require some considerable stretch of imagination and a certain suspension of criticism. It is, nonetheless, important for the belief structures of this particular Celtic revival in which the local is absorbed into ascribed universals.

Apologists of both revised paganism and pre-Catholic Christianity share several common themes. Paganism is literally 'of the earth', Celtic Christianity is valued for its prayers and poetry about the accompaniments of daily existence, one supposedly lived in a state of permanent cosmic wonder. Some of its most active proponents, such as Esther de Waal, have warned of the 'dangers of sentimentality' and their work benefits from rigorous modern scholarship, but they feed inevitably a readership whose members are largely unconcerned with such niceties.[17] Whilst the neo-pagans see themselves as rejecting centuries of oppressive Christian hegemony, the Christian rediscoverers see this indigenous Church as a refuge both from the hierarchical formalism and legalism of the Catholic West and Anglicanism, and as a focus for solitude and spontaneity, with a fundamental belief structure at odds with the liberal Churchman's denial of the objective nature of God. For Anglicans in particular, it also seems to offer a diffused ruralism which could replace the rapidly disappearing idealised country ministry once exercised by such models as George Herbert, John Keble and Hawker of Morwenstow.[18] At a time when formal Christian monasticism still declines whilst personal retreats grow, the Celtic eremitical models seem singularly attractive, albeit more read about than copied.

Tremoor Cross and Spring, Lanivet, in the Deanery of Bodmin
Source: Arthur G. Langdon, *Old Cornish Crosses*, 1896.

The emphasis, however, is less on structure than on spirituality. The rediscovery of Celtic Christianity depends heavily on the rhythms of its surviving writings and its making particular places holy. The resulting tourism is usually seen as a return to patterns of pilgrimage largely lost since the Reformation, but with more wholesome objectives than some mediæval journeys. For this, place and feature are more important than venerating reliquaries. The very earth itself is held to have absorbed something of the holy people who have lived there before. Whilst it does involve buildings such as Sancreed, St Just and so on, it is not solely dependent on them, at least in its Cornish manifestation. The popularity of the 'Saints' Way' between Padstow and Fowey, not to mention the widespread enthusiasm that attended the opening in May 1994 of the 'St Michael's Way' across the Penwith isthmus (part of the Council of Europe's Santiago de Compestella cultural route), is evidence of this.

SACRED SITES

This Celticism has certain key sites. As an alternative to Stonehenge's Druidism, many English people are drawn to Holy Island, Lindisfarne off Northumberland. Most influential in Christian terms has been Iona in Scotland, at least since its reconstruction began in 1938. This, with its attached religious community, functions almost as a British Taizé (a Burgundian ecumenical monastery attracting huge international youth pilgrimages) but plays on its much older roots. Its choice as the burial place of the late Labour leader, John Smith, after his tragically early death drew considerable media attention to its spiritual role.[19] The other main site is Glastonbury, with its complex overlays of mediæval piety, Arthurianism and rather more pagan geomantics.[20] Each has acquired a particular, and increasingly organised role for the mainstream churches as a pilgrimage centre, appealing primarily to the already committed.

There are, however, places where there is a more diffused sense of holiness. One such is the Lleyn peninsula in north Wales, opposite Bardsey ('The Isle of Saints'), which owes much to the poetry of R.S. Thomas, who provides both magnet and antagonism for the tourist.[21] The other is Cornwall, portrayed repeatedly as an almost accidental addition to the British mainland. In terms of Celtic Christianity, it functions as the hub of a world bounded by Ireland, Wales and Brittany rather than being linked with the English mainstream, a theme explored by E.G. Bowen in his significant *Saints, Seaways and Settlements in the Celtic Lands*.[22]

This separateness is actually strengthened by the extent to which perceptions of Cornish hagiography rely rather more on legend than on clear documentation. Cornwall lacks the Celtic poetic record such as exists for northern Scotland in the *Carmina Gadelica*.[23] In artefacts it offers no equivalent to the *Book of Kells* to provide an elaborate local aesthetic. What it does have is a very large number of rather small scale stone crosses, whose very restraint makes them somehow less awesome (but more mysterious) than their grander Irish or Scottish counterparts. It also offers a whole range of legendary lives of saints. One recent key text in the field, Shirley Toulson's *Celtic Year*, lists 46 of the many hundreds available as key figures for veneration.[24] That many of them do not feature in the official calendars of the Western Churches probably makes them even more attractive. Individuals such as Morwenna, Austell, Mollien and so on add greatly to the mystery of place and the mysticism it attracts. Is it with more than half an eye on the tourist potential that half of Toulson's list enjoys saints' days during the spring and summer months?

Grander legends reinforce this trend. One, that Christ came to Cornwall as a child, appears in many guises, most famously in William Blake's 'Jerusalem', but one of its recent tellings illustrates remarkably the mode in which legend is now exploited. In his locally-published *Cornish Mysteries* Michael Williams gives the benefit of the visit to St. Just-in-Roseland, but on these grounds: 'The fact is the sheer beauty of the place – it *is* a Garden of Eden – makes you believe *anything* could have happened here'.[25] This is teashop rhetoric, an incursion into the usual run of bleaker Cornish landscape writing of the picturesque more usually associated with the English mainstream. Such a construction allows the place to force the event, rather than the other way round.

In this identification of sacred place, the Christian values are often treated as an overlay on a more fundamental sense of the divine. Tintagel has had its Arthurian, or Merlinian (if such a word may be coined) potential exploited in many forms, not least since Arnold Bax challenged the English Musical Renaissance with the 'Celtic' wildness of his eponymous music.[26] St Michael's Mount, another supposed destination for the wandering young Jesus, fits a further mould: 'St Michael is the archangel associated in particular with the Age of Aquarius and therefore sites dedicated to him have particular significance for the New Age Pilgrim'.[27]

The author of that passage, Bill Anderton, also wrote of the Christian/ Pagan overlap, taking up an increasingly popular strain in guidebook writing, 'You will find... many examples of occult symbolism existing inside sanctified ground'.[28] The most commonly exploited of these magnets are Cornish holy wells, numbered in their hundreds. New Age teaching is strong on the healing values of sacred waters and quite happy to extend the historical overlay where it can. There has been a long sequence of antiquarian discovery, since Wilkie Collins visited Cornwall, with Victorian clergy and gentry carefully recording whatever the locals would tell them, and probably inventing where they would not.[29] The key text is M. and L. Quiller-Couch's *Ancient Holy Wells of Cornwall* of 1894, produced as a counterpoint to what they saw as the tendency of 'civilisation and progress [to] wipe away the old beliefs and superstitions'.[30] Their worries have proved misplaced. Guide books can be found throughout the area, often enhanced with OS grid references and information on parking and local pub lunches.[31]

Wells such as that of Madron are still visited regularly and customary forms of intercession, rags tied to twigs or rudely-made crosses, left there. But there are more than wells – the prehistoric sites, often loosely described as 'Celtic' despite their predating the Celts by centuries if not millennia, serve just as well. Crawling through underground *fogous* or the hole in Men-an-Tol appeals both to children and to those who may want non-specific spiritual healing as well as the curing of particular ailments, such as rheumatism, traditionally associated with the sites. Megaliths and stone circles, particularly in Penwith, have attracted considerable writing-up in this vein. To touch them, it is claimed, is to receive 'a tremble of ancient communication'.[32] Their 'institutionalised magic' is much reiterated, they are claimed to bind Druid and Christian together, a suspension of contrasting theologies if ever there was one, allowing Cornwall to be *the* place where 'the native gods remain constant as at the beginning'.[33]

By contrast it is worth mentioning Cornwall's other main role as a spiritual centre, one at first sight well removed from the views discussed above. It played a key role in the development of popular Methodism, that singular combination of Calvinism and ecstatic mysticism. There is, as far as can be judged, no study of the links between this and folk or implicit religion such as David Clark has provided for Yorkshire.[34] Yet the localism and de-centralised nature of early Methodism had much in common with the Celtic Christianity so recently rediscovered. Wesley and his local successors made links they might well have regretted with foresight when they preached in the 'Celtic' ruins of Chysauster. Methodists may come in smaller numbers than some of the other pilgrims, but their gazetteer for Cornwall excludes such fanciful notions and emotionalism with a doggedly factual listing.[35]

REFLECTION

In the spectrum of modern Celticism, Cornwall has come almost to represent a British Tibet; distant, valued by outsiders and threatened by an occupying power. When trekking in Nepal was opening up in the 1970s, a native Buddhist observed: 'Many people come: looking, looking, taking picture: Too many people. No good . . . Some people come, see. Good'.[36] It might serve to describe the impact of the neo-Celtic tourist on Cornwall as it tries to cope with an identity some of its residents have helped to create and a spiritual hunger which threatens its ascribed isolation.

ACKNOWLEDGEMENTS

An earlier version of this article was presented at the conference, 'The Romance of Place', held at the University of Exeter in April 1994. The author was grateful for the opportunity to read it there and for the helpful discussion which followed. He would also like to express his thanks to his colleague, Mary Stuart, for her valuable suggestions.

NOTES AND REFERENCES

1. M. Chapman, *The Celts: The Construction of a Myth*, London, 1992, p.214.
2. J. Lowerson, 'Golf And The Making Of Myths', in G. Jarvie and G. Walker (eds.), *Scottish Sport in The Making of The Nation*, Leicester, 1994, p.81.
3. J.K. Walton, *The English Seaside Resort: A Social History, 1750-1914*, Leicester, 1983.
4. J. Betjeman, *Summoned by Bells*, London, 1960, p.40; Posy Simmonds, *Mustn't Grumble*, London, 1993.
5. C. Thomas. *The Importance of Being Cornish*, Exeter, 1973.
6. R.S. Hawker, *Footprints of Former Men In Far Cornwall*, London, 1870.
7. A. Conan Doyle, 'The Adventure of the Devil's Foot', (first published in *Strand Magazine*, December 1910, pp.639 - 53), in *Murder on Holiday*, London, 1989, p.47.
8. Betjeman, 1960, p.40.
9. D. Clark, *Poldark Country*, St Teath, 1977, p.5.
10. A.G. Folliott-Stokes, *The Cornish Coast and Moors*, London, 1913.
11. J. Betjeman, *Cornwall Illustrated*, London, 1934, pp.l5-16.
12. A. Mee, *Cornwall*, London, 1937, p.l.
13. G. and S. Priestland, *West of Hayle River*, London, 1980, p.l2.
14. D. Val Baker, *The Spirit of Cornwall*, London, 1980, p.viii.
15. Chapman, 1992, p.224.
16. S. Toulson, *The Celtic Year*, Longmead, 1993, p.l5.
17. E. de Waal, *A World Made Whole: Rediscovering the CelticTradition*, London, 1991, p.12.
18. See A. Russell, *The Country Parson*, London, 1993; M. Hinton, *The Anglican Parochial Clergy: A Celebration*, London, 1994.
19. See, among others, *The Times*, 18 May 1994; *Sunday Telegraph*, 22 May 1994.
20. J. Lowerson, 'The Mystical Geography of the English', in B. Short (ed.), *The English Rural Community: Image and Analysis*, Cambridge, 1992, p.166.
21. R.S. Thomas, 'A Thicket in Lleyn' in *Experimenting with an Amen*, London, 1986, p.45, and 'Welcome' in *Welsh Airs*, Bridgend, 1987, p.21.
22. E.G. Bowen, *Saints, Seaways and Settlements*, Cardiff, 1977.
23. A. Carmichael (ed.), *Carmina Gadelica: Hymns and Incantations...*, Edinburgh, 1900, and E. de Waal (ed.), *The Celtic Vision: Selections from the Carmina Gadelica*, London, 1988.
24. Toulson, 1993.
25. M. Williams, *Cornish Mysteries*, Bodmin, 1980, p.68.
26. R. Stradling and M. Hughes, *The English Musical Renaissance*, 1860-1940, *Construction and Deconstruction*, London, 1993, p.157.

27. B. Anderton, *Guide to Ancient Britain*, London, 1991, p.208.
28. Anderton, 1991, p.ll.
29. W. Wilkie Collins, *Rambles Beyond Railways: Or Notes in Cornwall Taken Afoot*, London, 1851, p.44 ff.
30. M. and L. Quiller-Couch, *Ancient and Holy Wells Of Cornwall*, London, 1894, p.xi.
31. J. Meyrick, *A Pilgrim's Guide to the Holy Wells of Cornwall*, Falmouth, 1982; Anderton, 1991.
32. D. Val Baker, 1980, p.13 and p.33; J. Michell, *The Old Stones of Land's End: An Enquiry into the Mysteries of the Megalithic Science*, Bristol, 1974, (1979 edn.), p.32.
34. D. Clark, *Between Pulpit and Pew: Folk Religion in a North Yorkshire Fishing Village*, Cambridge, 1982.
35. T. Shaw, *A Methodist Guide to Cornwall*, 1991.
36. G. Rowell, *Many People Come, Looking, Looking*, Seattle, 1980, frontispiece.

CORNWALL'S TERRITORIAL DILEMMA: EUROPEAN REGION OR 'WESTCOUNTRY' SUB-REGION?

Alys Thomas

INTRODUCTION

> Geographically Cornwall is distinct from every other English county. It is surrounded on three sides by sea and separated from its only neighbour, Devon, by the River Tamar, still a significant physical and cultural divide. Viewed from Brussels, London and even Bristol, the far south west peninsula may seem remote and peripheral. In one sense it is, and for some that is a problem, whilst for others it is part of the great attraction to 'get away from it all'. Yet in another sense Cornwall is central to the north west seaboard of Europe, with a unique range of quality products and (that increasingly rare item) a strong local identity and community spirit.[1]

Cornwall's distinctiveness in terms of identity has only begun to be subjected to the full glare of academic scrutiny in recent years. However, the territorial isolation stressed by the County Council in the quotation cited above is being challenged on a number of fronts, notably the Bristol, London and Brussels perspectives which are listed as viewing Cornwall as remote and peripheral. This article explores the ways in which Cornwall's territorial identity is currently under threat against the backdrop of contemporary political trends and institutional innovation.

TERRITORIAL IDENTITY

The antiquity of Cornwall's territorial border, dating from Athelstan's settlement of 926, has always been of great significance as a determinant of Cornish identity. Philip Payton comments:

> For Cornwall, the importance of Athelstans's actions cannot be stressed too greatly. Not only had Athelstan established Cornwall as a geo-political unit, but also he had set it as the territory of the 'West Welsh' (the Cornish Celts) and defined its relationship with England.[2]

Of equal importance to defenders of Cornish difference and identity has been the continuity of the Tamar boundary and the constitutional status lent by the Duchy. These factors tend to be reinforced by Cornwall's physical isolation and perceived remoteness from the 'centre'. The Kilbrandon Commission on the Constitution stated in 1973: 'What they (the Cornish) do want is recognition of the fact that Cornwall has a separate identity and that its traditional boundaries shall be respected'.[3] Bernard Deacon has argued that modern Cornwall lacks strong core values of ethnic identity such as language or religion but both he and Payton agree that territory is probably the most significant core value. The threat to territorial integrity, therefore, is one which has far reaching implications for Cornwall's future not only as an institutional and political entity but also as a distinct cultural region.[4]

Payton and Deacon have argued that while literature on Cornish identity in the past has dwelt on a 'disappearing' Celtic heritage, a case can be made for the emergence of a contemporary Cornish cultural identity or rather a 're-invention' of Cornishness, assimilating the new with the old.[5] Payton has asserted that Cornwall's inherent peripherality led to a 'persistence of difference', claiming that Cornwall's industrial rise and relatively early decline and the subsequent emergence of a branch factory economy in the post-War period emphasised differences between a Cornish 'periphery' and English 'centre' and placed Cornwall 'firmly within the "multi-national" diversity of the British state'.[6] It is ironic that at a time when such strong arguments are being made for the strength and persistence of a distinctive Cornish identity Cornwall's territorial status is under attack from several different directions. The spectre of Local Government reorganisation looms over Cornwall as elsewhere with the possibility that the County Council, the most significant single Cornish institution, could disappear. Other Central Government initiatives, such as the Department of the Environment (DoE) 'New Localism' proposal, announced in November 1993, aimed at creating an administrative 'regionalism' based on a territorially extensive South West Region with a 'regional capital' in Bristol, treats Cornwall as part of a sub-region centred on Plymouth. Collaboration with Devon, particularly for the purposes of attracting European funding and for economic development are also felt by some to blur Cornwall's territorial identity. The European dimension has emerged as an influential catalyst to change, holding the potential for both threat and opportunity for Cornwall. The Euro-constituency issue, interregional co-operation and the hunt for European funding all have an impact in this area.

DEVONWALL – CONSPIRACY OR PRAGMATISM?

The demands of twentieth-century administration have been an important factor in seeing the territorial singularity of Cornwall challenged. As will be seen, contradictory demands of size exist in which, on the one hand, the Government has asserted that Cornwall is too small to be a region but on the other, is too large to be a unitary local authority. The consideration of Cornwall with Devon as a unit for particular purposes has therefore become commonplace. Writing in a comparative study of Brittany with Cornwall and Devon, Derek Hearl *et al.* commented that 'Cornwall and Devon undoubtedly "go together" in the minds of most British citizens and form a traditional area of England which has a more distinct identity than any other **group** of counties in the Kingdom'.[7] This view contrasts with those propounded by Payton and Deacon, among others, who identify Cornish difference by emphasising a Cornish identity based on territory and distinct industrial and post-industrial experiences which have left their imprint upon society in Cornwall. It is also worth pausing to consider whether the strength of a joint Cornwall and Devon identity should be measured on the basis of what 'most British citizens' think rather than the opinions of those citizens who actually inhabit the territories in question.

Co-operation between Devon and Cornwall is by no means a new initiative as a Joint Devon & Cornwall Committee was set up at the time of Local Government Reorganisation in 1974 and developed into an important forum, particularly for European issues. However, the pressures from Central Government and from sectors such as the newly privatised monopolies have led to an increasing level of co-operation. Devon & Cornwall was designated a NUTS II region by the European Community in 1988. In 1993 the Government put in a bid for Objective 1 Status for Devon and Cornwall which failed largely due to the fact that Objective 1 regions are designated as those whose GDP is less than 75% (a broad measuring stick) of the European Union average and the combined Devon and Cornwall GDP totalled 82%. Critics argued that Cornwall, with a GDP of 76%, was the victim of statistical invisibility and without Devon would have been better placed than Merseyside or the Highlands (both of which were successful in their bids) in achieving Objective 1 Status, and asserted that Cornwall should be designated a NUTS II region in its own right. Cornwall County Council itself had been working on a joint economic strategy with Devon and preparing its own submission in pursuit of Objective 5(b) status. The impetus supplied by organisations such the Westcountry Development Corporation (WDC), the Devon & Cornwall Development Bureau (DCDB), and the Devon & Cornwall Training & Enterprise Council (TEC) point to greater integration of Devon and Cornwall for economic development purposes.

This trend is resisted by those sections of the community which believe that Cornwall should assert itself as a distinct region in its own right. It is argued by critics of 'Devonwall' that the increasing level of co-operation between Cornwall and Devon is fundamentally detrimental to the interests of Cornwall.

In the 1988 CoSERG publication *Cornwall at the Crossroads* the authors noted that:

> the headquarters of virtually all of these 'Devonwall' institutions are located in Devon, most of them in Exeter or Plymouth. And this gives us a good idea of how 'Devonwall' would turn out. Devon would get all the advantages, Cornwall would lose on every count. Devon, with a million people, would always be big brother to Cornwall with half a million.[8]

It is asserted that a Devonwall approach further peripheralises Cornwall because the central focus of such a region would gravitate to the east, thus Cornwall's political and economic development would atrophy and options available to it as a distinct unit would be denied. Examples of current disadvantages arising from joint Devonwall initiatives are cited such as the preferential treatment given to Plymouth over Falmouth as a port[9] and the fact that Cornwall's linkage with Devon disguised the extent of Cornwall's economic disadvantage and prevented the attainment of Objective 1 status for European Structural Funds in 1993.

To a certain extent, however, the arguments about Cornwall as a junior partner in an economic and political partnership with Devon are secondary to the basic belief of many opponents of Devonwall trends that Cornwall's cultural distinctiveness should be recognised and Cornwall itself treated as a distinct unit. Thus CoSERG point out the special treatment accorded to Rural Wales and Scotland's Highlands and Islands, both of which possess development boards. In *Cornwall at the Crossroads*, the authors considered the establishment of the Highlands & Islands Development Board in the 1960s and the establishment of the Development Board for Rural Wales in the 1970s and their objectives of halting outward migration and safeguarding cultural identity. However, the authors expressed the view that the UK Government 'will clearly not sponsor a Cornwall Development Board (despite the fact that Cornwall has more people and arguably greater potential than rural Scotland or Wales)'.[10] What is interesting about the chosen contrasts with Scotland and Wales (and the Irish Gaeltacht) is the territorial dimension. The development boards in question only cover part of Wales and Scotland and are very much tied in with the dynamics of *linguistic* preservation; thus parallels are being drawn on the basis of culture rather than territory. As territory is considered to be the most definitive marker of Cornish identity, it is debatable whether these provide the most appropriate models.

There is some dispute about where the impetus for the Devonwall approach originates. Opponents claim that pressures from the private sector through agencies such as the West Country Development Corporation reveal a 'hidden political agenda' by some groupings within local government in Cornwall. It could be said that this is facilitated by the *ad hoc* approach of others in local government. This is typified by what opponents of Devonwall define as the paradox of strong support for a Cornwall-only Euro-constituency coupled with backing for a general policy of closer collaboration with Devon.

However, such arguments are disputed by claims that Cornwall is not by any means a junior partner in co-operative initiatives with Devon; thus, the transformation of the Cornwall European Office into a Devon and Cornwall operation in 1992 was not a 'takeover', as some argued, but an effective neutralisation of a rival and an assurance of Cornwall keeping the upper hand. However, this is qualified by the fact that pragmatic decisions are often influenced by external determinants. Despite support for the principle of a Cornish Development Agency the County Council came down on the side of the Devon & Cornwall WDC because it was clear that no support, financial or otherwise, would be forthcoming from Central Government for a 'Cornwall only' initiative. The authors of the Joint Economic Strategy Document took pains to stress that the linkage between Cornwall and Devon was primarily on the basis of economic need: 'Cornwall and Devon is (*sic*) characterised by strong and varied local and County identities. It is not one homogenous region. However, both counties need to restructure key industries, upgrade the infrastructure and provide more effective business support'.[11] Pragmatists, therefore, are not necessarily active seekers of co-operation or exponents of a 'regional' vision but it could be argued that the very nature of pragmatism implies a reactive rather than a proactive role to external circumstances.

A prominent voice for the Devonwall viewpoint is the *Western Morning News (WMN)* which consistently highlights the relative disadvantage suffered by what it terms 'the Westcountry' in comparison with Wales and Scotland which are in possession of clearly delineated regional (national) identities and Ministers in the Cabinet. There is a contradictory nature to the arguments put forward. For example, comparing the individual GDP figures for Devon and Cornwall individually against that of Wales as a whole ignores the fact that Wales is a larger unit made up of eight counties. Equally, as seen above, the charge of statistical invisibility is one which is made by critics of the Devonwall approach who claim that Cornwall's association with Devon disadvantages Cornwall. In short, the question of statistical invisibility works very much on the same basis as Russian dolls and can be something of a red herring in developing a case for regional policy in the current UK context.

There is a certain paradox in the nature of the pressure being exerted against Wales in particular by the Devonwall lobby. The *WMN* stated:

> The stark facts suggest that while Ministers want to centre power on Bristol, they are quite happy to see the cash speeding off down the M4 into Wales. The Welsh Development Agency has worked wonders in reviving the economy of the valleys, spending hundreds of millions of pounds of taxpayers' money to attract high tech firms and create thousands of jobs.[1]

It is significant that the article picks on Wales rather than Scotland. Recent upheaval within the WDA following a savage criticism of its administrative practices by the House of Commons' Public Accounts Committee has perhaps made the WDA an easy target on the basis that the money squandered on executive transport and suchlike should be diverted to 'more deserving' regions such as the South West.

THE EXPANDING REGION

Over many years Cornwall has been included in a broad South West region for various planning purposes. This region is vast, covering, for some functions, the counties of Cornwall, Devon, Somerset, Avon, Dorset, Wiltshire and Gloucestershire.[13] The South West Regional Planning Conference was set up in 1987 as a forum for discussing and advising on Regional Planning issues. In 1993 it published its advice to the Secretary of State for the Environment.[14]

The recent Government plans to integrate departments to create regional 'one stop shops' announced in November 1993 prompted particularly strongly voiced opposition from the *WMN*. The Department of the Environment initiative decentralises some of its administrative functions relating to transport, planning and economic development outside London in 'regional capitals'. The intention is that 20 existing programmes for regeneration will be brought under a single budget allowing for priorities to be 'set locally, in the light of local needs, and not in Whitehall'.[15] The designated 'capital' for the South West was named as Bristol. The reaction of the *WMN* to this proposal was notable in the manner in which it defended the interests of Devon *and* Cornwall against the concept of a wider South West region. It argued that the new regional capital should be based towards the 'far south west where it is needed the most'.[16] Remarkably, this was conceded by the Government, which announced the establishment of a Plymouth based office in May 1994. The concept of the 'far South West' in which Cornwall *and* Devon are perceived as a distinct and peripheral region of the greater South West presents a challenge, therefore, to the territorial identity of Cornwall.

There appears to be an increasing perception that the drive for inward investment coupled with a clear and co-ordinated regional context, as experienced in Wales, could be replicated in the English regions but it is questionable how clarity is to be achieved bearing in mind the fact that the English regions remain largely ill-defined. The complaint that Wales and Scotland do better from the Government is, to a certain extent, a valid one and one which the Government itself has picked up upon. In 1991 an article in *The Economist* noted that the then Secretary of State for the Environment, Michael Heseltine, was contemplating the importance of achieving regional balance in England and the need for a streamlined agencies to co-ordinate efforts at economic and industrial regeneration. The article concluded: 'He has been impressed by the Scottish and

Welsh Development Agencies, bodies that have a strategic overview (as well as a lot of government money). He would like an English Development Agency along the same lines'.[17]

In the case of the South West, while the Government made its announcement on 'New Localism' embracing a wide South West Region stretching from Cornwall to Wiltshire; the WDC, launched by Industry Minister, Tim Sainsbury, a month earlier, is based on Devon and Cornwall alone. A partnership of public and private sectors, the WDC claims to be 'the emergent strategic body to speak with one voice for the economic interests of Devon and Cornwall',[18] and asserts that 'an overall vision for Devon and Cornwall is essential if the Region as a whole is to prosper'.[19] However, critics argue that the fact that the WDC receives no Government grant means that it is in no position to fulfil a similar role to that of the WDA in Wales, or Scottish Enterprise in Scotland. However, the Devon and Cornwall Development Bureau, a local authority board, does receive part of its funding from the DTI for attracting overseas investment to Cornwall and Devon.

LOCAL GOVERNMENT REORGANISATION

There is irony in the fact that while Cornwall is considered by supporters of greater Devon and Cornwall integration to be too small as region, for Local Government Review purposes it appears it may be too big when measured against the Government's criteria as set out in the revised Local Government Commission Guidelines published in the autumn of 1993. The original Guidelines laid stress upon paying close attention to local feelings and stated that the Commission should not be tied to a uniform pattern for England as a whole. The revised Guidelines, however, speeded up the process considerably – Cornwall had been languishing in the fifth tranche of the review – and placed greater emphasis on the desirability of a unitary authority option. The County Council and the constituent Districts had, prior to this point, been united in favouring the *status quo* but the impression in the Guidelines that this option was not on the table led to some of the Districts breaking ranks and looking to two or three unitary authority options. The Local Government Commission paid an initial visit to Cornwall in January 1994 and formal submissions lodged in May 1994 included many attacking what was perceived as a very real threat to Cornwall's historic, territorial integrity.

The establishment of the Campaign for Cornwall in December 1993 was a direct response to the apparent break up of County and District consensus on the desirability of maintaining the two tier system. It was also felt that as the *status quo* was unlikely to be a realistic option the Campaign should throw its weight behind a single unitary option for Cornwall. Fears of a 'carve-up' hark back to the Redcliffe-Maud Report's recommendation for a 'Tamarside' unitary authority which threatened a takeover of South East Cornwall by

Plymouth City Council. The Campaigners claimed an initial victory following a preliminary visit by the Local Government Commission to Truro in February 1994 in ensuring that a single unitary authority option was on the agenda. However, the English Local Government Review has come under pressure from outside Cornwall with defenders of traditional counties such as Somerset challenging plans for division. Given the Government's current electoral vulnerability in the South West, in particular Cornwall, it is arguable whether it will choose to risk stirring up a populist campaign of opposition.

EUROPE

An important electoral test for the Government was the European election in June 1994. Cornwall and West Plymouth was considered to be one of the seats the Conservatives were most likely to lose to the Liberal Democrats and, as predicted, the sitting Tory (Christopher Beazley) lost heavily to his Liberal Democrat challenger (Robin Teverson) who achieved a 30,000 vote majority. Although the Liberal Democrats fared less well in southern Britain (with the exception of North Devon and Somerset) than had been anticipated, their success in Cornwall was remarkable. Significantly, perhaps, the Liberal Democrat campaign in Cornwall dwelt on anti-metropolitan issues (from water charges to the alleged need for a Cornish Development Agency), while the issue of the Euro-constituency continued to provide a focus for the articulation of quasi-nationalist Cornish sentiment. The inclusion of Plymouth with Cornwall had raised strong objections in the 1980s. It was thought that the extra seats awarded to the UK for 1994 would provide an opportunity to secure a Cornwall-only seat. In 1988 Cornwall had been significant in providing the strongest challenge to the proposed boundaries and had been granted an Inquiry.[20] The case put by those arguing for a Cornwall-only Euro-constituency was that the minimum electorate stipulated should be put aside and Cornwall should be subject to special geographical considerations such as those which applied to Northern Ireland and the Highlands & Islands on the grounds of distinct identity and geographical isolation. The same arguments were rehearsed in 1993. Speaking in the Parliamentary debate, Liberal Democrat MP Matthew Taylor stated:

> Cornwall has a separate identity with its own traditions, history, customs and language. Those attributes are firmly rooted in a Celtic past that bears more relation to Scotland and Wales than to Devon. There would have been objections if regions in Scotland or Wales had been linked with parts of England for the convenience of the review. It seems that Cornwall, which has a distinct and separate identity continues to be ignored. The European Union recognises that special regard must be paid to

> areas with strong regional identities. Indeed, the European Parliament's resolution is specific on that point and I believe that the boundary commission has failed to take an opportunity to observe that requirement.[21]

In 1993 the Cornish objections were matched in scale by those from other areas such as Norfolk and the North West of England. Despite a broad unity between local authorities and many other Cornish based bodies, the English Boundaries Committee rejected the case for a separate Cornish constituency and split Plymouth, leaving its Western half with Cornwall. The Euro-constituency issue raised important questions about the significance of identity. As noted above, Hearl *et al.* argued that Cornwall and Devon are perceived as having a joint identity by 'most British citizens'; however, the strength of feeling engendered by the Euro-constituency issue would appear to challenge this assessment.

Article 198a of the Maastricht Treaty established the Committee of the Regions which consists of representatives of regional and local bodies. Its function is to be consultative and advisory. Nevertheless, some regional authorities and bodies foster the hope that it may develop its role in order to have an input into the policy making process of the European Union and perhaps even to evolve into a second Chamber of the European Parliament. The German Lander originally brought pressure to bear on those drafting the revised treaty in order to cure what they termed the 'regional blindness' of the treaties as they stood.[22] Operating, as they do, within a Federal system in which the regions have a strong voice, a Europe based on the German model is therefore for many an attractive objective. However, the pattern of regional government in the Member states varies greatly and does not always correspond with the regional definitions employed for the purposes of European funding and in some states, such as the UK, no regional level of Government exists. The problem was recognised early on in the discussion and in reply to a query from an MEP, the DGXVI Commissioner, Bruce Millan replied:

> The great differences between the organisational and political regional structures in the member States can often be explained by historical factors. Such structures are the exclusive competence of the Member states. Therefore the Commission does not intend to establish a Community definition of what constitutes a region.[23]

The establishment of the Committee of the Regions and the debate about representation in Britain has served to highlight the issue of regional government in the UK and to illuminate the confusion which exists between functional/administrative regionalism and representative regionalism based on democratic devolution. Opposition victory on an amendment to the European Communities

Amendment Bill [known as the Maastricht Bill] ensuring that representatives on the Committee of the Regions should be local councillors prevented Central Government from appointing its own 'experts'. It was argued by Local Government Associations that the appointment of representatives by Central Government conflicted with the fundamental ethos of the Committee of the Regions, which was to allow for a more localised representation based upon the principle of *subsidiarity*.

Developments in Europe, such as the establishment of the Committee of the Regions, have opened up opportunities for European regions to play an increasingly assertive role in the European Union. However, for most UK regions, the rhetoric of regionalism does not square with the reality of the UK political system and its relationship with Europe. Cornwall County Council's *Strategy for Europe* published in 1993 cites its chief aim 'to retain the council's status and voice in Europe'.[24] The document stresses the vulnerability of Cornwall as a peripheral region and places emphasis on the need for co-operation with other local authorities and regions, in particular Devon, and highlights Cornwall's activities within interregional lobbying organisations such as the Conference of Peripheral and Maritime Regions and its Atlantic Arc Commission and the Assembly of European Regions. It is interesting that the original wording read 'to retain the council's status and voice in Europe **as a region**' but the decision was made by the County Council to drop the last three words. However, in the County Council's Draft Economic Development Plan which was circulated for consultation in early 1994, the 'vision' outlined is 'To establish Cornwall as a vibrant and prosperous European **region** which promotes a balance between a high quality environment and thriving economic base . . .'.[25]

This uncertainty appears characteristic of confused attitudes on the part of Cornwall County Council towards Cornwall's position within a shifting territorial context. The prospect of greater European integration and development of European institutions has posed a significant challenge to the Member states and their constituent parts. The UK response has been to juggle with limited definitions of *subsidiarity*. The establishment of the Committee of the Regions created significant problems in determining who should attend from the UK. Moreover, in England the lack of clearly defined regions posed even greater problems and representation has turned out to be a rather messy compromise which pairs members and their alternates on a party political basis rather than a regional one. Thus, the current Chairman of Cornwall County Council is paired with another Liberal Democrat councillor from the London Borough of Sutton. Those defending this arrangement assert that the aim of the Committee of the Regions is to provide a forum for local and regional voices rather than representation from specific regions. It is argued that it is the task of MEPs to provide territorial representation and the role of Committee of the Regions is to provide a voice for the regional and local tier of government across the European Union.

This interpretation leaves little room for the assertion of Cornwall as a European region in its own right. Those sections of the community who wish to promote Cornwall on the basis of its distinct culture and history, such as the Cornish Bureau for European Relations (CoBER) which has lobbied the European Parliament in order to achieve recognition and support for Cornish culture, are up against the pull of economic interests which claim that a Devon & Cornwall region offers the best opportunity for the development of a regional interest in an evolving European context.

CONCLUSION

The problem facing Cornwall in seeking to define itself as a region is the lack of a regional context in the UK. Scotland maintained a measure of administrative devolution through the persistence of its institutions such as its legal system and Wales has achieved administrative devolution on a gradualist basis since the nineteenth century. However, in these two cases *ad hoc*, piecemeal concessions have been made by Central Government in order to preserve central power as far as possible. The challenge of articulating regional concerns is one that has been gaining prominence in some parts of the country. For example, local authorities in the North of England have grouped themselves into the Assembly of the North. In the case of Cornwall the need to articulate regional concerns goes hand in hand with the attempt or desire to assert a distinctive cultural identity. In this sense, many want Cornwall to be seen as more than a region and want special recognition such as that accorded to remote sections of Wales and Scotland and Northern Ireland, as witnessed in the case of the Euro-constituency and arguments for a Development Agency.

Europe offers an opportunity to Cornwall to develop a distinct regional presence. However, in the absence of clearly identifiable Cornish-based institutions this task is made very difficult. The fact that Cornwall's territorial distinctiveness has already been compromised for certain economic and administrative purposes means that the pressure for 'pragmatic' joint action with Devon on behalf of Local Government and other bodies is increased. A reorganisation of Local Government which split Cornwall would further this trend as strategic planning functions currently carried out by the County Council would be passed on to joint boards which could conceivably cross the existing border. Certainly, the WDC would be poised to take a strategic role in economic development. To opponents of 'Devonwallisation', therefore, Local Government reorganisation is of crucial importance to Cornwall. It could be argued that some choose to regard it as an opportunity to establish a single and highly symbolic Cornwall Council which would be relatively powerful – particularly if Devon was split up into several small authorities. Such an arrangement would emphasise Cornwall's difference and claim to special administrative arrangements. Nevertheless, if the fortunes of Cornwall in resisting the trend towards increased Devon & Cornwall integration and putting across its case for a separate Euro-constituency are considered, then its fate at the hands of the Local Government Commission might look bleak. However, as seen above, the Government faces a strong electoral challenge from the Liberal Democrats who hold two of the Westminster seats and are close challengers in the other three. The party won control of Cornwall County Council in 1993 and in 1994 took the Cornwall and West Plymouth seat in the European Parliament. The Liberal Democrats, while espousing some of the 'pragmatic' aspects of Devon and Cornwall co-operation with regard to economic development, have not been slow to adopt a quasi-nationalist Cornish rhetoric on the matter of the Euro-constituency and in their resistance to a reorganisation of Local Government which would split Cornwall. The fact is that a populist Cornish identity exists, as identified by Deacon and Payton, which is focussed significantly upon Cornwall as a territory. In political terms the mobilisation of this populism could be decisive and may persuade the Government to err on the side of caution in the short term. However, populism is less easily mobilised against the pragmatic trend towards Cornwall's linkage with Devon at diverse levels, and it could be that this presents a longer term challenge to Cornwall's territorial identity.

NOTES AND REFERENCES

1. Cornwall County Council, *Cornwall – A Land Apart: Issues for the New Structure Plan*, Truro, 1993.
2. Philip Payton, *The Making of Modern Cornwall: Historical Experience and the Persistence of 'Difference'*, Redruth, 1992, p.46.
3. *Report of the Royal Commission on the Constitution*, London, 1973, para. 329.
4. Bernard Deacon, 'And Shall Trelawny Die? The Cornish Identity', and Philip Payton, 'Territory and Identity', both in Philip Payton (ed.), *Cornwall Since the War: The Contemporary History of a European Region*, Redruth, 1993.
5. Bernard Deacon and Philip Payton, 'Re-inventing Cornwall: Culture Change on the European Periphery', *Cornish Studies: One*, second series, No.1, 1993.
6. Payton, 1992, p.241.
7. Derek Hearl *et al.*, 'Politics and Government in the Far South West', in M.A. Havinden, J. Queniart and J. Stanyer (eds.), *Centre and Periphery: Brittany and Cornwall & Devon Compared*, Exeter, 1991, p.204.
8. Bernard Deacon, Andrew George and Ronald Perry, *Cornwall at the Crossroads*, Redruth, 1988, p.104.
9. CoSERG Pamphlet, February 1993.
10. Deacon *et al.*, 1988, pp.97-104.
11. Cornwall County Council, Devon County Council and Plymouth City Council, *Towards an Economic Strategy for Cornwall and Devon*, 1993.
12. *Western Morning News*, 10 November 1993.
13. Brian W. Hogwood and P.D. Lindley, 'Variations in Regional Boundaries', in Brian W. Hogwood and M. Keating (eds.), *Regional Government in England*, Oxford, 1982, pp.21-49.

14. South West Regional Planning Conference, *Advice to the Secretary of State for the Environment*, February 1993.
15. Department of the Environment Press Release, February 1993.
16. *Western Morning News*, 10 November 1993.
17. 'Regional Policy: Back in Fashion?', *Economist,* 20 April 1991.
18. Westcountry Development Corporation, *Strategy Report*, October 1993, p.2.
19. WDC, 1993, p.2.
20. Boundary Commission for England Local Inquiry, held at Bodmin, 12/13 July 1988.
21. *Hansard,* 15 February 1994.
22. Note from the Government of Nordrhein-Westfalen to other AER Regions, 12 September 1991.
23. Bruce Millan, reply to written question to the Commission, 18 June 1992.
24. Cornwall County Council, *A Strategy for Europe 1992-96*, Truro, 1993.
25. Cornwall County Council, *Draft Economic Development Strategy and Action Plan 1994-1999*, Truro, January 1994, p.18.

TOWARDS A CORNISH IDENTITY THEORY

Allen E. Ivey and Philip Payton

INTRODUCTION

What is the Cornish identity? Do the people who inhabit the territorial entity of Cornwall possess a distinct ethnic identity, or is the concept of 'Cornishness' a romantic myth constructed for the benefit of tourists and other seekers of the mystical and the foreign? For many years such questions were the province of literary fancy, with writers such as Denys Val Baker and Daphne du Maurier developing images of *The Timeless Land* and *Vanishing Cornwall*,[1] but of late the Cornish identity has received serious academic attention from sociologists, historians, political scientists, and anthropologists such as Bryant, Deacon, McArthur, Payton and Vink. Collectively, these social scientists have indicated that there is a distinct Cornish ethnic identity, and they have furnished an array of explanations to account for both its survival over time and its apparent recent reassertion.[2] Even *The Times* has asked, 'Are the Cornish an ethnic minority?',[3] while in 1994 the County Council could point to Cornwall's 'geographic, economic, historic, cultural and *ethnic* integrity'.[4] This article seeks to expand the debate by looking again at the notion of identity and providing a framework for considering alternative perspectives on the Cornish identity.

Multicultural theorists in the United States have argued that traditional social science discourse has been embedded in a Eurocentric perspective which fails to consider historical and cultural reality, a serious shortcoming when addressing the attributes and needs of, say, Native American or African-American individuals and communities. These multiculturalists suggest the importance of considering multicultural theory and practice from a frame of reference specific to each cultural/ethnic group.[5] It has already been pointed out how ingrained Anglocentric views of the United Kingdom have resulted in an educational, political and social system which is inevitably described from an English perspective and which not only equates 'Britishness' with 'Englishness' but fails to recognise territorially-based cultural diversity or a dichotomy between centre and periphery.[6] Thus a Cornish frame of reference, derived from the historical and cultural reality of Cornwall, would describe Cornwall and Cornish issues in a vastly different way from one constructed for England.

A multicultural view, however, does not reject Eurocentric or Anglocentric approaches; rather, the multicultural approach offers an integrating system for allowing various meaning-making systems to coalesce in a practical manner which is respectful of and responsive to cultural diversity. The issue of meaning-making is important. Vink has commented that consciousness of Cornish identity is 'acquired' through contact and conflict.[7] More generally, identity can be seen as a constructed meaning-making system for viewing oneself and others in a cultural context. There is certainly an English ethnic way of of construing the world and, if we admit a Cornish historical and cultural experience which is distinct from that of England, then there is also a Cornish ethnic way of doing the same.[8] In a sense, we are all 'ethnics' and our ethnicity provides us with spectacles through which we view our surroundings.

Summarising in 1990 the extensive literature on ethnic identity, Phinney concluded that:

> Tajfel (1981) defines social identity as 'that part of an individual's self-concept which derives from his knowledge of his membership of a social group (or groups) together with the values an emotional significance attached to that membership'. Some writers consider self-identification the key aspect; others emphasized feelings of belonging and commitment (Singh, 1977; Ting-Toomey, 1981; Taurel & Klein, 1977), the sense of shared values and attitudes (White & Burke, 1987), or attitudes toward one's group (e.g. Parham & Helms, 1981; Teske & Nelson, 1973). In contrast to the focus by these writers on attitudes and feelings, some definitions emphasized the cultural aspects of ethnicity, for example, language, behaviour, values, and knowledge of ethnic group history (e.g. Rogler, Cooney & Ortiz, 1980). The active role of the individual in developing an ethnic identity was suggested by several writers who saw it as a dynamic product that is achieved rather than simply given (Caltabiano, 1984; Hogg, Abrams & Patal, 1987; Simic, 1987).[9]

Building on Vink's 'acquired identity' concept and Phinney's literature review, we suggest that ethnic identity may now be defined as follows: *Ethnic identity* is an acquired sense of oneself and/or one's group as cultural beings, both emotionally and cognitively. It is a *process* of making meaning in cultural and social contexts and involves varying levels of identification and commitment. The *content* of ethnic identity relates to issues of language, behaviour, values, and knowledge of ethnic group history. Although an individual may be deeply influenced by such history, he or she is not necessarily aware of the power of this influence. Thus *ethnic identity development* often refers to the process of increasing individual and group understanding of previously unconscious forces (processes) and learning the facts of one's own cultural background (content).

This article focusses on the *processes* of ethnic identity and draws on cultural identity theory as a systematic form of meaning making. Originally conceptualised by Cross in 1971 and subsequently developed by a range of writers,[10] cultural identity theory may be described as a cognitive-developmental approach to identity development with a focus on an individual's cultural heritage.

THE NEED FOR A CORNISH IDENTITY THEORY

It seems likely that a coherent and widely articulated Cornish identity theory would lead to a better general understanding of the uniqueness of the Cornish within the United Kingdom. Such knowledge could lead to the more relevant and more effective delivery of human services such as education, housing, local government, counselling, and medical services, together with an enhanced sense of personal and group pride for both the indigenous and in-migrant Cornish. This might go a very long way to addressing the situation identified by the Commission for Racial Equality in 1992 in which a '. . . substantial number of indigenous Cornish people . . . feel disadvantaged compared with "incomers" in relation to class, income, housing, employment . . .', a situation in which one advisory teacher in Cornwall 'fully accepted the view that the Cornish are an oppressed minority, and found that recognition of this fact in her work had proved to be a useful introduction to multicultural and anti-racist education'.[11]

In the United States, Native American and African-American populations receive an education founded on Eurocentric values and beliefs. Very little attention, for example, is given to how history might be taught from a Native American or African-American perspective. Similarly, in Cornwall the Anglocentric focus of the National Curriculum makes it very difficult to teach history (or other humanities) from a Cornish perspective, despite the efforts of the Local Education Authority to accommodate Cornish Studies within the constraints of the Curriculum.[12] At best, Cornish Studies is presented as 'Local Studies'. And so, if the historical (and other) perspectives presented are almost always those of 'outsiders', then there are precious few opportunities in the education process for Cornish people to explore and gain an understanding of themselves as individuals and as a group. However, now that serious attention has at last been devoted to the study of Cornish identity and the special needs of the Cornish community, the stage is set for an empowering of the Cornish – 'empowering' in the sense that the Cornish can take an increased pride in their separate identity, can recognise how they have been affected and moulded by history, and – crucially – can take a greater part in planning for the future. It has always been possible to deny the existence of a Cornish identity (as recently as 1991 Denis *et al.* could claim that 'arguments based on the existence of an ethnic identity have a plausibility which is totally lacking in the far south-west')[13] but now a framework can be developed to affirm that identity.

MEANING-MAKING, CONSCIOUSNESS & CULTURAL IDENTITY THEORY

Meaning-making has been identified as a central factor in the development of a cultural identity. Ivey[14] has generated a developmental scheme of meaning-making based on Plato's celebrated observation in *The Republic* that the transition to enlightenment involves four levels of consciousness in which each level builds on previous perceptions of reality, preparing the way for the next higher level. Ivey points out that the progressions of knowledge portrayed in the 'Allegory of the Cave' may be construed as a useful framework for the generation of cultural consciousness. In Plato's allegorical story the prisoners in the cave thought that the flickering shadows in front of them was 'reality'. But as one prisoner was removed from his chains and taken out of the cave, he realised that what he had seen in the cave was not reality but only a perspective. However, as Plato notes soberly, if the former prisoner were returned to his fellows with news of the new truth, 'they would kill him'. The birth of consciousness is lonely and often fraught with real pain.

Cultural identity theory moves people from the 'cave' of naïve consciousness to awareness of self in relation to system. The parallels to the Platonic journey are not perfect but do suggest that coming to a new view of reality may involve some difficulty. As Cornford noted in his edition of *The Republic*, 'One moral of the allegory is drawn from the distress caused by too sudden passage from dark to light'.[15] So, too, the development of an individual's 'Cornishness' may involve difficulty and trauma, not least that occasioned by denial or even derision from others. As each stage of Platonic consciousness requires a new way of meaning-making, so each stage of movement in 'Cornishness' requires a new interpretation of the old 'reality'. With this in mind, let us turn to a more detailed examination of cultural identity theory and its implications for a specific frame for Cornish identity.

CORNISH IDENTITY & CULTURAL IDENTITY THEORY

A Cornish identity theory should have as its aim the generation of a positive sense of self and a positive sense of Cornwall's cultural history. However, cultural identity theory does not focus narrowly on an individual's own cultural heritage but examines the relationship between different cultural/historical backgrounds. Thus a Cornish cultural identity theory should enable a Cornish person to feel proud of self, proud of Cornwall, and ultimately proud and respectful of relationships with other groups. Cultural identity theory is not oppressive or exclusionary – rather, it seeks to forge new relationships with others for the future.

Five stages of Cornish identity have been selected as the framework of this theory. These levels are drawn from the work of Freire and Jackson and Hardiman.[16] Figure 1 presents the five stages as they are related to Platonic epistemological constructs:

Cultural Identity Theory & Platonic Epistemology

Cultural Identity Theory	**Plato**
Naïvety	Imagining
Acceptance - passive or active	
Naming and resistance - passive or active	Belief
-----------The *Line* between the world of appearances----------- ----------------------and the intelligible world----------------------	
Redefinition and reflection	Thinking
Multiperspective integration	Dialectic

FIGURE 1

In reviewing these five stages, it is important to note that rarely do individuals fit neatly within a particular stage. Most will straddle several stages, so that a Cornish nationalist, for example, might vacillate between the naming/resistance and redefinition/reflection stages. Certainly, resistance without reflection can be emotionally tiring but those who only reflect may never act, so that individuals may balance several stages simultaneously. Additionally, Parham has noted that it is possible to recycle through the separate stages several times in a lifetime, as one discovers new issues of identity or experiences renewed discrimination or derision.[17]

Naivety is the first stage of the theory. In the Cornish context, individuals may be unaware or at best dimly aware of any distinctions between 'Cornish' and 'English' ways of being. Cultural identity is not an issue. This level of identity would be exhibited amongst children who had not had an opportunity to study Cornish history and culture, and might occur in adults who would deny the importance or relevance of being Cornish in a predominantly Anglocentric society. In considering this stage, Jackson and Hardiman assert that this 'No social consciousness describes our condition when we are brought into this world. It describes the innocence that we bring to our socializers. It is from this perspective that we are taught our social group memberships and our social status as oppressed people'.[18] People move out of the naïvety stage when they discover their Cornish roots or when they encounter discrimination, especially when they encounter the 'Cornish paradox' – the insistence that Cornwall is part of England but the belief that the Cornish are 'not really English'.

Acceptance is the second stage. Jackson and Hardiman identify two types of acceptance, the active and the passive. Active acceptance may occur when a Cornish person decides to self-define as English, thus avoiding controversy or derision and seeking to self-develop (in accent, education, aspirations) as English. Such a person would be keen to leave Cornwall to 'get on' or participate more fully in English life, and might see Cornwall as 'backward' and the Cornish people as 'unambitious' or even 'incompetent'. The passive-acceptant individual is characterised by a self-deprecating knowledge that he or she is Cornish, perhaps regretting that 'I'm only Cornish, I can't do much' or insisting that 'It's too late, Cornwall can't survive the pace of change", attitudes similar to those encountered by McArthur.[19] Such a person might avoid contact with socially, economically and educationally better-equipped 'superior' in-migrants, leading to the 'informal social apartheid' detected by Deacon.[20] Needless to say, it would be possible for an individual to spend his or her own life at the active or passive acceptance stage. However, the active-acceptant individual may move to the next stage when confronted by even partial rejection (the 'Cornish paradox'), while the passive-acceptant individual may move as a result of encountering situations (a trip to Twickenham) or meeting individuals (a Cornish language enthusiast) who encourage a more self-confident expression of identity. Certainly, both types of acceptant will tend to be moved to a higher level of consciousness through increased contact with Cornucentric presentations of Cornish history and culture.

Naming and Resistance. Two emotions seem to be fundamental to this third stage of consciousness – anger and pride. For example, anger that in-migrants come to Cornwall with apparent ease while the indigenous Cornish are forced to leave to find work is balanced with a fulsome pride in Cornish rugby, the heritage of Cornish steam engineering, the Cornish language. As well as enthusiasm for Cornish cultural groups there may be sympathy for politicised organisations such as Mebyon Kernow, the Cornish Nationalist Party and the Stannary Parliament, or at least an insistence that the mainstream political parties should do more to accommodate Cornish issues. There will also be an insistence that Cornwall is not a 'county' but instead a Duchy, region or nation. There will be intense frustration with those Cornish people unwilling to move beyond the acceptance stage, while there will also be a desire by individuals to affect 'Cornish characteristics' – speaking with a Cornish accent, using dialect words, wearing identifiably Cornish clothing such as a rugby sweater or a tartan skirt.

However, many will prefer to be covert in this process, with critiques of Anglocentric perspectives only occurring in the privacy of the home or in other 'safe' situations. Anecdotal evidence suggests that this passive resistant situation is widespread in Cornwall but that because it is essentially private many Cornish people are unaware that their neighbours and friends feel as they do. Certainly, Cornwall has a long history of individualistic and quiet stoicism in the face of adversity, the quality of 'making do'.[21] It is worth noting that African-Americans felt much the same way in the 1950s and did not express themselves fully until the civil rights campaigns of the 1960s, an experience replicated in Northern Ireland where almost fifty years of quiet anger and frustration in the Catholic community was not vented until the late 1960s. A more distant comparison is that of Poland, where centuries of domination and partition by Germans, Austrians and Russians have bred a rugged but often introspective individualism.

There are individuals who may spend a good part or even all of their lives at this passive resistant stage. It is a safe place to be and it is hypothesised that this may be the predominant way of making meaning for most indigenous Cornish people. The naming and discovery of one's own ethnic and cultural heritage is a large project, particularly when one's history and language have not been taught in school and receive only secondary notice in even the local communications media. Moving from passive to active resistance involves considerable personal risk, with the public articulation of Cornucentric perspectives being criticised as 'extremist' or 'not representative'.

Reflection and redefinition. The central feature of this stage tends to be reflection, individually or in groups, on the nature or meaning of 'being Cornish'. Whereas the previous stage focussed on defining Cornwall on the basis of what is 'not English', this stage is more assuredly Cornucentric and seeks to develop an independent meanings system. At this stage of development, Cornish people can be expected to turn to a more sophisticated consideration of Cornwall past, present and future. Some may become interested in the Cornish language while others will concentrate on history, perhaps identifying 'key points' in Cornish history as an autodidactic exercise or to acquaint children and others with the basic facts of that history. There may also be attempts to present Cornwall as part of a Pan-Celtic world, drawing links and comparisons with Brittany, Wales, Ireland, Scotland and the Isle of Man. Significantly, at this stage individuals exhibit a confidence and pride in their Cornishness, and in seeking positive relations with the non-Cornish will expect to be treated with respect.

However, this reflective consciousness is essentially historical in its orientation, sometimes nostalgic for the Cornish past (before Cornwall 'was ruined' by modern development) and sometimes hesitant in confronting the present. Indeed, in discovering Cornish history the individual may encounter new sources of aggrievement or discomfort (for example, dismay at the repression of Cornwall after 1549, or regret at the passing of industrial prowess), returning to the naming and resistance stage. Alternatively, this same information may lead the individual to a renewed activism within the context of the next, multiperspectival stage of consciousness. An example of this might be the desire to set the Cornish identity in its international context, on the one hand pointing to an international Cornish identity embracing North America, Australia and elsewhere, and on the other placing Cornwall as a part of the Atlantic Arc and a wider 'Europe of the Regions'.

Multiperspective integration. At this level of consciousness the individual understands that each of the preceding stages has inherent value, and will draw from each of those stages as appropriate in a given situation. Here the Cornish person will attempt to utilise the best of varying cultural frameworks. In some situations the English tradition might be more effective than the Cornish; in others the emphasis might be Transatlantic or Commonwealth; in still others the approach will be clearly European. The interaction of cultural systems is appreciated. An English (or other) point of view is listened to with respect in the expectation of reciprocity. There is similar respect for other cultural traditions, both indigenous and immigrant, in the United Kingdom and Europe. There may be awareness of parallels between the Cornish experience and those of Native Americans in the United States and Aborigines in Australia. There will also be an acknowledgement that Cornish culture is not exclusive, and that special effort should be made to accommodate in-migrants.

CORNISH DEVELOPMENT THEORY & IN-MIGRANTS

For a variety of reasons, ranging from the relatively low cost of housing to the inherent attractions of the Cornish environment and the success of the tourist industry in marketing images of Cornwall, since the War large numbers of people have been encouraged to migrate to Cornwall from elsewhere – especially the South East of England.[22] While precise statistics are not available, it may be that post-1945 in-migrants make up as much as fifty per cent of the current Cornish population. Although it is not possible to make an absolute distinction between indigenous and in-migrant communities, not least because the Cornish-born offspring of in-migrants are in one sense indigenous, it is important to discuss how a Cornish identity theory might be applied to in-migrants.

Naïvety. Few in-migrants, except children, may be expected to be found at the naïve level of consciousness. However, some in-migrants may be naïve with regard to both Cornwall and their own ethnicity (only rarely is the nature of 'Englishness' discussed). While expressing satisfaction with 'living in

Cornwall' they will retain their Home Counties or other up-country way of construing the world and will be unaware of any contrasting or separate Cornish identity. The Cornish themselves will be seen as 'just one of us' and any attempts by others to articulate a separate Cornish identity will be met with puzzlement or even seen as a threat.

Acceptance. In-migrants at this stage tend to accept the *status quo*. They enjoy all the attributes of Cornish life but make it clear that they are English, not Cornish. The maintenance of hierarchial relationships between the two communities may be important, exemplified in the telling comment of one in-migrant who wrote that the Cornish were 'the postman . . . the milkman . . . the shopkeepers who are . . . a joy to pass a few words with to brighten up the day'.[23] Active acceptance on the part of in-migrants would emphasise the 'simplistic' or 'rustic' characteristics of the Cornish, while more passive acceptance might be in the form of Deacon's 'informal social apartheid'.

Naming and Resistance. At this stage in-migrants begin to accept that Cornwall is a distinctive region and that the Cornish have a separate identity. They recognise that Cornwall is beset by socio-economic and other crises, and may feel not only concern but also guilt – being 'part of the problem'. Some may decide to 'help the Cornish', maintaining their social and cultural distance, but a few will so identify with Cornwall that their experience of this stage is akin to that of the indigenous Cornish. It is at this point that the indigenous and in-migrant communities begin to merge. Environmental and socio-economic issues are often the starting point for indigenous/in-migrant alliances but some in-migrants will wish to go further, learning the Cornish language or undertaking genealogical research in a hunt for Cornish forebears. Single in-migrants may seek out potential indigenous Cornish partners. Many will feel that, 'In my heart, I'm Cornish'.

Reflection and Definition. Here the in-migrant comes to realise that he/she may also be disadvantaged as a result of living in Cornwall (poor employment opportunities for offspring, higher than average water and gas charges, low wages, and so on) and actively seeks alliance with the indigenous Cornish. This may lead to a wider understanding of 'centre' and 'periphery' within the United Kingdom, and of the role played by the English State in the acquisition of its periphery – including Cornwall. At this stage in-migrants may start to identify themselves as Cornish as well as English. Although the indigenous Cornish at this stage will concentrate on the meaning of 'being Cornish', the in-migrant may explore the special responsibility and opportunity of being English in a Cornish society.

Multiperspective integration. Here there is real resemblance between indigenous and in-migrant Cornish – in attitude, in aspirations, in enthusiasms, even in appearance as Cornish clothing and other symbolism is adopted, perhaps also in speech. In effect the two groups have become one, with both Cornish and English perspectives valued, each recognised as having a special place in local and larger society.

NARRATIVES & MEANING-MAKING

Through narration and *narrative schemes* we tell stories to make sense of our experience. Polkinghorne comments:

> narrative is a scheme by means of which human beings give meaning to their experience of temporality and personal actions. Narrative means functions to give form to the understanding of a purpose to life and to join everyday actions into episodic units. It provides a framework for understanding the past events of one's life and for planning future actions. It is the primary scheme by means of which human existence is rendered meaningful.[24]

Goncalves and Alves[25] point out that certain key 'scenes' in an individual's life experience are constructed as prototypes on which we build these narrative schemes. These prototypes then become the basis for organising life experience. Thus, for example, if a young indigenous Cornish person experiences 'scenes' in which Cornwall is denigrated, then we can anticipate a low level of Cornish consciousness. Similarly, a young in-migrant experiencing such a 'scene' might be expected to develop a denigrating view of Cornwall. Both indigenous Cornish and in-migrants face the issue of making meaning and telling stories about their experiences in Cornwall. The Cornish identity theory elucidated above assists us in postulating the narrative schemes which indigenous Cornish and in-migrants might develop at varying stages of cultural identity development. An example of this is Table 2 below.

SOCIAL & EDUCATIONAL IMPLICATIONS OF CORNISH IDENTITY THEORY

At each level of consciousness, educational and social needs are different. This has been noted in several discussions of general cultural identity theory[26] where it has been shown that in any interpersonal contact educators and others should be aware of the stages of identity development. However, traditional culturally blind education tends to see all individuals as the same; or, in a Cornish context, as being just 'English' like everybody else. Thus educational or counselling tasks avoid issues of cultural difference and may even seek to impose the values of the dominant perspective. By contrast, culturally aware educators and counsellors seek to meet their students or clients at their present level of cultural consciousness, expand that consciousness, and perhaps even seek to assist further advancements in awareness. In effect, there are two widely varying educational paradigms. The first, based on traditional approaches, ignores the possible social basis of an individual's problem and treats that person as *an individual*. However, the second model treats the person as *an individual who exists in a social system* and therefore includes consideration of socio-cultural issues in dealing with that person.

TABLE 2:

Narrative Schemes and Cornish Identity Theory

Issue	Indigenous Narrative Schemes	In-Migrant Narrative Schemes
Should Cornish history be taught in schools?	*Naive*. Not interested in history but the National Curriculum must be true.	*Naive*. Pride in being English, Cornish history not important.
	Acceptance. May be interested in Cornish history but accepts Anglocentric perspectives. Appreciates the occaisional mention of Cornwall.	*Acceptance*. Cornish history may have limited value as Local Studies.
	Naming and Resistance. Keenly aware that teaching of Cornish history is limited. May be aware that history is presented in an Anglocentric frame.	*Nameing and Resistance*. Sees that little Cornish history is taught and is concerned about Anglocentric frame.
	Reflection and Resistance. Becomes proficient in Cornish history from a Cornucentric perspective.	*Reflection and Resistance*. Seeks out Cornish history, sees it as vital component of Cornish education.
	Multiperspective Integration. Sees the value of multiple perspectives on history; keen to work with teachers on ways of teaching Cornish history.	*Multiperspective Integration*. Sees the value of multiperspectives on history; keen to work with teachers on ways of teaching Cornish history.

CONCLUSION

Drawing from cultural identity theories and the work of Freire,[27] Ivey has proposed that education and attendant areas of counselling and psychotherapy should be used as an empowering or 'liberating' process.[28] Helping individuals to see themselves in cultural context and in relation to history is critical to this process, and a 'psychotherapy as liberation' model may be considered a practical framework for implementation of a multicultural perspective. Certainly, in Cornwall the time is now ripe for the application of such an approach, not only in the teaching of Cornish history in schools but in many other facets of Cornish life too, and it is hoped that the Cornish identity theory outlined above may a first step in this process.

NOTES AND REFERENCES

1. Denys Val Baker, *The Timeless Land: The Creative Spirit in Cornwall*, Bath, 1973; Daphne du Maurier, *Vanishing Cornwall: The Spirit and History of Cornwall*, London, 1967.
2. Mary McArthur, 'The Cornish: A Case Study in Ethnicity', unpub. MSc, University of Bristol, 1988; Philip Payton, *The Making of Modern Cornwall: Historical Experience and the Persistence of 'Difference'*, Redruth, 1992; Caroline Vink, 'Be Forever Cornish! The Emergence of a Cornish Ethnoregional Movement in the Twentieth Century', unpub. University of Amsterdam doctoral thesis, 1993; Bernard Deacon and Philip Payton, 'Re-inventing Cornwall: Culture Change on the European Periphery', *Cornish Studies: One*, second series, 1993; see also chapters by Lyn Bryant, Bernard Deacon, and Philip Payton, in Philip Payton (ed.), *Cornwall Since the War: The Contemporary History of a European Region*, Redruth, 1993.
3. *The Times*, cited in *Cornish Banner*, 70, November 1992.
4. Cornwall County Council, *Cornwall - One and All: Submission to the Local Government Commission*, Truro, 1994, p.5; our italics.
5. J. White and T. Parham, *The Psychology of Blacks*, Englewood Cliffs, 1990; Allen Ivey, Mary Ivey and L. Simek-Morgan, *Counseling and Psychotherapy: A Multicultural Perspective*, Boston, 1993.
6. Payton, 1992, pp.7-9.
7. Vink, 1993, Summary.
8. See James Jupp, *The Australian People: An Encyclopedia of the Nation, its People and their Origins*, Sydney, 1988, p.119.
9. J. Phinney, 'Ethnic Identity in Adolescents and Adults: Review of Research', *Psychological Bulletin*, 108, 1990.
10. W. Cross, 'The Negro to Black Conversion Experience', *Black World*, 20, 1971; W. Cross, *Shades of Black*, Philadelphia, 1991; J. Helms, *Black and White Racial Identity*, Westport, 1990; Ivey, Ivey and Simek-Morgan, 1993; B. Jackson, 'Black Identity Development', *Journal of Educational Diversity and Innovation*, 2, 1975; B. Jackson and R. Hardiman, 'Social Identity Development Model', *New Perspectives*, 1993; T. Parham, 'Cycles of Nigrescence', *The Counseling Psychologist*, 17, 1989; J. Ponterotto, 'Racial Consciousness Development Among White Counselor Trainees', *Journal of Multicultural Counseling and Development*, 16, 1988; D. Sue and D. Sue, *Counseling the Culturally Different*, New York, 2nd ed. 1990.
11. Eric Jay, *Keep Them in Birmingham: Challenging Racism in the South West of England*, London, 1992, p.16; see also *Cornish Banner*, 70, November 1992.
12. Notably Ann Trevenen Jenkin (ed.), *Cornish Studies for Schools*, Truro, 2nd ed. 1993.
13. Michel Denis, Jean Pihan and Jeffrey Stanyer, 'The Peripheries Today', in M. Havinden, J. Queniart and J. Stanyer, *Centre and Periphery: Brittany and Cornwall & Devon Compared*, Exeter, 1991, p.38.
14. Allen Ivey, *Developmental Therapy: Theory into Practice*, San Francisco, 1986; Allen Ivey, *Developmental Strategies for Helpers: Individual, Family and Network Interventions*, Pacific Grove, 1991.
15. F. Cornford (ed.), *The Republic of Plato*, London, 1941, repub. 1982, p.227.

16. P. Freire, *Pedagogy of the Oppressed*, New York, 1972; B. Jackson and R. Hardiman, 'Racial Identity Development: Implications for Managing the Multiracial Work Force', in R. Vitvo and A. Sargent, *The NTL Managers' Handbook*, Arlington, 1983.
17. Parham, 1989.
18. Jackson and Hardiman, 1993, p.4.
19. Mc Arthur, 1988, p.75; see also Tom Tremewan, *A Builder's Life in Perranporth*, Truro, 1974, pp.103-104.
20. Bernard Deacon, 'Is Cornwall an Internal Colony?', in Cathal O'Luain, *For A Celtic Future*, Celtic League, Dublin, 1983, p.270.
21. Deacon and Payton, 1993.
22. Peter Mitchell, 'The Demographic Revolution', in Payton, 1993.
23. *West Briton*, 7 January 1985.
24. D. Polkinghorne, *Narrative Knowing and the Human Sciences*, Albany, 1988, p.11.
25. O. Goncalves and A. Alves, 'Prototype Narratives in Opioide Dependence', unpub. paper, University of Minho.
26. Sue and Sue, 1991; Ivey, Ivey, and Simek-Morgan, 1993.
27. Freire, 1972.
28. Ivey, 1993.

AN INTRODUCTORY NOTE ON THE WILDLIFE OF BRITTANY AND CORNWALL WITH SPECIAL REFERENCE TO THE LEPIDOPTERA

Adrian Spalding

INTRODUCTION

Present day visitors from Cornwall to Brittany will experience a sense of feeling at home, manifested by similarities in music and dance, numerous megaliths, shared legends such as that of King Arthur and Trystan and Isolde, a feeling of difference from the larger states of which they are a part. In fact, the cultural heritage of Brittany and Cornwall has many similar features, not the least of which are languages based on the same Brythonic roots. The languages of Breton and Cornish are closer to each other than to Welsh.[1] Many Breton and Cornish words are the same, e.g. bara for bread.[2] The similarities of the languages gives an indication of the common inheritance shared by peoples of both countries.

What the visitor to either country notices most must depend on their particular interests, but who can fail to see how the granite cliffs, drowned river valleys, saltmarsh and mudflats of the coasts contrast with the level heathland, granite outcrops, rich agricultural land and steep valley sides clothed in deciduous woodland of the inland areas? Place the visitor in either country away from people and roadsigns and he would find it hard to tell which he was in. The geology of Brittany[3] and Cornwall[4] is similar, even to the extraction of china clay by ECC on the central granite uplands of Finistère. (Bournerais, Pomerol and Tuiquier link together the wildlife and the geology of Brittany most effectively).[5] The climate in both countries is maritime, with warm wet winters and cool damp summers and the proximity of the sea is probably the dominant factor affecting the wildlife. Habitat types are also similar in Brittany[6] and Cornwall,[7] with expanses of lowland heath, sand dune, ancient woodland, upland grassland, maritime grassland, Rhos pasture, heath and cliff face habitat.

Within these habitats, Brittany appears to have higher species diversity than Cornwall. This is partly due to its greater size: Brittany covers about 33,700 square kilometres[8] compared with only 3,500 square kilometres for Cornwall (figures from the Cornwall Wildlife Trust). South-east Brittany is further away from the cooling influence of the sea than anywhere in Cornwall. Brittany's land-link with the huge Euro-Asian continent allows a constant exchange of species with the neighbouring lands, including recolonisation by species which have become locally extinct. Brittany has also probably lost fewer species due to human interference with the natural wild habitat because it has a smaller human population for its size. For example, the wolf (*Canis lupus*) was present in Finistère as late as around 1900,[9] but probably died out in Cornwall in the 13th Century.[10] The wild boar (*Sus scrofa*) still occurs in the Breton forests but disappeared from Cornwall a considerable time ago (the latest evidence is of bones from 1st - 3rd centuries A.D. but the wolf was probably present in Cornwall much later than this). The situation is complicated by the introduction and re-introduction (deliberate or accidental) by man of additional species. For example, the European Beaver (*Castor fiber*) has now been introduced into Brittany but the latest evidence for it in Cornwall is provided by remains from the early Iron Age.[11]

SPECIES RICHNESS IN BRITTANY AND CORNWALL

Brittany has many wildlife species that are not resident in Britain, such as the Bee Eater (*Merops apiaster*), the Common Wall Lizard (*Podarcis muralis*), the Fire Salamander (*Salamandra salamandra*), the Quimper Snail (*Elona quimperiana*, the Ilex Hairstreak (*Nordmannia ilicis*) and the Loose-flowered Orchid (*Orchis laxiflora*). There are many more species that occur in both Brittany and Britain but that have not been found established in Cornwall, e.g. the Natterjack Toad (*Bufo calamita*), the Large Marsh Grasshopper (*Stethophyma grossum*), the Glanville Fritillary (*Melitaea cinxia*) and the Scarce Emerald Damselfly (*Lestes dryas*).

During the last Ice Age, wildlife in Britain would have retreated from the advancing ice[12] or have died from the cold; other species might have been confined to the unglaciated parts of Britain. As the climate warmed, wildlife recolonisation of Britain occurred from mainland Europe as species crossed what is now the channel when it was still dry land. Many species failed to colonise or recolonise Britain before this land link was flooded about 8,000 years ago, although their presence in north-western Europe indicates that they could survive here, e.g. the Bow-winged Grasshopper (*Chorthippus biguttulus*) which occurs northwards to Scandinavia,[13] but which has not been recorded in Britain. Other species managed to cross the land-bridge but have not yet reached Cornwall; these were probably late post-glacial arrivals in Britain. There are many examples of these from the Orthoptera, whose distribution in Britain is well-known,[14] e.g. the Heath Grasshopper (*Chorthippus vagans*) and the Large Marsh Grasshopper (*Stethophyma grossum*). More recently, there has been considerable trade between the two countries for many centuries and it is likely that some wildlife species have been introduced into Cornwall from southern lands by the hand of man.

For some orders, we can count the number of species present in Brittany and in Cornwall (Table 1). Species richness increases from the north-west part of Finistère to the south-eastern Loire Atlantique where are found some species with a southern or Mediterranean distribution.[15] This distribution pattern shows clearly on maps and may be due partly to the warmer and drier climate experienced in the south-east. By comparison with France,[16] Bourgogne thought Brittany (especially Finistère) very poor for Lepidoptera, mainly because of the geological situation, the constitution of the soils and the absence of the particular plants to provide food for larvae.

TABLE 1:
Numbers of species present in Brittany and Cornwall

group	Brittany	Cornwall
nesting birds	172	107
mammals	56	37
reptiles & amphibians	26 - 28	8
orchids	36	18
grasshoppers & crickets	45	14
dragonflies & damselflies	52	22

(approximate figures only, taken from a variety of sources including Monnat (1973) and the CBRU)

COMPUTER MAPPING IN BRITTANY AND CORNWALL

Computerised mapping of species in Brittany is apparently still in its early stages compared with Cornwall, but there are good distribution maps for example of orchids,[17] amphibians and reptiles,[18] and unpublished maps of Odonata compiled by Alain Manach. There is also an excellent account, with distribution maps, of the nesting birds of Brittany.[19] The Museum National D'Histoire Naturelle in Paris has published several atlases (e.g. for beetles, mammals, birds) for the whole of France. These include species recorded in

Brittany, but the maps are too large scale to give detailed distributions (for the Orthoptera[20] each distribution dot covers an area of about 20x27km.). Detailed knowledge of the distribution of Lepidoptera in Brittany is limited so that Philippe Fouillet writes, 'Il n'existe pas actuellement de synthèse permettant de juger du niveau de rareté en Bretagne occidentale des Lépidoptères nocturnes . . .'.[21] He goes on to write that so much more is known about species in Britain. In Cornwall we are lucky to have access to the ERICA database in the Cornish Biological Records Unit (CBRU) at the Institute of Cornish Studies, which has information on over 22,000 species in Cornwall and the Isles of Scilly.

BUTTERFLIES

There have been 4,677 species of Lepidoptera recorded in France[22] compared with just over 2,500 in Britain and Ireland.[23] This difference is a function of several features, especially the greater habitat and climatic diversity in France. Brittany has more butterfly and moth species than Cornwall, with about 78 species of breeding butterfly in Brittany[24] compared to 39 breeding species in Cornwall.[25] Tiberghien[26] notes that in Brittany there is a mix of species associated with five different biological zones, so that we find 'eurasiatiques, holarctiques, Méditerranéo-Asiatiques, occidentale et espèces d'Europe et Afrique du Nord'. It is not surprising, therefore, that of these 78 species recorded in Brittany, 39 (50%) do not occur in Cornwall and 26 (33%) do not occur in Britain.

The greatest difference between the butterflies of the two countries is probably found in the south-eastern corner of Brittany, where the climate is warmer and drier. Several butterflies occur here which are not found in Britain, such as the Meadow Fritillary (*Mellicta parthenoides*) (which has small isolated populations in Brittany). Its distribution in Brittany is poorly known as it is difficult to identify with certainty without genitalia dissection. The Tree Grayling (*Neohipparchia statilinus*) was once widespread in the southern half of the peninsula[27] but is now probably confined to south of Rennes.[28] Other non-British species occur widely over Brittany. These include the Pearly Heath (*Coenonympha arcania*) (much less common than the similar Small Heath (*Coenonympha pamphilus*) which was recorded in the south-east by W.J. Griffith (at one time assistant *conservateur* of the museum in Vannes) over 100 years ago.[29] It is now probably declining but still has scattered populations in western Brittany. The Black-veined White (*Aporia crataegi*) is to be seen regularly in Finistère flying fast from flower to flower; this butterfly was common in south-eastern England at one time but is now extinct in Britain.[30] The Idas Blue (*Lycaeides idas*) (never recorded in Britain) has scattered populations in west and central Brittany, especially on heathland.[31] There are many local forms in France, forming clines with intergrading forms;[32] the one found in Brittany has been given subspecific status (ssp. *armorica*) by Leraut.[33] The Short-tailed Blue

(*Everes argiades*) and the Long-tailed Blue (*Lampides boeticus*) were both recorded by Bourgogne[34] in Finistère, but the Long-tailed Blues were probably migrants. Both of these species have been found in Cornwall as migrants.[35] The Baton Blue (*Pseudophilotes baton*) is very localised in Brittany, flying in two broods in May and again in July and August. This and the following species have never been recorded in Britain. The Large Chequered Skipper (*Heteropterus morpheus*) is found in damp areas especially peat moors in a scattered distribution including the Monts d'Arrée. It occurs in the Channel Isles, where there is a tiny colony in Jersey.

Other butterflies occur in both Brittany and Britain. The Speckled Wood (*Pararge aegeria*) is represented in both Cornwall and Brittany by the northern form ssp. *tircis*, which has pale yellow wing patches. The ssp. *aegeria* (with orange wing patches) almost reaches southern Brittany where it forms a cline with *tircis* on the boundary between the two subspecies.[36] The Bath White (*Pontia daplidice*) occurs rarely in Brittany as a breeding species,[37] but is seen in Britain only as a rare summer migrant: 57 are listed on the ERICA database at the CBRU as having been recorded in Cornwall this century. In contrast, the Swallowtail (*Papilio machaon*) has never occurred in Cornwall, despite its image being used on tourist literature to advertise the attractions of the Lizard Peninsula. In Brittany, it appears to be increasing and this species has been found on the north coast of the Crozon Peninsula in some numbers, nectaring on Thrift (*Armeria maritima*) plants in a saltmarsh. In Britain, this species is confined to the Norfolk Broads and it is a different, darker subspecies.[38] The Large Blue (*Maculinea arion*) is especially interesting. Once the symbol of CTNC (now the Cornwall Wildlife Trust) and the British Butterfly Conservation Society (now Butterfly Conservation), this species has always been closely associated with Cornwall, where huge numbers used to fly in summer in the northern coastal valleys. Extinct in Cornwall since 1976,[39] the Joint Committee for the Conservation of the Large Blue Butterfly hope to reintroduce this butterfly to at least one of its former sites in Cornwall. The Large Blue was abundant in certain localities in Brittany in the early part of this century,[40] but 30 years ago Bourgogne knew of only three sites in Finistère. It is unlikely that any sites for this lovely butterfly are now left in Brittany.[41]

MOTHS

It is more difficult to generalise about moths, partly because there are so many more of them. There have been some 2,400 moths recorded in Britain and Ireland,[42] with at least 1,487 having been recorded in Cornwall.[43] There is no definitive list of the moths of Brittany (in fact, most regional lists soon become out-of-date as new species are discovered within the area), but there are certain to be many more species here than in Cornwall, for the same reasons as for the butterflies. However, there is little published work[44] and most papers in the

French journal *Alexanor* are about central and southern France where species diversity is higher. The *Faunistica Lepidopterorum Europaeorum* project has been set up to provide up-to-date distribution maps of the European macrolepidoptera[45] and will eventually place the Breton records within the European context.

Tiberghien[46] suggests that in Brittany euroasiatic species predominate over the Mediterranean-Asiatic, Atlantic-Mediterranean, Holarctic, European and cosmopolitan species. Aljundi[47] recorded 188 species of Noctuidae near Rennes and divided these species according to their international distribution (Table 2). It has been calculated that out of these 188 species, 14 (7%) have never been caught in Britain, 18 are recorded occasionally or regularly as migrants (9%) and 43 (22%) have never been recorded in Cornwall. Direct comparison of moth-trapping sites on granite cliffs in Finistère and Cornwall showed a low level of similarity and much lower species diversity for the Cornish site.[48] In a further small sample catch on the Breton coast,[49] the author found that 9% of the species recorded had not been found in Cornwall. Further south in France the difference in species present seems to increase, e.g. out of 99 species recorded in the Lot area, there were 29 (29%) species unknown in Cornwall.[50]

TABLE 2:

Noctuidae recorded by Aljundi at Rennnes (1975-78) sorted according to their international distribution

Biological region	No. of species
Euro-Asiatic	107
Mediterranean-Asiatic	46
Holarctic	17
Atlantic-Mediterranean	12
Cosmopolitan	5
Subtropical	1
Total	**188**

Particular habitats, common to both countries, show differences in species abundance and diversity. The central heathland areas in Brittany seem to be particularly productive. The author recorded 1,200 moths (59 species) during one night on the Monts d'Arrée heaths,[51] including 621 True Lover's Knot (*Lycophotia porphyrea*). This would be an exceptional night's catch in Cornwall. The Rhos pasture sites are also apparently more productive than their Cornwall (or Devon) counterparts (for example a catch of 92 species in one night in the Monts d'Arrée on 6 August 1991). Wolton & Trowbridge[52] found these pastures similar to the British ones in both their plant and animal communities. The only moths they recorded were the Forester (*Adscita statices*) and the Narrow-bordered Bee Hawk-moth (*Hemaris tityus*), both associated with damp pastures in Britain.[53] There seems to be a high degree of similarity between the lepidoptera of Rhos pastures in Britain and Brittany; during several catches in a wet meadow in Brittany the author recorded only one non-British species – the Orache Moth (*Trachea atriplicis*). The maritime habitats of both countries also appear to have a great deal in common, especially with the Noctuidae such as the Sand Dart (*Agrotis ripae*) on the sand dunes. Other species are rare in Cornwall but widespread in suitable habitat in Brittany e.g. the micro-moth *Bucculatrix maritima* which is uncommon in Cornwall but found on Sea Aster (*Aster tripolium*) in saltmarshes in Brittany.[54]

Some species occupy different niches in Brittany from Britain. Thus the Speckled Footman (*Coscina cribraria*) is confined to heathlands of the New Forest in Britain but is common on the Breton coasts where it is well-camouflaged on the lichen-covered granite rocks; the British moths are a different sub-species. The Brussels Lace (*Cleorodes lichenaria*) is abundant in woodland in Cornwall, where it feeds on lichens growing on trees; in Brittany the larvae have been found feeding on the lichen *Ramalina siliquosa* growing on the cliffs. Records of Brussels Lace from the Kynance Cove area indicate that its larvae may be associated with a cliff habitat here as well.[55] The Beautiful Hook-tip (*Laspeyria flexula*) is another woodland species in Britain and has only been found three times in Cornwall. In Finistère the adults can be found on the coast, where the larvae probably feed on lichens in the extensive blackthorn (*Prunus spinosa*) thickets covering the cliffs.

Some moths are extending their range and may well reach Cornwall at some time. *Harpyia milhauseri* is a southern species in France but now possibly breeds in Brittany. It has no English name as it has only twice been recorded in Britain (never in Cornwall) as a migrant. The Latin Moth (*Callopistria juventina*) is common on the bracken-covered slopes in Brittany; like the preceding species it has been moving northwards in Europe.[56] It is very likely that it could survive in Cornwall if it were deliberately introduced but may reach here under its own steam.

However, the Channel appears to be an effective barrier to the dispersal of European species to Cornwall. For example, the Pine-tree Lappet (*Dendrolimus pini*) occurs abundantly in conifer woods in Brittany and France where it can be a forest pest[57] and has been recorded on the Channel Isles.[58] Despite this, it has only been recorded twice in Britain[59] and rarely if ever crosses the sea. The Alchymist (*Catephia alchymista*) occurs in Brittany, an interesting out-station for a central European species,[60] but nearly all the migrant records in Britain are in the south-east, suggesting that the sea between Brittany and Cornwall is too wide for migrant moths to cross with ease.

NAMES FOR LEPIDOPTERA

The nations of Continental Europe generally make no scientific distinction between moth and butterfly as we do in Britain. Thus the words *Schmetterling* (German), *papillon* (French) and *mariposa* (Spanish) can mean either butterfly or moth. Particular night-flying species can be referred to by adding *nocturna* (Spanish) and *de nuit* or *nocturne* (French) or by using the separate German word *Nachtfalter*. Similarly in Breton the word *balafen* (plural *balafened*) refers to any lepidopteran. There are several local variations of another word for butterfly in Breton – *ealic doue* (meaning God's little angel) and for moth – *ealic doue noz* . There appear to be no Breton words which refer to particular species. In Cornish, the word *tykki-dyw* (literally God's beautiful thing from the 'Late' Cornish form *tegen Dyw*) means either butterfly or day-flying moth.[61] Night-flying moths are called *tykki-dyw nos*. The old Cornish word in *Vocabularium Cornicum* (written before the thirteenth century) gives *Gouthan* for moth (*goedhan* in Kernewek Kemmyn); this is given as equivalent to the Latin *tinea* (meaning gnawing worm from larvae destructive to clothes).[62] There are no old Cornish names for individual species, although new names (generally based on literal translations of the common names) have been created for 28 species found in Cornwall.[63]

ACKNOWLEDGEMENTS

The author would like to thank Francois de Beaulieu for his hospitality and for imparting his knowledge of Brittany's wildlife and Pierre le Floch for his help with moth-trapping and with the Breton language. The author would also like to thank Chris Haes for information on grasshoppers of Brittany.

NOTES AND REFERENCES

1. P.B. Ellis, *The Story of the Cornish Language*, Penryn, 1990.
2. D.B. Gregor, *Celtic: A Comparative Study*, Cambridge, 1980.
3. S. Durand & H. Lardeux, *Guides Géologiques Régionaux: Bretagne*, Masson, 1984.
4. R.M. Barton, *An Introduction to the Geology of Cornwall*, Truro, 1964.
5. M. Bournerais, C. Pomerol and Y. Turquier, *La Bretagne du Mont-St-Michel à la Pointe du Raz*, Lausanne, 1985; M. Bournerais, C. Pomerol and Y. Turquier, *La Bretagne de la Pointe du Raz à l'estuaire de la Loire*, Lausanne, 1986.
6. F. de Beaulieu, *Nature en Bretagne*, Douarnenez, 1991.

7. R. Bere, *The Nature of Cornwall*, Buckingham, 1982.
8. M. Renouard, *Guide to Brittany*, Rennes, 1993.
9. J.-Y. Monnat, *Bretagne Vivante*, Colmar-Ingersheim, 1973.
10. F.A. Turk, 'Notes on Cornish Mammals No 2.', 1960.
11. R.T. Brooks, 'The Rumps, St Minver, Interim Report on the 1963 excavations. Report on the animal bones by R.E. Chaplin and J.P. Coy', *Cornish Archaeology*, 3, 1964.
12. P. Crawford, *The Living Isles*, London, 1985.
13. H. Bellman, *A Field Guide to the Grasshoppers and Crickets of Britain and Northern Europe*, London, 1988.
14. J.A. Marshall and E.C.M. Haes, *Grasshoppers and Allied Insects of Great Britain and Ireland*, Colchester, 1988.
15. J.-Y. Monnat, 1973.
16. J. Bourgogne, 'Observations sur les Lycènes des Landes du Finistère', *Alexanor*, 1, 1960.
17. B. Bargain, F. Bioret and J.Y. Monnat, *Orchidées de Bretagne*, Brest, 1991.
18. B. Le Garff, 'Atlas des amphibiens et des reptiles de Bretagne', *Penn ar Bedd*, 17, 1988.
19. Y. Guermeur and J.-Y. Monnat, *Histoire et Géographie des Oiseaux Nicheurs de Bretagne*, Aurillac, 1980.
20. J.-F. Voisin, *Atlas des Orthoptères de France*, Paris, 1992.
21. P. Fouillet, *Étude de Peuplements Entomologiques des Landes du Cragou: Importance pour la Gestion du Site*, (unpublished report), 1992.
22. P. Leraut, *Liste Systématique des Lépidoptères de France, Belgique et Corse*, Paris, 1980
23. J.D. Bradley and D.S. Fletcher, *An Indexed List of British Butterflies and Moths*, Orpington, 1986.
24. The author has calculated this figure using L.G. Higgins and B. Hargreaves, *The Butterflies of Britain and Europe*, London, 1983, and M. Chinery, *New Generation Guide to the The Butterflies and Day-flying Moths of Britain and Europe*, London, 1989 as guides.
25. A. Spalding, *Cornwall's Butterfly and Moth Heritage*, Truro, 1992.
26. G. Tiberghien, 'Faunistique Et écologie des Principaux Groupes d'invertébrés sur le site de Beauvais-Chatenay (Station Biologique de Paimpont à Plelan le Grand Ille et Vilaine). Part 1: Presentation, Rhopalocères et Hétérocères Vernaux', *Bulletin de la Société Scientifiques de Bretagne*, 57, 1985.
27. C. Oberthur and C. Houlbert, *Faune Entomologique Armoricaine*, Rennes, 1912.
28. R. Essayan, 'Contribution Lépidoptérique Francaise à la Cartographie des Invertébrés Européens', *Alexanor*, 13, 1983.
29. T. Bezier, 'Catalogue Raisonné des Lépidoptères Observés en Bretagne jusqu'en 1882 par W.J. Griffith', *Bulletin de la Société Scientifiques et Médicale de l'Ouest*, XI, 1902.
30. C.R. Pratt, 'A modern review of the demise of *Aphoria crataegi* L.': the black-veined white', *Entomologist's Record and Journal of Variation*, 95, 1981.
31. Bourgogne, 1960.
32. L.G. Higgins and N.D. Riley, *A Field Guide to the Butterflies of Britain and Europe*, London, 1970.
33. Leraut, 1980.

34. Bourgogne, 1960.
35. A.M. Emmet and J. Heath, *The Moths and Butterflies of Great Britain and Ireland*, Volume 7, Part 1, Colchester, 1989.
36. Higgins and Hargreaves, London, 1983.
37. Tiberghien, 1985.
38. J.A. Thomas, *The Butterflies of Britain and Ireland*, London, 1991.
39. J.A. Thomas, 'The Return of the Large Blue Butterfly', *British Wildlife*, 1, 1989.
40. C. Oberthur and C. Houlbert, *Faune Entomologique Armoricaine*, Rennes, 1912.
41. Bourgogne, 1960. The author is indebted to J.A. Thomas for information on the current status of the Large Blue in Britain.
42. Bradley and Fletcher, 1986.
43. F.H.N. Smith, 'The Cornish Lepidoptera, Some Figures and Facts'. *CTNC Newsletter*, 59, 1992.
44. R. Rahn, C. Dufay and A.K. Aljundi, 'Atlas des Lépidoptères Noctuidae de Bretagne, *Sciences Agronomiques Rennes*, 1979.
45. P. Svendsen & M. Fibiger, (eds.), *The Distribution of the European Macrolepidoptera. Volume 1:Noctuinae*, Copenhagen, 1992.
46. Tiberghien, 1985.
47. A.K. Aljundi, 'Contribution à l'étude des Lépidoptères Noctuidae du Bassin de Rennes', PhD, Université de Rennes, 1980.
48. A. Spalding, 'Some Moths of the Reserve Michel-Herve Julien, Cap Sizun, Brittany', *The British Journal of Entomology & Natural History*, 2, 1989.
49. A. Spalding, 'Moths in Brittany and Cornwall', *Entomologist's Record and Journal of Variation*, 103, 1991.
50. A. Spalding, 'Observations on the Lepidoptera of one site near Cahors, France', *Entomologist's Record and Journal of Variation*, 98, 1986.
51. A. Spalding, 'A Snapshot of the Moths of the Reserve Les Rochers du Cragou', unpublished report, 1991.
52. R.J. Wolton and B.J. Trowbridge, *'The Occurrence of Acidic, Wet, Oceanic Grasslands (Rhos pastures) in Brittany, France*, Peterborough, 1990.
53. A.M. Emmet and J. Heath, *The Moths and Butterflies of Great Britain and Ireland*, Volume 7, Part 2, Colchester, 1991.
54. P. Leraut, *Les Papillons dans Leur Milieu*, Maxeville, 1992.
55. A. Spalding, 'A Further Note on *Cleorodes lichenaria* Hufn., the Brussels Lace', *Entomologist's Record and Journal of Variation*, 101, 1989.
56. J. Heath and A.M. Emmet, *The Moths and Butterflies of Great Britain and Ireland*, Volume 10, Colchester, 1983.
57. I. Novak, *A Field Guide in Colour to Butterflies and Moths*, London, 1980.
58. T.D.N. Peet, '*Dendrolimus pini* L. the Pine-tree Lappet (Lep.: Lasiocampidae) in Guernsey', *Entomologist's Record and Journal of Variation*, 101, 1989.
59. R. South, *The Moths of the British Isles*, London, 1961.
60. J. Culot, *Noctuelles et Geometres d'Europe, Vol II*, Svendborg, 1917-1919, reprinted 1987.
61. K. George, *Gerlyver Kernewek Kemmyn*, Callington, 1993; similar spellings are current in the Unified and Modern forms of revived Cornish.
62. A.M. Emmet, *The Scientific Names of the British Lepidoptera, Their History and Meaning*, Colchester, 1991.
63. A. Spalding and L.E.T. Jenkin, 'Cornish Names for Moths', *Entomologist's Record and Journal of Variation*, 100, 1988.